CONFESS, CONFESS, CONFESS

The True Story of a Prisoner of War

By Nick A. Flores

Turner Publishing Company
Publishers of America's History

www.turnerpublishing.com

Author: Nick A. Flores
Graphic Designer: Amanda J. Eads

The materials were compiled and produced using
available information; Turner Publishing Company and
Nick A. Flores regret they cannot assume liability for
errors or omissions.

Library of Congress
Control Number: 2003103262

ISBN: 978-1-68162-328-3

Limited Edition

Table of Contents

Author's Note

I was compelled to write this story so the American people would know first hand of how we lived in the POW camps and also to pay tribute to those who gave their ultimate sacrifices for freedom.

Up until 1993, there was very little information known about life in the POW camps. Men pushed their mental and physical powers to survive. Unfortunately they died of malnutrition, disease, or yellow fever due to the lack of medical treatment. I saw men cry as they died in my arms. Some of these were veterans of World War II, and some were just barely eighteen years old.

I hope that our country's future generations don't have to witness what I did as a POW. I pray that history won't repeat itself.

Nick O'Dell

Semper Fi

Acknowledgments

It's been over 10 years of hard work to make *Confess, Confess, Confess* a reality. I could never have done it on my own. My deepest appreciation to Peter Tsouras for inspiring me to detail my life on the pages of this book. A special thank you to Walter E. Boomer, General United States Marine Corps Retired; Captain Phillip Rogers, United States Marine Corps; and Dallas Meehan, Lieuteant Colonel, USAF Retired for their contributions to this book.

I would also like to thank, from the bottom of my heart, Marijane Kolher-Flores, Michael A. Flores, Wilma Flores, Jim Wood, Daron Kolb and Don DeArmond Jr. for their many hours of hard work and dedication on getting the book ready to publish. This book would never have become a reality without the love, prayers and support of my family and friends. Thank you so much.

A special thank you goes to the staff of Task Force Russia, who were very supportive to my cause.

Dedication

I dedicate this book to the memory of my
loving mother and father,
who inspired me with the teachings of the Bible
If you have the Lord in your heart,
anything is possible.
To the memory of the POW/MIAs
who gave and those that gave their
all for what we all have today,
and to their families and loved ones.

Freedom is not free.

IN 1993 I HAD THE PRIVELEGE of helping to set right a terrible injustice of forty years ago. It was one of those bureaucratic bungles for which no one individual could be held accountable. Much worse, when they happen in large organizations, redress is oftentimes difficult. This is the true story of Nick Flores, one of the heroes of the Korean War, who was given a general instead of an honorable discharge upon leaving the military, despite his acts of courage as a prisoner of war. The offending technicalities were a few minor infractions that appeared on his otherwise blemish-free record. Further, these incidents had occurred before his departure for Korea. In his book "Confess, Confess, Confess," Mr. Flores writes in an unimpassioned way about this experience, implying no rancor or bitterness. (There are not many among us who could feel the same way.) His account of the tribulations of war is honest, straightforward and very understated. Those who have served in combat will be amazed by the calmness of his tone in light of all the hardships he and his fellow POW's endured. And while decades have elapsed since that time, he portrays his wartime experiences in vivid detail, capturing the dread circumstance of being a prisoner in war-wracked eastern Asia with the immediacy of the moment. What shines through most strikingly in this story of pain, courage and torture is the character of Nick Flores: a *good* man and a *good* Marine. A good man because he places the welfare of others over his own. A good Marine because he never gives up! The country for which Nick Flores so proudly fought finally recognized him in 1993, and I had the honor of presenting him with a Prisoner of War Medal and an Honorable Discharge -- righting the wrong of forty years ago. But I will not give away the whole story and instead allow you, the Reader, to have the pleasure of discovering how this event comes about. By all accounts I am lucky to have been a witness, our country blessed to have men like Mr. Flores.

Walter E. Boomer
General United States Marine Corps (ret.)

Preface

Amidst the forgotten heroes of "The Forgotten War," there arises the saga of one hero who finally has found recompense for years of injustice and abandonment. The story of Nick A. Flores is a singular one for a variety of reasons. First of all, he was an exceptional figure in the North Korean Prisoner of War camps, a realm of the war that has not produced a plethora of Homeresque giants. Secondly, his brazen escape attempts landed him quite accidentally in an enigmatic investigation which is still mysteriously being unraveled today. And lastly, his personal story of justice accomplished coupled with belated recognition for his heroic deeds make his journey of pain all the more special and rewarding. The story of Nick A. Flores is the story of a simple man who cherished his country and his Corps and who did his utmost against incredible odds.

– Captain Phillip Rogers, USMC

Introduction

June 25, 1950 — During the early morning hours, the armed forces of Communist North Korea opened a massive artillery barrage along the entire width of the 38th Parallel which constituted the international border between the two Koreas. The assault began in the west and continued eastward for more than an hour. The forces of the Republic of Korea (ROK) were utterly surprised. So too were the small numbers of American advisors who were attached to ROK Army. The artillery barrage was followed by the North Korean People's Army (NKPA), leading the way with approximately one hundred and fifty Russian-built T-34 tanks followed by well equipped and well-trained divisions of NKPA infantry numbering some ninety thousand combat troops. The major North Korean thrust was in the west of the Korean peninsula, toward Seoul, the capital of South Korea.

South Korea's army, considerably smaller than that of her Communist neighbor, and not as well trained and equipped, was unable to stem the onslaught. By June 28, Seoul had fallen, and across the peninsula, everywhere south of the Han River, the South Korean army was in full retreat.

Meanwhile, within hours after the invasion of South Korea, the United Nations, at the urging of the United States, called for an immediate cease-fire and the withdrawal of North Korean troops from South Korea. North Korea ignored the resolution. Two days later the Security Council asked United Nations member states to come to the assistance of South Korea.

The United States was the first to react. Even before the UN resolution, President Harry S. Truman directed General of the Army Douglas MacArthur, commander of U.S. occupation forces in Japan, to ensure the safe evacuation of United States civilians and to supply weapons and ammunition to South Korea. The following day, June 26th, MacArthur,

with the concurrence of national authorities, directed U.S. air and naval forces to support South Korean ground units. MacArthur's ground forces in Japan consisted of four under-strength Army divisions composed largely of inexperienced, undertrained men, lacking in heavy weapons, softened by the "fat cat" life of occupation duty.

After the fall of Seoul, North Korea's forces paused briefly to regroup, then resumed their drive southward. United States units were sent into the piecemeal – the worst possible was to engage an advancing enemy. The result was predictable. They too were driven into retreat. By the end of July the remnants of South Korea's army and the United States units sent to bolster them, were pressed into small rectangular area surrounding the port of Pusan at the southeastern tip of Korea. Here they dug in, and with reinforcements pouring in by the hour, established the "Pusan Perimeter," stretching about one hundred miles from north to south and about fifty miles from east to west. It was their last line of defense.

Undaunted, MacArthur made plans for a daring counterstrike: an amphibious assault far to the rear of the North Korean lines at Inchon, some thirty miles west of Seoul. MacArthur's plan envisioned a breakout from the Pusan Perimeter to coincide with the surprise invasion of Inchon and the recapture of Seoul. The Eighth Army advancing from the Perimeter would constitute a "hammer" that would pound retreating Communist units against the "anvil" of the Inchon-Seoul forces.

"D-day" for the assault on Inchon was set for September 15, 1950. The assault force would be led by the experts in amphibious operations, the First Marine Division, commanded by Major General Oliver Prince ("O.P.") Smith, backed up by the Army's Seventh Infantry Division. With supporting units, the force numbered some seventy thousand men organized into the X (Tenth) Corps under the command of Major General Edward Almond.

The invasion began as planned. Supported by air strikes and by naval gunfire, including the sixteen inch guns of the recently de-mothballed *USS Missouri*, the Marines hit the beach around 6:30 in the morning. Later in the day, other Marine units went ashore, and by the early hours of the following morning, had secured their objectives at an incredibly small cost in casualties. Twenty Marines were killed, one was listed as missing in action (and presumed dead), and fewer than two hundred others were wounded. Two days later, the Army's 7th Infantry Division began coming ashore. X Corps, spearheaded by the First Marine Division, recaptured Seoul on September 28, 1950.

Within days, the Allied invasion force now had the benefit of close air support operating out of Kimpo, and on the 20th of September, the Marines began their drive toward Seoul itself, some twenty miles from the landing at Inchon. The battle for Seoul entered its final stage on the 24th. The following day would be exactly three months since the North Korean invasion of the South began. The X Corps commander, Major General Ned Almond (who had "promised" MacArthur that Seoul would be taken on the 25th), released publicly to the press that Seoul had been liberated. The next day, both he and MacArthur from their respective headquarters, officially announced in separate communiques, the "liberation of Seoul." They were premature. Most of Seoul was still under North Korean control, and Marines were still engaged in dangerous work of routing them out street by street. Indeed, fighting was still going on when General MacArthur and President Syngman Rhee held liberation ceremonies in Seoul on the 29th.

Inchon was MacArthur's "finest hour." During liberation ceremonies in the capital city, Seoul, South Korean President Syngman Rhee referred to General MacArthur as "the savior of our race." North Korean forces were demoralized and on the run. With the successful breakout from the Pusan Perimeter, the "hammer" of General Walker's Eighth Army began to pound the retreating enemy. By the beginning of October, with the exception of a few pockets from which North Korean forces operated in guerrilla fashion, all of South Korea had been liberated. The Korean War had lasted a little more than three months. It might have ended then and there. The question was, should United Nations forces stop at the 38th Parallel, or advance to a new, more defensible boundary between South and North Korea? Or should they press the attack all the way north to the Yalu River in order to effectively reunite the two Koreas under the American-sponsored regime of the South? Inherent in the latter course was the risk of reaction by either China or the Soviet Union, or possibly both.

In the glow of victory and with the headiness of success, the American Caesar made it clear what his preferences were. The Russians were bluffing. If the Chinese intervened in their masses, they would be terribly "slaughtered" by our air power. Here was a chance not only to "contain" Communism, but to roll it back decisively. Here also, was a chance for a Democratic Administration to prove its resolve, and that it wasn't "soft on Communism." America's allies, most notably the British, were less sanguine about pressing the attack into North Korea. But there was little doubt that the U.S. position would prevail in the United Nations as it was constituted in 1950. Moreover, the pace of events dictated that decisions be made rapidly. So, in the rush of military maneuver following the success of the Inchon-Seoul campaign, and the breaking of the North Korean siege of UN forces within the Pusan Perimeter, the United Nations accepted the American-sponsored resolution (suitably ambiguous to appease the concerns of her less convinced allies) that "all appropriate steps be taken to ensure conditions of stability throughout Korea," which was the basis for pressing the attack into North Korea. This decision would lengthen the war by nearly three years. Now the order of business was just how to orchestrate the invasion of the North. General Walker, the senior field commander in Korea, and his staff conceived one plan calling for the consolidation of all UN and ROK forces under his command. Then he would launch coordinated attacks northeast and northwest from Seoul, while ROK units advanced northward along the east coast. The main line of resistance would be systematically pushed north, while ports along the coasts and airfields in the interior would be secured for resupply. Such a plan also had the advantage of allowing UN and U.S. national authorities to respond to any Chinese or Soviet reaction as necessary.

In the meantime, however, MacArthur had conceived his own plan. In the first place, he would not relinquish direct control of the X Corps which had successfully pulled off the Inchon amphibious invasion. This decision, contrary to Army doctrine, effectively divided the major elements of American ground forces in Korea into separate commands. Furthermore, his plan called for yet another amphibious operation by X Corps, this time on the east coast of North Korea. This operation, in turn, not only separated the two field commands geographically, but also created a logistical problem of monumental proportions. Because of the tidal conditions at Inchon, only the Marines would embark there, while the Army's 7th Division would truck (and march) southeastern to Pusan for embarkation. The landing site of the amphibious invasion was the North Korean port of Wonsan, with D-day set for the 20th of October.

But, because of the tremendous logistics involved, including the need to clear Wonsan harbor of mines, ROK units took Wonsan by land before X Corps could go ashore in what turned out to be an "administrative landing." Originally, MacArthur's plan called for X Corps to attack across North Korea from the east coast landings, eventually taking Pyongyang, the North Korean capital. But even before X Corps was loaded aboard ships, 1 Corps (advancing as part of Eighth Army), was deploying for an assault on Pyongyang. This did not deter MacArthur. He merely redirected X Corps toward a new mission; one that would have grave consequences for those who took part in it. They would attack not west, but north; to the Yalu and the border with China. Their route of attack, especially that of the Marines, would be by way of a landmark now famous in American military history; the Chosin Reservoir.

On the 16th of October, there were more than twenty five thousand other Marines of the First Marine Division. About the same time, the Army's 7th Infantry Division was preparing to embark from Pusan, on the southeastern tip of South Korea. The X Corps was on its way for another MacArthuresque amphibious landing, this time on the east coast of North Korea. The two hundred fifty ship armada arrived off Wonsan Harbor on the 19th of October.

Mine sweeping for the Wonsan landing, which had begun on the 8th, was still underway. In fact, on that very day an ROK vessel, the YMS 516, disintegrated in a terrific explosion which occurred in the supposedly cleared lane. This prompted Admiral Struble, Joint Task Force commander, to delay the administrative landing until all the mines had been cleared from the lane, a task estimated to take another three days. In the meantime, the entire fleet would reverse course every twelve hours, steaming back and forth off the eastern coast of Korea.

On the afternoon of 19 October, just after the first turn about occurred, a rumor that the war was over, swept through all two hundred fifty ships, and for the rest of the day, the troops rejoiced at the "news." It was exhilarating to have been in combat, and now with prospects of more fighting just over the horizon, it came as a relief to learn that it was over.

But when the fleet came around again, heading north instead of south toward Pusan, reality began to sink in. Noncoms and junior officers informed their troops that there had been no truth to the rumors. The landing was still on! And then when the news spread that the reversals in course were to await mine sweeping operations, the Marines became bored with the monotony of the wait, and dubbed the tactical maneuvers, "Operation Yo-Yo."

Finally, on the 25th of October, after twelve days of frustration, Operation Yo-Yo came to an end when the fleet arrived in Wonsan Harbor and prepared for an administrative landing that evening and continuing the next several days. The Marines were further chagrined when they learned that not only had they been pre-empted by ROK forces that had taken Wonsan two weeks earlier, but even Bob Hope and Marilyn Maxwell beat them to their objective, when they performed a USO show on the evening of the 24th. The administrative landing was not completed until October 31. By then, four thousand seven hundred thirty vehicles were moving across the beaches.

The Motor Transport Section set up their truck compound near the Division Command Post, about a mile north of Wonsan. The truck compound was located in a school yard, from where the drivers could begin trucking supplies from the Wonsan piers to various units within the Division. Within a few days, the trucks were ordered north to Hamhung, about sixty road miles up the east coast of North Korea. Hamhung was an important transportation center and had a population of more than eighty five thousand in 1940. It was only a few miles from the large port city of Hungnam, and the fairly modern airfield of Yonpo to the south. It is also on the coastal route connecting North Korea with Soviet Russia. Only one hundred miles to the northwest was the Yalu River, the border with Manchuria (China), over which some thirty five thousand Chinese "volunteers" had already crossed into the mountains of North Korea during those same weeks in October when X Corps was sailing from Inchon and participating in Operation Yo-Yo.

On the 23rd of November, Thanksgiving Day, the trucks delivered all the trappings of a traditional feast to the units within their perimeter. The menu that day included shrimp cocktail, stuffed olives, roast turkey with cranberry sauce, sweet potatoes, fruit salad, fruit cake, mince pie and coffee. And the war news was heartening too! Only the day before the Marines learned that the 17th Regiment of the Army's 7th Infantry Division had reached the Yalu River at Hyesanjin in the northeast. And despite scattered reports of the presence of Chinese soldiers in the vicinity of the Marines, not a single "ChiCom" had been encountered by the Army in its advance to the border. A victorious peace seemed within grasp. It was truly a day for giving thanks.

Just a few days after Thanksgiving on the 27th of November, the Marines began their advance north to the Yalu. Their route of attack would then take them to the southern edge of the Chosin Reservoir, and then northwest to Mupyong-ni and from there, north to the Yalu. Meanwhile, the 7th Infantry Division would advance from the east side of Chosin Reservoir north to the Yalu. Earlier, on Thanksgiving Day, the 1st Battalion of the 7th Marines led the advance, enjoying a belated holiday feast on the 24th.

– Dallace Meehan
Lieutenant Colonel, U.S.A.F. Retired

Chapter One

The Road to the Marines

The Russian colonel, an intelligence officer, walked to where I was sitting helplessly blindfolded, with my arms around the back of the chair, handcuffed. He asked me angrily, "Why don't you confess?" Responding in the way I had been trained to do, in such an eventuality as I now found myself, I interrupted by saying, "I am Nick A. Flores, United States Marine Corps, 1091431." I got a powerful slap for saying that. He continued asking me, "Where is your parachute? Where is your squadron based?"

I replied hastily, "Sir, I am not a pilot." He then added, "If you are not a pilot, why are you wearing a pilot uniform? You are lying to us. We will punish you for lying to us. You are a pilot and you must confess! Confess! Confess!"

He then slapped me on the face with the back of his hand. As a result, he must have cut my lip because I felt someone blot my mouth with what felt like a towel of some kind. They just did not believe what I told them. I knew then, that there would be more unrelenting questions to follow. It was then that I thought: "What in the hell was a Mexican boy from Del Rio, Texas doing in Manchuria?"

As I, Nicanor Abraham, learned in later years, being born in the early thirties was not the most welcome sight for the Flores family of five. It was another mouth to feed. I entered the Flores family on March 20, 1931 and though I was an added burden, there was a lot of excitement in the household.

My birthplace was Del Rio, Texas, a small town near the Mexican border, one hundred and fifty miles southwest of San Antonio. My dad and mom owned a gas station/grocery store, but due to the Depression my father was forced to close the store. He gave too many people credit that could not pay. We moved to San Felipe, on the other side of town, where mom and dad bought a house and dad took a job at Montgomery Ward.

My mother and father were strict. My dad was a sharp dresser, always clean – even his days off from work. He stood about five-foot-eight, husky build, and his hair had started to recede when he was seventeen. On his round face was a ready smile. Everyone in town knew him and he was well liked and respected by the people he worked with.

As for my mother, she was the apple of my eye. She stood four-foot-six, very pretty with light complexion, as we all were, and she kept herself slim and trim. She wouldn't hesitate to let anyone know that she was a housewife. She never went to where my father worked because she believed that a woman belonged at home.

My dad would never go anywhere without my mother except to work. Our entire family went to church together each week. I never heard them raise their voices to one another nor did I hear them argue. My parents had a beautiful relationship.

San Felipe was where I spent my childhood. This is where my father became a member of San Felipe's first Board of Trustees. When I was eight years old, besides attending school, I worked at a slaughterhouse, mowed lawns in the neighborhood and still had time to play cowboys and indians.

When I think back, those years were the most exciting and growing times. I was always doing something to bring money home. My contribution to the family was most welcome because by this time I had a younger brother, Armando. I also had two sisters, Graciella Irma and Suzie, and an older brother Paul.

Irma and I were very close. She stood five-foot-five, slim build, long brown hair and brown eyes to match. She was the typical tomboy; she would rather play sports with the guys than pick up a doll. She was very outspoken, and would let you know what was on her mind. In school, Irma was on the track team.

In 1941, tragedy struck our family. It all started in 1940. Irma had been practicing for the two-hundred-meter run. After running her heart out, someone handed her a soda pop. After drinking approximately half of the can, she collapsed. She was immediately rushed to the hospital, where she was diagnosed with acute pneumonia. Several days later, spots were found on her lungs. New diagnosis – tuberculosis. Devastation overtook our family. The doctors recommended my parents put her in San Angelo Tuberculosis Center, in San Angelo, Texas. She stayed there six months, after which time the doctors told my parents that there was nothing more to do for her. It seemed that the tuberculosis had gone, or was in remission. My father had mentioned to the doctors that the family was planning on moving to California. The doctors told my father that the weather and climate might do Irma some good.

Dad had heard that California was the place to go, especially if one had a family. The opportunity was there for the whole family to work in

My baby picture at 6 months old.

the fields picking fruit and vegetables. There was good money to be made! When school closed for the summer, we headed for California. It took us four or five days to get to San Jose.

Dad was looking forward to making a lot of money, so after a short time we started picking peas, then pears, prunes, and green beans. We had not been in California very long when Irma came down with pneumonia. Back into the hospital she went, this time in San Jose, where she struggled for life for three weeks, until the pneumonia took her life at the young age of sixteen. I will forever miss her.

A short time later dad decided that since we were still in school, he would get a job at Del Monte which was close to our home. A few months after Irma passed away, we went back to Del Rio for a couple of years. In 1942, I met my first love, her name was Carolina Esqueda, "Mito," and it was love at first sight.

Mito was a pretty girl with the prettiest brown eyes. She was very light complected, her hair was shoulder length and was brown and curly. She was very athletic and she joined the cheerleaders so that she would be able to see her school football team, the San Felipe Mustangs. Her personality was cheerful and fun, and a tomboy. If she saw some boys playing football or basketball, she would ask if she could play. I would go to the corner near her house and wait for her to carry her books to school. We had a beautiful relationship. We just loved each other very much, but later found out that her mother was against it.

One evening after her mother had talked to the sheriff and principal about them not letting us see each other, Mito and her best friend decided to run away from Del Rio. They came by my house that evening and Mito whistled for me. I came out and she said, "My love, I am going away. My mother forbids me to see you anymore."

I told her, "You are not going away without me" and then we left Del Rio via Hwy 80. We got a ride to San Antonio where we slept on the side of the road. It was here that I started thinking about my mother and the words that she spoke to me often.

She said, "Abraham, sit here son. I want you to know that when you go somewhere alone, there is someone up there that you can talk to," while pointing to the sky. "Don't ever forget, son. If there is anyone that can help you, it is God. Talk to him and he is ready to listen."

When we woke up, we started hitchhiking and eventually, a couple heading to Dallas picked us up and they let us out on the outskirts of the city. From there we found our way to the road leading to Texarkana. By this time we were very hungry and decided that we would have to find work, so we started asking around. Luckily, a truck with a lot of people in the back stopped and asked if we wanted to pick cotton. That was an offer we could not pass up. After a few days of picking cotton, we were paid, so on our way we went. We passed by Clarksville, Tennessee, Evansville, Indiana, and ended up in Gary, Indiana. On our ride to Gary, in another truck, the driver learned that we were runaways during our conversation.

Once in Gary, the driver called the police and that is how we were apprehended. Unknowingly to us, an All Points Bulletin had been issued on us. We were taken to the police station and from there put on a bus for Del Rio. When we returned home, I was grounded as my punishment. Not long after I came back home, dad and mom said, "Let's go back to California." We moved without my seeing Mito or saying anything to her about leaving Texas. I did not want to go to California and leave Mito; I loved her so much.

In California, I attended thirteen different schools. Every time we moved with the harvesting of fruit or vegetables they took me out of one school and put me into another. In 1945 I got a paper route and cut lawns during the evenings and on weekends. My paper route was delivering the *San Jose Mercury News* early in the morning. Mom would wake me up at 4:30 a.m. and we both would fold the papers for delivery. At 5:30 she would make me a cup of cocoa, give me a cinnamon roll, then off I would go to deliver my papers and after doing that, I would go to school by 7:45.

I used to ride my bike by the post office on the way to the *Mercury News* office and I would see a poster that said "I WANT YOU." I stopped my bike and I kept looking at this man who said "I WANT YOU." Next to that was a poster that said "JOIN THE MARINES." I parked my bike and just stood there looking at the man dressed in a blue uniform, holding a sword with white gloved hands and wearing a white cap. I studied it for a few minutes and I said, "That's what I want to be, a Marine." I got on my bike and went to the newspaper office where I took care of my business, then went by the post office to look again at the Marine, and the man that wanted me. I then hurried home and when I got to my house I could not wait to tell mom.

I ran in the house and said, "Mom, at the post office there's a man that points at me and says he wants me!"

"Where is this man?" she asked.

I said, "At the post office."

"Wait until your father comes home from work and you tell him about this man." Mom was not very happy of what had happened and especially about the man.

At five o'clock that evening, dad drove up and got out of the car. Mom did not wait until he got into the house, she stopped him on the porch. "Pabilto, we have a problem. Abraham says there is a man who wants him. He says that the man points a finger at him and says 'I WANT YOU.' He also says that he is there every day."

Dad was a little reluctant to believe what I had told mom, so he questioned me too. Before he could say anything back to mom, she said, "Come and eat dinner and when we get done, we are going to see about this man who wants him."

While dad is eating, he looks at mom and slightly turned his head to look at me and then says, "What does he say when you go by there?"

"I WANT YOU," I responded.

"Nothing else?" asked dad.

I said, "No."

We finished dinner and my sister asked, "Where are you going?"

Mom replied, "Business," with a loud voice. With dinner over, my mom told my sister to pick up the dishes and that we would be back in awhile. Dad put his hat on. My folks were visibly tense. We piled in the car and I sat in the back. There was not a word spoken all the way to the post office. We got to St. James Park, which is across the street from the post office. Mom says to dad, "Go and see who it is and why he wants my son. Ask his name so we can give it to the authorities." At that time I did not know what dad and mom were suspecting or why they were mad.

Dad and I got out of the car then walked across the street, 1st Street, and we stopped on the sidewalk where I said, "There he is, dad."

As we got closer, dad chuckled and when we got to the poster he let out a big laugh and asked, "Is this the man?"

I replied, "Yes sir." Then he went into hysterics laughing. "Dad," I said, "I want to be one of those guys," pointing to the poster.

Dad says, "He is a Marine."

I replied, "When I grow up, I want to be a Marine. Okay, dad?"

He grabbed me by the hand and we headed for the car, without me saying anything. He said, "I want you to be a Marine."

We got back to the car and as dad reached for the handle on the car, he bent his body from the waist down, just laughing. Mom yells, "Pablito! What's so funny?"

Dad says, "You know who wants him? There is a poster with Uncle Sam on it and he is trying to get men in the service and he is pointing a finger at whoever gets close to the poster. It says 'I WANT YOU.' Uncle Sam represents the United States, meaning our country wants you to join the military service."

Mom had looked unsatisfied by my father's explanation, but as it was a poster, there was no danger. As I sat in the back seat, I thought I would probably get grounded for this wild-goose chase.

When we got home, dad explained what was out there and mom finally agreed that I would make a good Marine. A little later, my dad sat there and explained to my sister and brothers what had happened. After that, I went by there every day and I would say, "Uncle Sam, I am going to be a Marine. You want me. You got me." I was determined that one day I would become a Marine.

While in San Jose, I was cutting lawns, had my paper route and was going to school. I also made many a trip to the store for mom, which usually meant I would buy some candy with whatever change was left. That was a real treat, plus it made going to the store, which took time away from my many other daily adventures, seem worthwhile.

I did not like staying in one place for long, nor did I like not being busy if that led to me getting in trouble. Trouble seemed to be my middle name.

Well anyway, after a few months of doing my thing, tragedy entered our household again. This time it was Gramma Flores. The cable read, "Pablito. Mom dying, come quick." That didn't set very good with my father, as you can imagine. He was devastated. He quickly notified his employer and left for Del Rio. My father loved his mother dearly and waiting for the outcome of his mother's condition was heartbreaking. There were several legal papers and other things to get in order, since he had bought the house for his mother.

Before my father had left for Del Rio, he had made my oldest brother, Paul, head of the house. That in itself didn't set right with me. It didn't take long for me to become his 'go-fer.' Authority had quickly gone to his head. With all the "new authority" going on, I rebelled.

One evening, my brother and I had a big fight about who was the boss. In the end, my mother backed up Paul one hundred percent. Even at this point, I was reluctant to give in. I decided to think about all this and in no time at all, I came to a conclusion – get out of town. One evening I got real mad and headed for town. Not to run away, mind you, but to think things over, again. As I sat in St. James Park, I was trying very hard to be open-minded about the whole problem but in less than five minutes, I was thumbing a ride to Del Rio, Texas.

It wasn't like this was the first time that I ran away. The first time I had two girls with me and made it from Del Rio to Gary, Indiana. Going from San Jose, California to Del Rio was nothing. Somehow, I felt like I was destined to travel. While standing there, with darkness descending, I got a little scared. I quickly reminded myself that I had done it before, so I could do it again. I zipped up my jacket, said a small prayer, then started thumbing to the unknown.

A few hours had passed, as well as several cars, when I started to think this would be as far as I would be going when a car pulled over on the shoulder of the road. A nice man said, "Jump in." As I did just that, he asked where I was going.

I told him, "Los Angeles, and from there, Del Rio, Texas."

The very nice, soft spoken, older man quickly said, "I'll take you as far as Los Angeles and then you can go on your way to Texas."

I replied, "Thank you." Getting to Los Angeles was nothing; getting out was another thing.

The following morning we arrived in Los Angeles. I had fallen asleep and when I woke up, I was ready to go. I was dropped off on Highway 101 and did not know which highway would get me to Phoenix. Luckily, after an hour or so, I got a ride with a middle aged man and his family. He wanted to know where I was heading. I told him, "Phoenix."

He told me, "Well, you are a lucky boy. That is where we are heading." We arrived in Phoenix and the man asked if I was hungry. He was planning on stopping to eat.

I said, "Yes sir, I am."

After finding a restaurant, everyone piled out of the car and entered the restaurant. After a relaxing and filling stop, we all headed for the car. "Where are you going?" he asked.

I quickly said, "El Paso, sir."

"I will drop you off at an intersection that heads south," he said. That hit my ears like a shot in the arm. I was feeling very encouraged and raring to go.

It did not take us long to arrive at the drop-off point. The man steered the car to the side of the road and said, "This is it. Now, you take care of yourself." He reached in his pocket, brought out his hand and outstretched it to me while saying, "You use this fifty cents when hard times come your way. If you get hungry, use this money. OK?"

I said, "OK. Thank you sir."

After closing the car door, they sped off and I was alone again. I might add, a little on the scared side. However, it was too late to turn back now. At this point, I did not know which highway would take me in the right direction but stuck out my thumb anyway.

After a few hours, a vehicle stopped alongside the road. I walked up to the car where a man dressed as a preacher asked me, "Where are you going son?"

I looked up at the sign next to me and I told him, "Globe, Arizona." With a slight smile, he said that was where he was going. At the time, I wondered where Globe, Arizona was but letting this nice man take me there seemed the right thing to do. We headed down the road and I saw a lot of cactus, rocks and a very lonely highway. As we approached an intersection, he slowed the car down and said, "Son, I am going to leave you here. I have to see some people at this ranch, but I'll be back in a few minutes."

I said, "Sure," with assurance that he would be right back.

Here I was, all alone, darkness was engulfing me and I could only hear the sounds of wild animals off in the distance. I looked in both directions and not a single headlight could be seen. I sat on the pavement and exclaimed out loud, "Now what?" While I sat there, I started thinking about mom. I wondered how she was doing with her son running away. I told myself, "She shouldn't have taken Paul's side." This was the only thing I could think of to justify my running away. It made me feel good to know I was doing the right thing.

As I sat trying to figure out my next move, a thought came to mind. My mother always told me, "Son, when you find yourself alone, don't forget there is someone always ready to listen to you. Christ our Lord is always ready to listen. He is there to help you." With that thought, my fears became ever so slight.

Still no preacher, and I was all alone in the desert. I came to the conclusion that I better hit the road. I got up, stretched and then started walking to Globe. After a few hours had passed, I took a look behind me and saw the moon shining so bright. It seemed to be lighting my way to Globe. Continuing my walk, on the white line, I was startled by the howling of coyotes. There hadn't been a noise to be heard before this. I started looking around and noticed how eerie the cactus looked. Like they were coming toward me. I yelled out, "Is anybody out there?" My body started shaking, and then the coyotes started howling again. For unknown reasons, I started whistling but the coyotes didn't stop. I said, "Lord, I hope you're out there. These coyotes sound like they are hungry."

I kept walking and keeping a watch behind me. Those cactuses kept getting closer, so I thought; and this made me a little fearful. A few minutes later I noticed a pair of headlights. That was a relief to know I wasn't alone on the road. No sooner had I thought this when the headlights disappeared into thin air. Did someone go off the road or make a U-turn? I started using bigger steps, and then I turned around and went backwards to make sure no one was following me. The coyotes still made their presence known. A few times I howled back, hoping they would think I was one of them. I don't know how much time passed but I was almost to the top of the hill. I was getting very thirsty but was not going to venture out into the wilderness and try to find some water. I convinced myself to get rid of that thought.

Up ahead was a car parked along side of the road. I quickly sat down on the pavement and tried to come up with a plan of action. I figured there were three choices; one would be to keep walking as if no one was there; or two, go around the car on the opposite side of the road; or three, walk up to the car, knock on the window, and ask them to wake up and please take me to Globe. Ideas number two and three didn't seem the right thing to do so I chose number one.

I started walking and in no time, I was next to the driver's door. I did not expect anyone to be awake so when I heard, "Hi kid. Where are you going?"

I started to shake in my shoes. I answered, "Globe."

He told me, "I took the wrong turn and ended up here. I was tired so I thought I better rest here."

"I saw your headlights about two hours ago and thought the car would be gone by now," I said.

"Come on," he said, "I'll give you a ride to Globe." After driving a few hours, we reached Globe where he dropped me off and then went on his way.

"So this is Globe, Arizona," I told myself as I looked at the big city with population of two hundred. I needed to find a place where I could rest. That did not take me long and once I sat down, I realized how tired my feet were. I also looked at my shoes and saw that they had seen better days. My left shoe was pitiful. The sole was gone and the right shoe was not much better. The sole on that one had come lose up to the heel, and every time I took a step, it flapped.

I felt hungry – no, starving is the better word for it. I hadn't had anything to eat for about fourteen hours. I reached in my pocket for the fifty cents the man gave me in Phoenix. Still holding on to the coin, I asked,

"What can I buy with fifty cents?" I paused for a few minutes then came to one conclusion. Save the fifty cents for hard times in case they should arise.

I got up and looked at the road. It sure looked like the one I had just come from. One good thing about it, it was daytime and no howling coyotes. The cactus was still there, but not moving. I then started on my next lap to the unknown. I picked a spot where I would be seen but not in the way of traffic.

I started thumbing a ride and I walked out of the big city of Globe, Arizona. I guess no one was leaving Globe, for I ended up walking five to six miles without anyone stopping. I continued on and then I felt my left foot getting hot. I looked down and realized that the sole of my left shoe had come off. The top lace of my shoe was still hanging on. I then looked on the side of the road for something to wrap my foot with. As I left the pavement in search of cardboard or a rag to tie my shoe, I looked towards Globe and to my surprise, I saw a pickup truck coming into view. I rushed back to the pavement, hopping on my right shoe, keeping the left foot up in the air. With all the commotion going on, I accidentally hopped into the thorns of a cactus. I fell down, tears in my eyes, then tried to remove the thorns out of my foot. While doing that, the pickup that I had spotted earlier, stopped. A man got out of the truck and asks, "Are you having problems, son?"

While wiping the tears away, I told him, "Kind of."

"What are you doing out here in the desert, by yourself?"

"I am heading for Del Rio, Texas."

He reached out, took a hold of my arm, lifted me up and helped me to the road. "Well son, I am not going that far but I'll take you as far as Tucson." With an odd expression on his face, he said, "You have been walking for a long ways. You have worn out your left shoe and the right one is ready to go too."

"Yes sir" was all I replied.

With the conversation over, I hobbled to the truck and away we went. Down the road a ways, the man commented, "You look tired and sleepy."

My answer was, "Yes sir."

"Here, take this cushion and lay it by the door. Get some sleep because you have a long way to go."

I told him, "Thank you, sir." I realized that I was tired and hungry, but when you consider how far I had gone, I wasn't in to bad of shape. About five hours later, we reached Tucson.

As I woke up, he asked me, "Are you hungry?"

"Yes, sir!" Those were beautiful words to my ears.

He pulled into a restaurant parking lot and stopped. While getting out of the car, he asked me, "What would you like to have?" Before I had a chance to answer, he asked, "What about a hamburger and a cola?"

"That sounds OK," I replied.

He went in the restaurant and in no time, he came out with a hamburger for each of us, plus a cola for me and he had coffee. After we finished eating he said, "I'll drop you off on the road to El Paso."

I thanked him for the ride, the food and the sleep that I was able to get. Once we arrived at my drop-off point, we shook hands. I told him, "You know what? I am going to be a Marine when I grow up."

His reply was, "You'll make a good one, no doubt about it. So long, son, and good luck." We shook hands once more then I got out of the truck. After waving so long, he drove off.

I crossed the highway in front of where he let me off and I saw a sign that showed the mileage to El Paso, two hundred and ninety miles. To me, that might as well have been around the world! I took another look at my feet and realized that the upper part of my shoe had come off. It was just dangling so I pulled it off. I moved to the corner of the road and I started thumbing a ride.

It took three rides to get to El Paso. When I got there, I noticed that the Mexican kids were barefooted. With the shape of my shoes, I fit right in. Outside of El Paso, I thumbed a ride. Some people picked me up. They asked me where I was going. I told them Del Rio, Texas. The man driving said, "We're going to Dallas, so we will drop you off in Van Horn. Is that okay?"

"Yes sir. That is good enough."

Three hours later, we pulled in to Van Horn. I was dropped off next to a sign that let me know I had three hundred and five miles left to go. After my ride took off, my stomach let it be known that food was needed. Lucky for me, a car pulled over and a man rolls down his window. He asked, "Are you going to Del Rio?"

With a big smile, I yelled, "Yes, sir!" I couldn't wait to see Mito and tell her that I was going to be a Marine. I sure had missed her.

The man told me, "Hop in" and I didn't hesitate. No more thumbing a ride for this kid. Before we started on our journey to Del Rio, he filled up his gas tank. On our way we went. He asked me, "What's your name?"

I looked at him and answered, "Abraham."

"Abraham is in the Bible, isn't he?" he asked in a loud voice.

"Yes sir."

"What are you going to do in Del Rio?"

"I am going to see my father."

While the conversation had been going on, we both noticed the sky getting darker in front of us, and lightning was noticeable. A few hours passed and we noticed sprinkles on the windshield.

He said, "It looks like we're going to get some rain." No sooner had he said that when a downpour started; I mean cats and dogs. The wipers couldn't get the water off the windshield fast enough. He slowed down, which made me feel better.

We reached Sanderson, which was about one hundred twenty miles from Del Rio. The streets were getting flooded. The man exclaimed, "Let's get some gas and get the hell out of here! We need to cross the bridge before it's washed away." After getting the fuel, we took off like scared rabbits. About thirty miles down the road, he stopped on a hill. The lightning was scary and the thunder was loud. He then said, "Let's wait here and see if the storm passes!" The storm never did let up, so we continued on to Del Rio.

We came upon some flooded areas of the road, but by going very slow, we were able to cross. Thankfully the current wasn't severe yet. About an hour later we came upon Devil's River, now called Big Canyon, and the water level was very close to flood stage. Another three feet and it would have washed the bridge away. We stopped about one hundred feet from the bridge and it was a frightening sight. I was scared and I could tell by the look on his face that he was scared also.

He asked me, "You want to cross it?"

I replied, "That's up to you."

"If we stay here much longer, the bridge will be washed away and we'll be stranded. We are going to have to cross now."

"Let's go," I told him. We both prayed.

The bridge was approximately one hundred eighty feet long. Once across, you went up a hill where the water wouldn't wash you away. He backed up the vehicle a hundred feet, then floored the gas pedal. Away we went, at a high rate of speed, looking in no other direction but straight ahead. The lightning was illuminating the way, with wind pushing the vehicle side to side. We never slowed down and when we got to about thirty feet from the bridge, we saw the bridge swaying side to side. At that moment, my heart was in my throat. We were almost across the bridge when I felt the bridge sway. I prayed to myself, "Lord, please get us across."

Before long, we were headed up the hill and then a feeling of relief came over us. We knew our mission had been successful. He stopped the car at the top of the hill. We both prayed, trying to get ourselves together after that frightening experience. I asked his name and he replied, "Raymond." I wanted to know because he had just safely brought me through a terrifying ordeal.

We continued on and soon came to the town of Langtry. Judge Roy Bean got his start from here, as the legend goes. We were advised from some local towns people that parts of Highway 90 were flooded. We continued on our way to Del Rio, being ever so cautious. An hour and a half later, we were in Del Rio. Raymond asked me where I would like to be dropped off and I told him the outskirts of town. On our way to that destination, we saw sand bags in front of stores, stacked high. The sidewalks were not visible due to the water level. We were forced to drive slow because of six to eight inches of water on the road. When we finally got to the intersection where I wanted to be dropped off at, I was only six blocks from home.

It had been nine long days since my adventure started and was it worth it? Yes – every minute. I learned to survive, deal with the elements, and had experienced fear. I met some wonderful people who had been there to lend a hand to someone in need. I had endured through the difficult times and I managed to end up in Del Rio with my fifty cents still in my pocket.

I bid Raymond farewell, as he put his arms around me. "You are a brave kid, Abraham. Thanks for your company to Del Rio. It was a great trip. Thank you."

I wished him luck and said, "I hope we get to meet again some day. Take care of yourself and go with God. So long." He sped off headed to San Antonio.

The rain was coming down steady and I was soaked. It took me about thirty minutes to walk to my house, putting the time close to midnight. I knocked on the front door with no answer. I am shaking from head to foot, "Come on dad, open up," I yelled. I soon heard footsteps and then he opened the door.

"What are you doing here? Your mother is worried sick about you running away." Then I saw a grin form on his face and he let me in. I took off my wet clothes, handed them to my father, and then he put them by the heater to dry. I wrapped a blanket around me in hopes of getting warm and so I would stop shivering. I slept next to my father.

In the morning, I put on my dry clothes. My father left for town and once again I was on my own. I couldn't wait to see Mito. Heading toward the door, I remembered that I did not have any shoes. Just then, my father returns home because the whole downtown area was flooded. He noticed that I was ready to head to the front door and he asked, "Where are you going?"

I replied, "To see my friends."

"No," he said, "You stay here and wait till the water goes down and then you can go."

I eventually saw Mito and my friends. I was happy once again. I also learned that a friend of my father was going to drive up to Sister Bay, Wisconsin, to pick cherries. That sounded like an adventure that I would like to participate in, so I convinced my father that the best thing to do would be to let me go along with his friend. He reluctantly gave me his permission to go.

I was fourteen when I picked cherries in Wisconsin. When my father's friend and I arrived at the cherry farm, we went right to work. After one day, I knew that picking cherries was not my thing. I realized that it took a lot of them to fill a bucket. When I made up my mind, I took off for Del Rio once again.

I was luckier this time in getting rides. After two different rides, I ended up in the outskirts of Oklahoma City. As I am thumbing a ride, walking along the highway, I didn't see any cars coming. This was a great time for a break. While I sat there resting, I heard a train whistle which sounded like it was coming in my direction. The tracks were only a block away. A thought came to my mind. I had never ridden a train as a hobo, so I said to myself, "Why not?" The train sounded to be moving slowly, so I walked to the train track, waited patiently for the train with suitcase in hand. I soon saw a rail car with the door open. I walked along with the train, with plans to first throw in my suitcase and then I would jump in. No problem throwing my suitcase in, but when it came time for me to jump in, the train had started going faster. By the time I had gotten up the nerve to jump, the train was going too fast. All I could do was stand there and wave good bye to my suitcase.

Well, I got a ride to San Antonio and then to Del Rio. My father was in Del Rio and he asked me, "Why are you not picking cherries?"

I told him, "They were too small. It took a long time to fill a bucket, so I quit and hitchhiked back here."

My dad let me stay with him a week, and I got to see Mito again. We saw each other almost every day. When my father decided to send me back to San Jose, I told Mito that I would be back.

I went back to San Jose on the bus, and when I arrived my mom said, "Don't run away anymore. You have to go to school." I told her I would not do it again. I was "sentenced" to school for two more years. I got to the tenth grade and I asked mom and dad if I could join the Marines. They said they would think about it. Dad was still in Del Rio and said he would be coming home in two weeks. Mom said, "When your dad comes home, ask him if we can sign for you to join the Marines." Well, he came back, and with their blessings they signed and I was on my way to becoming a Marine at seventeen.

Chapter Two
Destination: Korea

I was sworn in on December 14, 1948. I was to depart to San Francisco in four days and then report to San Diego Recruit Depot. I, along with twenty other recruits, left by train and arrived that evening. I realized then that my dream of being a Marine had finally come true. Boot camp in the Marine Corps is not easily forgotten. For some eighty-plus recruits, it was hard to take; the toughness, the loneliness that leads to getting homesick. For me, I had already experienced tough times as I was growing up.

It was during the first day of training that I would lose my birth name. My drill instructor was asking for our complete names and when he got to me, he asked, "What is your name?"

I replied, "Nicanor Abraham Flores."

With a loud voice he shouted back to me, "If you think that I am going to call you Nicanor Abraham Flores, you are mistaken. From this day forward, you will be called Nick A. Flores! Is that understood?"

I had no choice but to say, "Yes, sir."

In March of 1949, I graduated from basic training as a private first class (Pfc.). A few of the important things I learned from my Marine training were self-esteem, to be self-sufficient and to take pride in being the best. I also learned to be tough and do whatever it takes to stay alive. If there is something to be done, do it without expecting someone else to do it for you.

After basic training, I spent my ten-day leave in Del Rio and saw Mito every day. This went all to fast and had come to an end. From there I took a bus to Camp Pendleton Marine Corps Base, Oceanside, California, home of the 1st Marine Division. While on the bus, I remember people looking me up and down. This did not bother me for I was so proud of my dress blues. I felt so good about what I had become. I arrived at Camp Pendleton on March 25, 1949. I was assigned to Headquarters Company, 1st Service Battalion, 1st Marine Division.

That evening the recruits were lined up in a single file. A 1st lieutenant and staff sergeant picked every other man for motor transport drivers while the others were to be "frog men" in the under water demolition unit. I was pleased to be chosen a truck driver as that had been my first choice. Our driver's school started the following week, lasting about two and a

My graduation picture after I had finished basic training.

*Combat training for maneuvers
at Camp Del Mar in California.*

*On leave after graduation
from basic training.*

half weeks. During this training, we learned to drive a variety of military vehicles, especially the low-boy used to haul tanks and heavy equipment.

Now that I had been assigned officially to Motor Transport Section of Headquarters Company, 1st Service Battalion, my job started. I would truck supplies to various units within the Division. They expected our trucks to be kept in tip-top shape. We were to check the oil before ever considering mounting the truck. We also did all the maintenance such as washing the truck. Tires were to be kept clean and they must have the correct amount of air pressure.

Every Friday morning, at 0900, was vehicle inspection. We were to be ready, standing by our truck when we saw the company commander and motor transport sergeant come into view. After the inspection, if we had passed it, they would dismiss us. This usually occurred about 1500 hrs. Whoever had been dismissed would make a dash for the barracks to shower and shave, for going on pass. For those who did not pass inspection, they were grounded and spent the day cleaning trucks and the Motor Pool grounds, standing guard duty, or working at the mess hall.

Early in 1950, my unit and two-thirds of the First Marine Division were introduced to an exercise called maneuvers. They were held at Camp Del Mar, just across the road from Camp Pendleton. Some of us inexperienced Marines didn't have a clue what the maneuvers would be like. We would play war games, eat C-rations and pretend we were in a real war. We landed on the beach at Del Mar. This was our introduction to amphibious landing. Little did I know how useful this training would become. All that we trained for would be put to a test in a place called Inchon on September 15, 1950.

Toward the last days of May, the unit was told that in June there would be a General Inspection, including dress blues, in order to help celebrate the making of the movie, "Sands of Iwo Jima," starring John Wayne. The orders were as follows; all dress blues were to be cleaned and pressed, all brass emblems, buckles and buttons were to be polished, shoes to be spit-shined and cap and gloves cleaned to "snow white." They would inspect rifles, so they needed to be properly cleaned. Last, lockers should be in proper order. Good luck! For the next two days, we prepared for the big event.

For three to four hours, I and the rest of the Marines, formed up on the parade ground, stood at "parade rest" and "attention," and then we "passed in review" in front of the grandstand. The host officer was the camp commander, General Craig, who was accompanied by none other than John

Wayne, John Agar, Forest Tucker, and various other Hollywood dignitaries and Marine Corps brass. Unfortunately, the day was hot and humid, and several Marines passed out in the heat. I had been fortunate enough while a young man to be exposed to tremendous heat out in the fields where our family picked vegetables and fruit.

During my stay at Camp Pendleton, I wrote Mito quite frequently but would not receive letters from her. The reason for this was not one that I could find so I kept busy. During the weekend passes where I did not go home, I would often pull duty for someone that had been willing to pay me for the weekend pass. When I was not pulling duty, I would run errands to the PX, (Post Exchange), to get sandwiches and drinks for the guys shooting dice and playing poker. They always gave me more than enough money to cover items. When I returned with the requested items, they told me to keep the change. During a month's time, I would end up making almost equivalent to my Marine Corps pay. This had been an arrangement that worked well for all concerned!

On the weekends when nothing was going on and I had a weekend pass, I would go see my family. My transportation was either the bus or hitchhiking. Occasionally using the bus system, I arrived back to base late by fifteen minutes.

On one specific weekend I had gone to San Antonio since it was a long weekend, but took longer to get there and return. I ended up at base two and one-half days late! This was due to being in an accident involving the car that stopped to pick me up while I was hitch-hiking. I had spent most of those two and one half days in the hospital although the Marine Corps did not seem to appreciate this fact. As a result of my lateness, I was confined to base, forfeited twenty dollars a month for two months, and pulled extra duty such as working in the mess hall or whatever I was ordered to do. Thinking back on that time, I did not realize that these infractions would cause such suffering and severe consequences for the rest of my life.

On June 25, 1950, my brother Paul got married. The reception was held at mom and dad's house, and I was among those that attended. It was late afternoon when I received a hand delivered cable from the 1st Marine Division, stating that I was to report immediately back to base. I very quickly gathered my things, bid everyone farewell and left for the base.

Returning to the base, I was told to get my truck and gear ready to be shipped out to Kobe, Japan. Everyone was excited to be going overseas. In the next three weeks we took trucks to San Diego Harbor to be loaded aboard a ship. We had worked hard each day and night to get the equipment in shape; changed oil, put on new tires if needed, got out tarps for the trucks and made sure the engines were in tip-top shape.

After that was finished, we were told to get our gear together, clean our rifles, and send home belongings that were not going overseas. On August 17, 1950, we embarked aboard *USS Meigs* and sailed the next day for Kobe, Japan. Many of us had never been on a ship, and our stomachs were not cooperating very well. We spent fifteen days of leaning over the rails and vomiting.

We arrived and disembarked at Kobe on September 1. During the nine days we were there, we bought souvenirs to send home, wrote letters and mingled with the Japanese. On September 10, we boarded the *USS Union*. All passes were canceled and no one was allowed to leave. The next day we loaded food, fuel, and all the provisions that we were to use once we landed in Korea. There was scuttlebutt that we were to land in Inchon. That was news to us as some of us had not heard about Korea until they mentioned that North Korea had invaded South Korea. Some did not know where it was.

I know, through many conversations, that many of us were excited that we were going to war. After all those exercises and maneuvers, we were going to find out if we learned anything from it. A few days after sailing, we were told that we would meet with the other ships at the location where we were to make the landing at Inchon. We arrived the morning of September 13. This was the first time I had seen the concentrated naval might of the United States. These ships were all sizes and shapes but the most memorable was "Big Mo," the Battleship *Missouri*. We stood at port-side saluting the ship as she got in place to fire her sixteen-inch guns. It seemed that the whole world shook when they went off. By the evening of the fourteenth, there were rocket ships firing at the Inchon beaches. All ships were firing their guns. What a sight to remember!

Unbeknownst to us at the time, General McArthur and his staff had decided that the island of Wolmi-do, at the mouth of Inchon harbor, was to be taken before the main landing because the enemy garrison there might be able to disrupt the landing. So the Navy gun boats fired on Wolmi-do most of the night and the following morning. By this time Wolmi-do looked like a huge bonfire.

That evening after we ate dinner, we were all briefed on the landing and given our instructions. I then went up on deck to see the ships firing at the location where we were to land. It looked like the Fourth of July, especially with the ships firing rockets. Most of us had never seen such a spectacular demonstration of American firepower. After watching the fireworks, some of us went down below to the third deck, which was our quarters.

Gunny Sergeant Edward Opiot was our transport sergeant. He was a veteran of World War II, a Marine who went by the book; expected the best from us and demanded excellence out of his drivers. He stood about five-foot-six, mustached and all the proudness of being a Marine showed. He wore his clothes tight, with creases in his shirts and pants. He was a gentle man that could become stern when necessary and he very seldom was angered by any mistakes we made. He would simply take you aside, then explain to you what you had done wrong and how to correct it.

I went up to the second deck, after a few minutes of resting, to check on my truck. I wanted it to be in good running condition when I made the landing. After starting it and making sure the nightlights worked, I checked the tires. Having completed this, I went down to my bunk and was told we would get our instructions about the landing in the morning.

The following morning, Sergeant Opiot, accompanied by Warrant Officer Givens, who said, "Okay, this is it. This is the moment you have been waiting for. The landing is to be at 0530 and as of this minute, the ship's guns are pounding the heck out of the beach. So what I want to express to you is to be alert, listen to commands, and for God's sake, keep your rifle at your side at all times no matter what – your life depends on it. It's a new experience to a lot of you Marines. You have never been in a real war. Just remember what you learned on maneuvers at Del Mar Beach. This will be the last time I see a lot of you, so be calm and use your head, don't be stupid and try to be a hero. Let's bow our heads in a moment of silence." He then said, "Amen" and walked away.

We stood at attention as he left, and Sergeant Opiot asked us to stand at ease and that he had a few words to say to all of us. He started by saying, "You were trained to take orders, don't try to do things on your own. This is a real war. You can get killed out there. This is what we will be doing: Lights will go out at 2000 hours, you get some sleep if you can" as he chuckled and grinned. "The morning reveille is at 0300 hours. You will be at the mess hall by 0330. At 0400, I want you to get your gear together and put it in your truck. You then get on top deck and you wait for your truck. When your truck is brought out, you will be called on the loud speaker. It will be lowered onto the landing craft. You will go down on the nets, and you will mount your truck, and you will then start your truck immediately, as they release the cables. You will put on the emergency brake and don't turn off the motor. As soon as you're loaded, the landing craft will go to a location; circle till all the landing craft have been loaded with trucks, supplies, and the troops; then you will approach the beach when the flares go off to signal the go ahead for landing."

Just then someone asked, "What happens then as we hit the beach?" Sergeant Opiot replied, "And then you're on your own."

Everyone then said, "Thanks a lot!"

"That's it men. Good luck and be careful. God be with you. Now you're dismissed. Get some rest and try to get some sleep."

After being dismissed, a lot of us went topside to watch the fireworks. The ships were pounding the beach with everything they had – cruisers and the battleship "Big Mo" continued to make themselves known. The aircraft carrier *Boxer* was also there with her jets and Corsairs; they were taking off and doing bomb runs into Inchon factories. We could see the city of Inchon aglow. It was getting dark and it was a spectacular scene with all the fireworks flashing from the guns pounding the beach. I decided that I had seen enough so I went down to the lower deck, to my bunk. I decided to write a letter to my mother and father to let them know I was okay. I wasn't afraid of the landing – I was more preoccupied thinking "what if." What if my truck stalls when the ramp goes down or if I get hit with all this ammo on my trailer, then what? The lights on the lower deck flickered to let us know we had ten minutes before lights out. It was at this time I decided I would talk to God and tell him that I was going to leave my life in his hands. If it were for me to die for my country, let me die as a Marine and with honor, and let my country and parents be proud of me. As I was saying my prayer, the lights flickered again.

Henry E. Ellis and Grady M. Stroman were across the aisle from me. Nearby were Theodore R. Wheeler and Leon Roebuck. Little did I know that Theodore (Ted) Wheeler would become an inspiration to me in the near future. Ted had arrived at our outfit just before we shipped out to Korea when the reserves were called from Arkansas. He was a husky five-foot-ten kid, with red hair and a thick moustache. He resembled Stalin. Ted had a heart of gold and was always ready to help anyone in trouble. He was liked by everyone that came in contact with him. His nickname became Arkie.

Ellis asked me, "Are you scared?"

I replied, "Not really, I'm only concerned about my truck stalling at the landing!"

Just then Stroman said, "Well, we'll see what happens in the morning." The lights went out and he said, "Good night you guys and good luck." We decided to get some shuteye, but of course, we couldn't get any sleep with all the commotion going on out there with the ships firing away. It was a very restless night, but some of us were able to get a few winks between booms and the rocking of the ship.

Reveille sounded and it seemed so loud like there was a bugle going off in my ear. After getting dressed, many of us headed to the mess hall where we ate bacon, ham, eggs, pancakes and had milk or coffee to drink. Most of the guys were through eating when Sergeant Opiot came in. He told us, "Okay men, as soon as you are finished, you are to go get your packs, ammunition and weapons. Make sure you load your rifle before loading your truck.

A day before the landing we had been issued three bandoleers with twelve clips of cartridges each. Sergeant Opiot was very specific. "As soon as you are loaded on the landing craft, take your M1s off safety. If not, you will have problems."

As he finished talking to us, we all went to our bunks and got our packs ready. By this time it was 0400, and we went up on deck and stood in a platoon formation. Sergeant Opiot said, "When your truck is called by number, you start going down the net. Now don't forget what I said. As the truck is loaded, start your motor, warm the engine and you stay put. When you hit the beach there will be someone there to tell you where to go, so there won't be any confusion. There will be a banner with Headquarters, 1st Service Battalion, and there will be an arrow where to park. Get out of the truck, take your M1 and leave the truck running, then take cover. I will be there as soon as all the trucks are unloaded. Once again, good luck." Sergeant Opiot knew that he had a lot of young Marines on his hands. A lot of us had no experience so he kept repeating commands hoping they would sink into our heads.

It was 0500 hours. They had unloaded a few trucks and then came my name on the loud speaker. "Nick Flores, your truck is ready."

Someone in the column said, "Okay Nick, give them hell."

I replied, "If the gooks get in my way, I'll run them over." They all laughed.

The weather was cool, hardly any wind that I can remember, as I was going down the net to my truck. I had a hell of a time getting down because my M1 wouldn't stay on my shoulder. It kept hitting my forearm and almost made me fall off the net. God forbid that you fell down and

Landing craft circling before landing at Inchon.

landed on the landing craft forty feet below. With the truck loaded, about thirty Combat Marines joined me on the LCVP ready for the landing, and then I didn't feel so alone.

I started my truck, then took my M1 off-safety. As I was doing this, the LCVP left the side of the ship. We joined the rest of the landing craft that were circling, waiting for the rest. So we too waited for the flare to proceed to the beach.

As we circled, we saw the flare go up, and the LCVPs made a few more circles and lined up in waves. It was grand. Nevertheless, I can't remember exactly where I was, yet there I was in the middle of it all! Bullets and mortar fire were coming from the beach. I just sat there, grabbing the wheel of my truck and revving the motor so as not to have it stall on me.

This section of the beach was known as Blue Beach. I saw a LCVP explode in flames right before my eyes. Marines were jumping into the water hollering for help, and there was nothing any of us could do but just keep on going. I could see fire about one hundred feet past the beach where the ships had been firing on Inchon. It was still dark at 0540 hours. The skipper of the LCVP yelled at us and said, "Okay fellows, this is it."

I heard him, and said, "Lord, bless these Marines who are undertaking the task of landing for the cause of freedom." As I finished, I felt my heart in my throat, pounding away, and a thought flashed through my mind and I wondered, am I going to be the next fatality? I then said, "I know you won't forsake us in this time of need, Lord."

As I finished my prayer, the ramp went down and the Combat Marines that were with me hit the beach and I followed. Going over the ramp I saw a Marine with a small flashlight signaling me to drive forward and to the left, about one hundred fifty yards from the beach. I stopped the truck and grabbed my M1 as some bullets hit my truck from beyond where I parked. The beach was cluttered with Marines, some hurt and yelling, "I've been hit." As I was taking cover I could see the tanks coming off the LCVP. As they approached the beach their guns were shooting at forward Korean positions. Then I saw the tanks with flame throwers. That's a sight to see in real life. Dawn broke. We saw wave after wave of landing craft unloading heavy equipment: bulldozers, tanks, graders, supplies of ammo, food, clothing, and medical equipment, as well as F-86 Sabres flying in forward position and dropping napalm.

My heart finally started to beat normally as daylight started to break, and I knew I was going to be all right. I looked up and said, "Thanks."

Landing at Inchon – first wave of Marines, 5:31 a.m. September 15, 1950.

Chapter Three

The Chosin Reservoir

After securing Inchon, we were trucking supplies to the perimeter of Ascom City and then Kimpo Airfield. We were working day and night for the Marines who were moving to take Seoul.

We were trucking from Inchon where they were unloading the LST and bringing the supplies to the beach. It was a hectic operation; the Marines were advancing very rapidly and our company of trucks couldn't keep up with the supplies of ammo, fuel, C-rations and the supplies that the Division needed. We were driving sixteen hours straight.

On September 28, at the truck compound, we heard the good news that the X Corps and Marines had taken Seoul. While this was going on, Henry Ellis and I were to haul food supplies to Kimpo Airport. When I got there, I realized that my cargo consisted of Hershey bars and Baby Ruths. The guys unloading these cases of candy bars slipped a box of Hersheys into my cab. I was very thankful for this kind gesture. It beat the heck out of C-rations! After trucking day and night, we had lost track of time. They had released me from duty for eight hours of sleep time and after only five hours of shuteye, they told me that South Korea was back in our hands. The X Corps and the Marines had reached the 38th Parallel and pushed the North Korean Army back to that line. This news gave a lot of us the feeling that our mission had been completed and the next step would be to load all the equipment, personnel and head for Inchon. There, we would, as the rumor had it, head for Wonsan. The excitement mounted as they told us to pick up all equipment, gas drums, water tanks etc. We would be hauling the material to the beach for loading aboard ships and LSTs. After the cleanup had been completed, we loaded our trucks and sailed out of Inchon Harbor. Aboard ship the scuttlebutt fueled and before long the feeling was that we would be heading home – wrong. We departed from Inchon, Korea, on the *USS Union* AKA 106, on the 17th of October. We disembarked at Wonson, Korea, on the 26th of October. After getting to Wonson, we set up our compound near the 1st Marine Division Command Post (CP).

While we were there, unloading the equipment, we noticed the temperature had changed drastically. It was cold, and soon we were told to put on our parkas, and they would soon issue cold weather boots. After getting settled in our compound, they sent us to the quartermaster to pick up our cold weather gear.

We were given orders to set up at the school ground, near the CP. This would facilitate the transportation of supplies to and from the CP and the division units. We had been very lucky to have been selected to be at the school, as it was only a quarter of a mile from the CP.

After completing the task of trucking supplies from Wanson, only a few days had passed and we were to move to Hamhung. There we would set up at a school outside the city limits, where Headquarters Company, 1st Service Battalion was housed with 1st Tank Battalion and Supply Company. The school made a good base for our trucks as it was accessible to the roads in every direction as well as to and from the city of Hamhung. The school playground was large enough to hold about thirty trucks and also jeeps and trailers. We were housed in schoolrooms, six men to a room.

Thanksgiving day was the 23rd and we made a run to Hamhung to get supplies for the great day of Thanksgiving. We distributed supplies to different outfits that were within our perimeter. When that was finished, the division indulged in a Thanksgiving feast of turkey with all the trimmings.

On November 25, 1950, we were told that we must gas up our trucks and get them in good running condition. We were to make a run to Hagaru-ri and when they gave the orders, we would pick up our supplies and the MPs.

Our 1st sergeant got us together and read off the names of the drivers who would go on the run to Hagaru-ri. Corporal Wheeler, Pfc. Ellis, Pfc. Stroman, Pfc. Roebuck and I were called. On the morning of November 28, 1950, we left Hamhung for Hagaru-ri with the convoy commanded by Major Seeley of Division Headquarters. Warrant Officer McCool was also with us. We reached Koto-ri where the 1st Marine Regimental Command Post was, and other convoys were waiting to go to Hagaru-ri. They informed us that we could not go ahead to Hagaru-ri or back to Hamhung; we were to stay there and wait till they formed another convoy. It was cold, so we tried to keep warm by going inside the tents that had been set up for the drivers. There were Army and Marines that came from Hamhung in convoys that were also told to stay. That night we settled down at Koto-ri.

The next morning, November 29, the men were standing around fires trying to stay warm. When the cook yelled "Chow down" there was a mad dash to get breakfast. Although we received small portions of powdered egg with toast, it sure hit the spot. Since everyone was drinking coffee, the cooks could not keep enough made. Finally, we completely ran out.

As we are sipping our last swallow of coffee, we heard someone yelling, "The road is clear. The road is clear. Man your trucks." As we headed for our trucks we heard, "Gather around here men."

This voice was from Colonel Chesty Puller, Commander of the 1st Marine Regiment. He had a few campaigns under his belt, was stocky built, very aggressive and had a style of his own like no other. He spoke to us with pride, determination and authority, "I don't care if the Army is going or not, but we, the Marines, are going at any cost! Our Marines need those supplies now, so let's get to it."

All truck drivers made a mad dash to their trucks and Sergeant Pettit gathered his military police, who were going to set up a stockade in Hagaru-ri. Sergeant Pettit and I were told to roll and that we would be the lead truck. That did not sound good to me or my passengers. This was about 1200 hours on November 29, 1950. About two to three miles out of Koto-ri, we came up behind an Army convoy that had encountered enemy fire, so together our convoys headed for Hagaru-ri, fighting some snipers as we moved to our destination.

A little ways down the road we were fired upon, so we stopped the convoy and returned fire. Someone yelled and pointed, "They're over there in that ravine." We all started shooting in that direction. Consequently, our return fire made them retreat. Without hesitation, the Major said, "Mount up" and we went toward our destination.

Due to the snow and ice on the ground from previous storms, traction was limited so we were forced to continue at a slow pace. As the convoy moved north to Hagaru-ri, about four miles out of Koto-ri, we came under sniper fire. I was in the lead truck and Sergeant Pettit was my passenger. Sergeant Pettit was a tech sergeant (gunny) for the MP Co. in Korea, and all-Marine. He stood about five-foot-ten, thin and very light complected with scattered freckles. He served in Tarawa and Saipan, and had become a POW under the Japanese for two and a half years. His friends knew him as Tex, which was an appropriate nickname for a man who was born in Brownsville, Texas and spoke with an obvious Texas accent. When he spoke to you, you were never unsure what he had said for he was direct and looked you right in the eyes. As we were slowly moving, Sergeant Pettit asked me if I had some coffee to which I said, "Yes." I then reached for my canteen and handed it to him. The Sarge grabbed the canteen and poured himself a cup of coffee. As he did that, he lifted the canteen and asked me if he could pour me one. I said, "No thanks, Sarge." It was cold and though a cup of coffee sounded good to me, it was not the proper thing to do, as I was having a rough time keeping the truck on the road with both hands. The road was icy and a slippery mess so we had to keep on the center of the main supply route. This main supply route had been designated as the road our trucks were to travel to transport all needed supplies for our troops at the Chosin Reservoir. There was only two feet on each side of the road so if you veered too much off the road, you would end up in two feet of snow with ice on the sides of the gully.

As Sergeant Pettit was taking a mouth full of coffee, we heard a "bang" like metal hitting metal and then we realized that the engine had stopped. The truck was just rolling without power. After a few seconds Sarge said, "What was that Nick?"

I replied, "I don't know but I think the engine was hit." The Sarge told me to get it going as I tried to turn the motor over but nothing happened.

I tried everything to get the engine started but without success. In those few seconds we heard more rifle fire and then we knew the enemy had zeroed-in on us. They hit the windshield and some bullets hit the door narrowly missing Sergeant Pettit. He then heard the MPs in the rear of the truck, yelling "Let's get the hell out of here and take cover." They scrambled to the snow taking cover in the ditch next to the road.

Sergeant Pettit and I furiously tried to get the truck engine to start. Just then we saw mortar rounds falling about thirty to fifty yards from the truck, then the truck behind me blows its horn for me to move. He starts pushing on the trailer, hooked up to my truck, trying to push me off the road. Just then Sergeant Pettit yelled, "Let's get the hell out of the truck!" We were scrambling to get our gear while opening the doors. In those seconds, a mortar round hit close to the truck and trailer, capsizing it, as we fell to the ground.

I fell on the crest of the ditch, and that is when I felt my back snap with pain. I also felt a sting in my arm but everything was happening so fast that I did not realize shrapnel had hit me. As Sergeant Pettit and I are scrambling on the ground, looking for cover, we dashed to the ditch then crawled about thirty feet to the rear of the convoy, which was getting fired upon from the ridge.

Approximately half way down the ditch toward the rear of the convoy, we heard an explosion. Turning in that direction we saw the truck that was pushing mine off the road, had received a direct hit. It was on fire, as was my truck. By this time we had lost sight of the tanks that had been in front of us. The Chinese were smart because they knew we could not turn around so they knocked out the first and last truck in the convoy.

Things were in total chaos. Bullets were flying everywhere, trucks were burning, and men were yelling that they had been hit. Not many of us had been prepared for this. Most of us were horrified and scared. As dusk settled in, the sunlight leaving us, we scrambled to take cover on the west side of the convoy behind the trucks and equipment that were not burning. All we could do was retaliate and take cover wherever we could. The Chinese knowing that we probably could not get out of the ambush, kept the barrage of mortar and machine gun fire. Due to the snow on the ground and the glare from the trucks burning, the Chinese who were dug in at the hill beyond the railroad tracks had us zeroed-in.

While all this is happening, we were trying to figure out how to stay warm. This was not going to be easy as the temperature was thirty below and dropping. The chill factor added great adversity to our situation. After six hours of the sporadic fire fight, the situation was evidently taking its toll on the men. The casualties were devastating.

A bugle sound of attack was heard and Major McLaughlin said, "Here they come men. Keep on your toes." We knew then that our ammunition was running low. The guns and rifles were freezing, and were not working. Our hands were so cold we almost could not hold the rifles. The gunfire kept on a few more hours when someone said, "They're all over this side. The west side." Though the Reds were crawling, we could see them and we turned half the men to the west to cover our flank. The bugle sounded again, which made us all very nervous. Mortar rounds were falling close by and one hit a weapon's carrier full of ammunition for the recoilless gun, just seventy-five feet from where we were.

Major McLaughlin yelled, "Someone move that truck away from that burning one before we blow up!" Someone jumped on the truck to move it back, but silhouetted by the light of the fire, was hit. Since the truck was on fire, the gas tank would soon explode. I saw the Marine get hit and fall out of the truck. I was ten feet away and knew if I didn't move it that would be the end for all of us. I decided that if I crawled to the running board, the illuminating snow would not silhouette me. I began to crawl from the west side, reached the truck, put it in reverse and hit the starter. The truck started to move back, with me right along the side and could get it to a safer distance. Luckily, it had all gone smoothly.

I moved to another position. My hands were numb, so I got inside one of the trucks that was in front. I urinated, then poured it on my hands. As I was doing this, I happened to look out the window and to my amazement, I saw two Chinese crawling in the ditch. I knew they were Chinese because of their white snow suits. So without making any noise, I slowly rolled down the window. Of course, I was afraid but I knew it was something that had to be done. I grabbed my semiautomatic carbine and slowly took aim at the Chinese as they were getting past the door. I pulled the trigger and to my surprise all it did was click. Then I was horrified. I put the window up very slowly until it was shut, then started taking the weapon apart. While in boot camp, you were trained how to take your weapons completely apart, blindfolded. You would do this until you had mastered it. The training was good, as it saved my life.

So back to the truck and the task at hand. By this time the two Chinese were five feet in front of the truck. I finished putting my weapon together and again rolled down the window, took aim and fired. They did not move anymore, as they received about twelve rounds of my carbine.

Just then I got to thinking that I should get out of the truck in case the Chinese fired more rounds at the trucks on the MSR (main supply route). I looked around making sure the coast was clear then I made a mad dash for the rear of the convoy. There I was approached by an officer who asked me to relieve the soldier who was manning the Browning Automatic Rifle (BAR) on the truck beside me. I followed orders but it was cold. The BAR was shooting in short bursts and was freezing up. As I stood there firing, we could hear the sounds of *banzai* bugle attack so I fired in that direction. This action did nothing to silence the sound.

Just then Ellis came up behind me and said he was there to relieve me. Bullets were flying everywhere and the Chinese were giving us everything they had. It had not been but a few seconds after I handed the BAR over to Ellis, he was about to fire when they hit him with a bullet right between the eyes. He fell backwards and I tried to hold him up; he was dead and I could do nothing for him. By this time everyone was running out of ammunition and the weapons were freezing up. The Army and the Marines were getting worried because we were seeing a lot of dead and wounded. Major McLaughlin was also very concerned at this point.

It was about 0400 hours on November 30, the temperature thirty degrees below zero with a wind chill that made it fifty below. The men were exhausted, ammunition was all but gone, weapons were misfiring due to the extreme cold and men were wounded and dying. Those who didn't die of gunfire just froze to death. Winning our way out of this ambush would take a miracle.

All Major McLaughlin wanted was time. He felt assured that help would come from the rear echelon. During this time he sent two MPs to take a jeep and find help. Even knowing the odds, they had to try.

Major McLaughlin found out all too soon that the two men had not made it out. The Chinese captured them and sent one of them back to tell

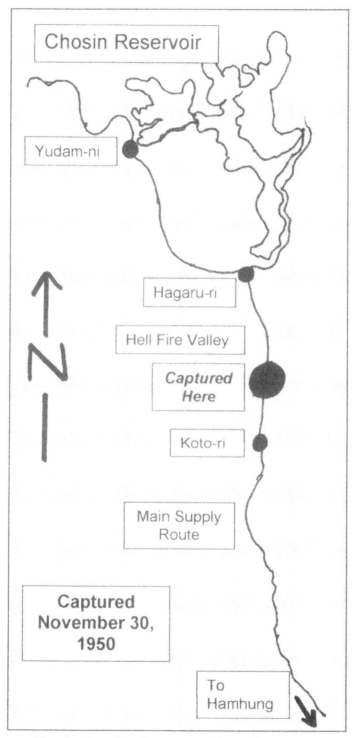

Map showing where I was captured in Hell Fire Valley.

our officer-in-charge to surrender, but Major Seeley and Warrant Officer McCool told the Major to stall, that help was coming from the 1st Marine Regiment Command Post at Koto-ri.

Major McLaughlin was still trying to stall even after the failed attempt to get help, but decided in the meantime to talk with the Chinese Officer regarding the terms of surrender. The major had consulted with other officers and told them the Chinese would send all the wounded and dead back to our front lines if we surrendered. If not, they would kill us all. When the officers looked around and saw the dead and wounded and were then told the Chinese had three thousand men to our one hundred and fifty, they agreed that surrender was inevitable.

After reaching the decision to surrender, Major McLaughlin told the Chinese officer that we would accept their terms of surrender. The Chinese told us to put down our weapons which we did after disassembling them. The Major then told us to load the wounded and the dead on trucks capable of being driven back to Koto-ri, the 1st Regiment Command Post, where we had been the day before.

At 0530 hours, the Chinese put us in a single file, searched us and took all our valuables, including wallets. While I was standing in line, I realized I had a .45 strapped to my waist. Ted Wheeler, standing next to me, said, "Nick, get rid of your .45 or they are liable to shoot you." I got scared and slowly dropped my .45 inside my parka and let it drop into the snow and buried it – carefully. I was shaking from fear that the Chinese soldier would see me drop the pistol.

As we were getting frisked, I was looking at the terrain, so if there was a chance to escape, I would know which way to go. When I looked to the rear of the column, I noticed some commotion going on between a Chinese officer and one of our men. The Chinese officer was trying to confiscate the man's camera. I later found out, to my amazement, that the man with the camera was none other than Frank Knowles, the correspondent and photographer for Associated Press.

There were GI bodies among the Chinese casualties all over the hillside. Some were still moving. I watched as the Chinese killed these men solely because they could not stand up or walk. After this incident, the Chinese would let us pick up those that were still moving to see if we could help them. To our dismay, some were too shot up; they were beyond help.

I could see hundreds of Chinese in foxholes, some manning machine guns. This brought back the realization that the Chinese had been waiting for us and that they had been dug-in for days before our arrival.

We began heading east toward the slope, near the railroad tracks. There were houses that had belonged to Korean families before they had been evicted. The Chinese put us in groups of ten to twelve men. The lieutenant, Sergeant Pettit, Corporal Wheeler, myself and all the other men in our group were all bunched up. It was so cold. There were some large holes in the exterior walls through which the wind howled. I looked at the kitchen and realized there were only two guards. I noticed a hole behind us that a person could climb out. We noticed that just outside the Chinese had piled all our confiscated weapons.

I turned to Sergeant Pettit and said, "Sergeant look at all those weapons."

He replied, "I saw them."

This was the first time I really thought about escaping. The front lines were only one or two miles away. F-86 jets were flying missions and Marine choppers were all over. From the house we could also see emplacements all over the hills. It looked like half of the twenty thousand Chinese Volunteers were waiting for us. I had come to the conclusion that escaping at this time would be impossible. So again, I took the time to look around at the surrounding landscape, so if the chance to escape presented itself, I would at least know what I had to deal with.

That afternoon a Chinese officer came to our hut and told our group that we were going to move out soon. When he left, we wondered aloud where we were going to end up. From our hut we could hear Marine choppers cruising above. As we tried to look, the officer told us to step outside because we were moving out. While getting in line outside the hut we saw hundreds of Chinese roaming around and picking up their dead and stacking them in a pile like cords of wood.

The Chinese gathered the remainder of the POWs and instructed us to form two columns. They placed guards along both sides. The officer-in-charge told us to move on, so we then started our "great journey" to the unknown. While moving in a northwesterly direction, we came upon some dead and wounded soldiers from the United Nations and some Chinese. I saw some men laying in the snow yelling for help. Because they could not get up or would delay the march, the Chinese shot them with machine guns. So inhumane. We tried to help but the Chinese gave us a look and shook their heads. "Don't help" was the message. I counted six or seven POWs putting the wounded onto stretchers.

Just as we crossed the road where they had ambushed us, we came upon bodies of our men just lying in the snow. The reality of war stared us right in the face. Most of our trucks had been hit and were still smoldering. Only a few remained intact. It was at this time that I noticed that other POWs were joining our column. There must have been thirty to forty Marines in our truck, with Army units behind us. All in all, two to three hundred men in the long convoy consisting of approximately thirty five trucks. It was getting colder and our faces felt the icy wind coming from the north. It must have been twenty to thirty below zero. With the winds blowing like they were, the chill factor was somewhere around forty to forty-five below zero. Our breath was turning to icicles on our mustaches and eyebrows. The dead could feel no pain but we sure could. Nonetheless, we had to keep walking. Some POWs were still dazed at what had happened. Most of us were still "wet behind the ears." I was only nineteen and a few others were somewhere between eighteen and twenty years old.

As we are approaching the mountain, about three hundred yards from the main supply route, we were going to start up a hill where the snow was knee deep. We were very concerned about what was going to happen to us. We were hungry, scared, tired and freezing. The wind was so cold it seemed to go right through our parkas. When we started climbing the mountain, we noticed how slippery it was. The officers told us to watch our step and make sure it was a firm one. It was going to be a slow march and it would take a long time to get to the top.

By the time we reached the middle of the long climb it seemed as if we had other POWs join in the column. There was very little talking as the Chinese had told us no talking while in the column, but somehow we could sneak a couple of whispers and ask, "How you doing buddy?" Sometimes you got an answer but other times you didn't. Some of the men were worse than others, as the lucky ones could walk but the unlucky had to be carried on stretchers. I did not know why some of our men were shot where they lay and why some were allowed to be put on stretchers. The trail we were on was very hard traveling as it was wide enough for only one person.

The column came to a halt. This was a blessing because the men couldn't have walked to much farther as the ice on the boots was caked solid and this made the boots very heavy and difficult to lift your feet to keep going. Someone passed the word from the front of the column on back that we were to take a break for a few minutes. The Chinese officer was coming along the column and telling us, "Rest. Rest," while motioning us to sit on the ice and clean our boots or what have you.

We all took a break. Some POWs just lay back against the embankment while some just sat down and rested. Others fooled around with their boots and tried to get the ice off. All in all, you could see the pain in their eyes and on their faces, just looking straight ahead into space with ice all around their faces. Maybe they were thinking of their loved ones back home or their buddies that didn't make it. Maybe wondering if they were strong enough to make it themselves to wherever we were being taken. The Chinese officer in charge yelled, "Lets go" in English. We all got up very slowly, trying to get our bearings and try to come to the realization of where we were.

As we walked up the mountain on the narrow trail, I looked over and saw a sheer drop of at least one-hundred fifty feet. Ted Wheeler, just behind me, told me, "Be careful because the trail is steep and a misstep could be curtains for you."

My back was hurting something awful, about which I complained. Ted kept telling me, "We'll be on the top of the mountain soon." I knew he was saying that so I would not give up. After awhile, I turned around to see how the men on the stretchers were doing and they weren't there anymore. The men who were carrying the stretcher said the wounded GI was dead so no use carrying a dead man, so they dumped him down the mountain. I was not able to pass judgment. Maybe I would have done the same thing.

As we marched, slipping and sliding, we seemed to be climbing Mount Everest, with no end in sight. Just one mountain after another. We were all tired, cold and hungry, but the Chinese kept on making signs to keep going. Our legs were getting cramps and yet you did not dare stop because all they had to do was pull the trigger and you would be dead, then rolled down the mountain. That would solve their problem.

After four or five hours, we finally came to a flat area on the mountain when we heard "rest" up in front of the column. Then the Chinese officer in charge said, "We rest a few minutes."

We talked between ourselves and some said, "I'm too tired to go any further. I'm hungry."

I turned around and told Wheeler, "I can't go anymore. I hurt so bad I can't go another step."

Ted replied, "Hey Nick, just think when we get home, your mother is going to cook us enchiladas, rice and refried beans. Man, don't give up. We'll tell your mom to fix us some bean burritos with flour tortillas. How does that sound?" It was like a shot in the arm, it sounded so good. I had something to look forward to.

I owe him a lot because he kept me going when I wanted to give up. It was a blessing that he was there. I learned later in years that he had moved to Phoenix, Arizona.

Our rest stop was over too soon. They told us to move on, though some people did not want to keep going. It had been very tiring and strenuous coming up the hill, especially walking on ice. When our leg muscles cramped, we would quickly bend down to massage them. The opportunity wasn't as often as we would have liked for fear of holding up the line and or being shot.

The Chinese officer told us that there were only a few more miles to go, then they would feed us. I remember that we stopped and were put in some shelters. Ted, myself and twenty other POWs ended up in a barn that had bales of hay. We were hungry and cold. You could hear the wind whistle outside. The last meal we had was at the 1st Marine Regiment C.P. on November 29, in the morning.

As we were looking for a place to sleep, the conversation turned to how nice it would be to get some shuteye. I climbed to the top of the hay that was about five feet from the ground. I dug a crack between four bales and pushed myself down to where my shoulders were the only thing visible. Ted was about three feet from me and Sergeant Pettit was twenty feet from me in the opposite corner. Someone in the group made a comment, "This is just like sleeping at the Hilton!"

We could hear the Chinese talking outside. New guards had replaced them. By this time a few minutes had gone by and most of the POWs had gone to sleep. When dawn broke, we woke up to boiled potatoes, dirt and all, but they were hot and it sure felt good in our stomachs. At least they were warm and filling. Then we heard the whistle blow so we knew it was time to move on.

The Chinese were moving us as far as they could from our front line because about every two to three hours a chopper would still come by and check on the column of POWs. Our captors would stop us in our tracks and take cover so the choppers would not see us. As we took cover in the brush, I again thought this was the time to escape. Jenneni and I happened to hide in the same place. I told him, "Let's not go back in line. Let's wait and we'll escape and head for the front lines." Jenneni was from New York and in the 24th Regiment 7th Division. I would say we were within ten miles from our troops. We were rested and with a little luck, we might make it.

Our luck ran out about fifteen minutes after the column had left. One of the Chinese soldiers, who was one hundred feet behind, spotted us and returned us to the rest of the POWs. Sergeant Pettit asked me where I had gone. I told him that another POW and I had hid in the brush when the Marine chopper came by us as we were supposed to do.

As the walk to camp continued, we came upon some American jeeps and a few trucks that had either been bombed or shot up. I don't recall what outfit they were from, but while passing the vehicles, two Chinese guards had picked up a dud mortar round. Surprisingly enough, they started throwing it up in the air. Someone yelled, "Hit the dirt!" so we did. They kept on doing it and we just lay there, trying to take cover far enough away as not to be close when or if it exploded. Finally, one of the officers saw what they were doing and yelled at the guards. I presume it was to stop and get back in the column.

As we marched up and down hills, across ravines and creeks that were frozen over, we rested only minutes at a time. The attitude for the day was weary, tired, cold and hungry. This had become an everyday occurrence. We had been walking for miles, stopping for a brief rest, then continuing on. It felt, at times, to be endless. With every step one took, one less encouraging thought. Would the bunch of us ever be warm again? Would we ever taste "real" food again?

A few days later, we heard the sound of jets so close that we became scared. We looked up at the F-86s, saw they belonged to us and they waved the wings to let us know they were there. It was a welcome sight, just knowing that we had not been forgotten.

We got back to our marching. In about an hour, we saw what might be a railroad station or junction, at which the Chinese were pointing to, saying something to the officer. We walked to the building and were told this is where we would rest. The day had worn itself out, with dusk approaching and the weather not getting any warmer. The Chinese decided there were too many choppers and jets still overhead, so we would continue to travel at night.

After getting settled in our temporary shelter, we started looking for our buddies. We inquired about who was and was not among us. If they were not there, the question became, what happened to them?

During training back home, the men were told that after their rifles, their feet were the most important because our feet would sweat, becoming wet, and with the cold weather we must change our socks often. I had four pairs so I changed them periodically so as not to get frostbite. Some men did not have any extra pairs, so I would lend them mine. After you took off the wet socks, you would put them inside your tee shirt to dry them out with your body heat.

As the day lingered on, they fed us, but we did not question what our chow would be because we could see the pots full of potatoes. As it ended up, that would be our diet for a while. We took full advantage of this time to get our much needed rest.

After being there a few hours, we heard the jets come by and saw them wave their wings again. Flying so low, I guess they were keeping an eye out for us and trying to see in what direction the Chinese were taking us.

Unknown to me at the time, this was two years to the day that I joined the Marine Corps; I joined December 14, 1948. The telegram to my family reporting me missing in action was received on the 14th of December 1950.

It was an enormous blow to my family. I would learn later, that adding to the heart-wrenching news, my mother was in the hospital recovering from a hernia operation. My father, after receiving the telegram, got the family together and told them about what the telegram said and their mother must not know about it until she has recovered from her operation. He had decided to call mom's doctor and let him know what devastating news they had received. He also discussed with the doctor, his concerns about telling mom at the hospital. He agreed that it wasn't the right time for her to hear anything upsetting.

That very same day they received the news, they went to see my mother at the hospital. The way it was related to me, the devastation showed on every one of their faces, even though they were trying very hard not to let it. The moment the family walked into the room, my mother immediately knew something was wrong. As my father got close to her, she asked, "Something happened to my son, didn't it? Don't lie to me. I want to know what happened to him and I want the truth."

Put on a spot, my father told her, "Honey, we just received a cable from Washington, telling us that Abraham is missing in action. That means they don't know where he is. However, they mentioned in the telegram, that they would keep us updated on any new developments." My mother lay there very silent, tears running down her face, lost in a world of a missing son. My father and family did not stay very long afterward, as they thought it best that my mother get her needed rest.

Once my mother came home, neighbors would come over and visit. When the subject of me came up, they would tell my mother to leave it in the hands of God. That God had taken me to heaven and I am now with God. My mother would tell them, "No. My son is coming home. I know, because God told me he would be coming home."

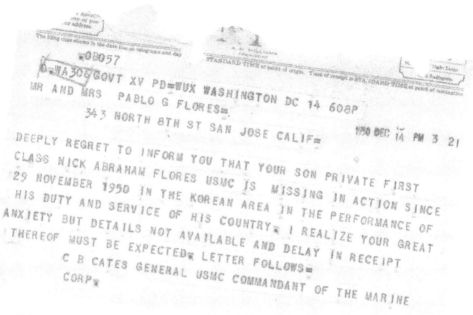

08057

NA30GGOVT XV PD=WUX WASHINGTON DC 14 608P

MR AND MRS PABLO G FLORES=

343 NORTH 8TH ST SAN JOSE CALIF=

DEEPLY REGRET TO INFORM YOU THAT YOUR SON PRIVATE FIRST CLASS NICK ABRAHAM FLORES USMC IS MISSING IN ACTION SINCE 29 NOVEMBER 1950 IN THE KOREAN AREA IN THE PERFORMANCE OF HIS DUTY AND SERVICE OF HIS COUNTRY= I REALIZE YOUR GREAT ANXIETY BUT DETAILS NOT AVAILABLE AND DELAY IN RECEIPT THEREOF MUST BE EXPECTED= LETTER FOLLOWS=

C B CATES GENERAL USMC COMMANDANT OF THE MARINE CORP=

*Telegram sent to my parents
announcing I was Missing in Action.*

From the day of her release from the hospital, my mother went to church every day, rain or shine. She lit a candle and then prayed for my safe return. Along with her, the family had taken the news hard but my father was trying to keep his emotions from showing. More often than not, he was unable to do this. My sister would find my father in the garden, watering the plants, thinking of me and unable to hold back his tears. My oldest brother Paul had approached my dad, telling him not to worry because he was going to join the Marines and then look for me. He did try to join but was refused because of a finger he had lost in an accident.

My mother's faith in God, her belief that God would bring me home and the need for the family to feel this way was what helped her through it. She was often heard to say, "If anyone can make it, Abraham will make it."

Before we moved on, the sick and wounded were checked-on to make sure they were all right. We tried to make them as comfortable as we could. It was about 1930 hours, and they told us to prepare to journey to another temporary camp.

Walking at night and resting during the day continued for a few more days. We stopped in some places for just one or two days. We had been on

Our deathmarch to "Destination Unknown." (Sketch by Nick A. Flores)

the road for two to three weeks. We finally came to the temporary camp. The Chinese had been ready for us, as we could see the Chinese cooking and we could smell the food, which was like a dream come true. Looking at each other, we all asked, "What's this? Our camp?"

Just then, the officers answered, "No, it's a temporary camp. We will be here for a few days."

They assigned us ten to fifteen men to a house where we would spend a week to ten days. The date was approximately the 21st or 22nd of December. The Chinese brought wood to the huts, so we could build fires to keep warm. They had a unique way to warm the huts. They built tunnels with two exits, one at each end of the house. Flat rocks were used to cover the top of the tunnel, one or two inches of mud spread evenly to create a floor. Then a fire was built at one end so the heat would travel through the tunnel, heating the rocks and coming out the other side. The result was a warm house.

When we settled in our little hut, we chose one man to be in charge and look out after the rest. He was to get the food, and when there was a lecture, or something the Chinese wanted to know, they would call all the designated squad leaders to assemble. In turn, we would be told what was happening.

They delivered good news. It was close to Christmas and we could write our families. Excitement was in the air just knowing we were going to let our families know we were alive and well.

Throughout this, men were taking the burlap wraps off their feet. Some had frozen toes, while others were still bleeding from their wounds. One of the officers, Major McLaughlin, asked the Chinese for medical care and doctors. They responded, "At this time there are none available." They asked our officer, "Were there any medical corps men among us?" To our disappointment, there didn't seem to be any, so we did with what we had. Some men had kept their first aid kits, which had a few band-aids and bandages so we were able to take care of some wounded.

While eating dinner of rice and potatoes, Officer McCool was going from house-to-house telling everyone to change their socks or they would suffer from frostbitten toes. The weather was still bitter cold as winds had picked up and temperature had fallen to twenty-eight below. Some men who were on stretchers never showed up at this camp. They had died on the march.

Sometime during the march, the winds would pick up to twenty or thirty miles an hour, which made visibility poor and just plain moving became unbearable. Your beard would turn to ice and then the perspiration from walking would also freeze. It was hell. A few men had given up. They threw themselves on the ground saying, "I can't go on. Let me die here." Of course, we would not let them, even if it meant that we had to carry them. At times like this you wondered if you were going to be next.

All these thoughts came to us as we were resting in the huts. What the Chinese had planned for us, we didn't know, and we didn't care; just so long as we could rest and take care of our feet and bodies. This was a blessing from God that we stopped because we were so tired and cold. Just as we bedded down, the Chinese blew their whistle, which meant go to bed. You could not help but overhear the conversation and comments about the march. Some would say they had been cold. Others had been ready to give up. Another would say, "Did you see those guys dump the guy on the stretcher?"

A GI would respond, "He was dead. You don't carry a dead man on a stretcher when you don't know whether you're even going to make it."

Before we started to go to sleep, Ted and I had chosen one corner to sleep together so our combined body heat would keep us warmer. Others paired up the same way.

The next morning, December 22nd or 23rd, we were awakened by the whistle around 0730 or 0800 hours. It was still very cold, somewhere around thirty below. We were told to assemble. The Chinese officer in charge of the column said that we were to eat, then they would talk to us and issue writing paper. Sitting in the hut, eating rice and drinking hot tea, we wondered why the sudden good treatment. We did not ask, but the GIs welcomed it as it was better than walking on the ice in bitter cold.

We were given paper and pencils to write our letters. Little did we know that we would be told what to write. The Chinese officer in charge was telling us to write that the Chinese Peoples' Volunteers were treating us good, feeding us good, taking good care of the wounded and they had given us all the essentials for our well being for daily life as a POW. Most of us did not want to go along with writing that; that we were getting good treatment. Sergeant Pettit told some of us that if we wanted our letters to get through, we had to say just that. He also said that at least our parents would know we were alive. After the letters were written, they were collected and then taken to the Chinese officers camp headquarters.

A couple of days went by and an Army officer came around with a petition for us to sign. I remember him reading something like: The American Imperialists were killing innocent women and children, and

'...Pray for Me,' Writes S.J. Marine, Red POW

LETTER BRINGS HOPE – Pablo G. Flores and his son Paul read letter received from Marine Cpl. Nick Flores, Pablo's son captured in Korea Nov. 29. Letter was written in prisoner of war camp somewhere in China. It was first word Nick was alive. (From the *San Jose Mercury News*)

that we had no reason to attack North Korea, that we were fighting for the DuPonts, Fords and so forth. Below that the petition read that the Chinese were treating us good, feeding us well and that we were dying for a false cause.

I had read in the *Stars and Stripes* that early in the war some POWs denounced the U.N. forces and that we were war mongers. Also, some had been tortured to the brink of death because they would not sign a petition declaring that America was the aggressor. Maybe this was a good thing that the Chinese had us because the Korean Peoples' Army were killing all their POWs.

We knew that what we were to write in our letters was a bunch of propaganda as we were told by some officers and if we signed the petition, we would have to suffer the consequences. Many of us did not sign it. They also gave us reading material, newspapers and books but that communist literature also was full of propaganda.

It was now December 24th. Everyone was excited about it being Christmas Eve and we were going to celebrate Christmas the following day. I remember that the Chinese Peoples' Volunteers had fixed rice, pork and crackers. They had planned all this and fixed it especially for us. We had church services by a chaplain in our group. We were really thrilled about the whole day of Christmas.

On December 26th the same old routine returned; lectures, read books, eat dinner and rest some more. There had been scuttlebutt going around that a few POWs were going to be sent home and that got everyone excited about who was going and who would be staying behind. The Chinese had us gather for an assembly and we suspected that this was to tell us who would be going.

Ted Wheeler from our hut was fortunate enough to be leaving. I cannot remember anyone else from our squad. The men who would be leaving were getting ready. I don't recall how many POWs were exchanged. Nevertheless, it happened a little after Christmas or just before New Year's Day.

After the chosen guys had left, you could see and feel the sadness by the others that were not so lucky, including me. Don't get me wrong. I was happy that some were going home and especially Ted. I kept thinking who would take care of me? Ted had looked after me from day one of the march, and now I had to go it alone, along with the others.

Sergeant Pettit was among the POWs that were staying. He and I had become good friends. We had been together since Hamhung, where the convoy had originated. I had looked for the other drivers from 1st Service Battalion but to no avail. I stayed with Sergeant Pettit and we became traveling buddies on the three-month march to Camp 1. As for marching, it was that time again to the dismay of all.

The weather was still twenty or thirty below and the wind was blowing fifteen to twenty miles an hour. We rested but weren't equipped with the right type of clothing for these conditions. As we made the "march" we saw Chinese troops along the way. It seemed like all the millions of Chinese that were in China were there in Korea. As we walked by them, some would smile, laugh and react like we Americans were fighting a losing battle. I observed that some of these people had wooden rifles made to resemble real weapons. Many of these Chinese, I would estimate, were only fifteen or seventeen years old.

As our march continued north, our column had gotten smaller due to all the POWs that were chosen to leave in Little Switch. Through the first day of the march we had lost some on stretchers and were forced to leave from twenty to thirty men in different places due to their wounds and frostbite. By this time, after leaving Kangee, the Chinese only had approximately one hundred and eighty POWs left in the group.

It seemed like a never-ending journey. The POWs that had wrapped their feet with burlap were complaining to the guards that their feet were too heavy with ice and they could not walk fast. This complaining was not doing any good. The guards did not understand English and all they responded with was *pali pali* which meant "hurry hurry." Anyway, the burlap wraps on our feet were frozen with ice and this did make it difficult to move the feet very fast. The chill factor must have been fifty below. Consequently our eyebrows and mustaches had turned to icicles. Our arms and hands were so cold that we could not bend them at the elbows to put them inside our parkas. As we approached the next temporary camp, we could see the fires from about one hundred yards away. Some Chinese soldiers were around the fire keeping warm.

Sergeant Pettit was behind me and he came by my side and said, "Hey Nick, we're going to warm up as soon as we get to those fires, so when we get there, change your socks and check your toes for frostbite." Just then the guard told him to get back to the column.

It seemed like the Chinese were expecting us. Surprisingly, some of the fires we saw had pots of millet seed and sorghum seed cooking on top. By this time it was a welcome sight because it made you feel like there was hope for us after a cold and miserable march. As the column stopped, the Chinese soldiers started to count-off men to a hut. We knew that rest and food were forthcoming. Some men were showing signs of relief. We started talking with each other while waiting to be escorted to the huts. Of course, we were hungry so we were looking forward to getting our hands on some food.

The huts were warm and there were straw mats on the dirt floor. When we got settled in our spaces, we started to peel off some of our heavy clothing including the parkas and especially take our boots off and those who had burlap wraps on unwrapped their feet.

Explaining the feeling of being in that hut is very difficult. The different attitude reflected on the faces of the POWs, after being on the march with the wind chill factor of forty to fifty below zero. A few minutes had passed when an officer came in our hut and told us to pick someone to get the food for us. There were fifteen men in our hut. Sergeant Pettit was alongside of me, sitting on the floor. He then rose and introduced himself and said, "I am Sergeant Pettit. Anyone want to volunteer to get the food? My toes are frozen and he hadn't finished saying what he was going to, when someone in the corner said, "I'll go, Sarge. My name is Smitty and I still have my clothes and boots on."

Sergeant Pettit said, "Thanks."

They fed us approximately an hour after getting settled in the hut. The food came and with it were fifteen small bowls. Smitty took the job of dishing out the food with a large sized wooden spoon. After he did that he started handing each of us a bowl with one potato in each bowl. There were no utensils so we had to use our fingers. The menu was millet seed, sorghum seed and boiled potatoes. The food was hot and that is all that mattered because we were cold and hungry. Someone in the hut said, "I'm a farm boy and I used to feed my chickens this stuff!"

Chapter Four

Camp One

Two weeks had passed since leaving the temporary camp, stopping at various towns to sleep and eat. We had climbed mountains, crossed valleys and traveled roads on our way to our unknown destiny. The Chinese were letting us travel during the day as we were so far north that the fear of UN helicopter or jets flying overhead was not present.

February was now upon us. I, as well as the others, found out after one POW asked the Chinese officer in command of the column what the date was. The weather was cold, still ten or twenty below zero. Some of the guys in the column were getting weaker and falling down. When this happened, the Chinese guards asked us to get them up. It was not as if we wouldn't but we were just as weak and it was difficult to pick up someone who didn't want to get up. Several minutes later we had managed to pick up one fallen buddy and get him back in the column. I often heard cries, such as "Let me die" and "I can't go any further, let them kill me," from men that had reached their breaking point. Everyone has one, unfortunately. The hunger and cold was taking its devastating toll.

After a few hours, one of our officers went to the Chinese officer and asked to please rest for a few minutes or he would lose some men in the column. We then heard a whistle and soon the word was passed along that we were going to rest for twenty minutes. As I sat down, Sergeant Pettit came over to me and asked, "How are your feet?"

I said, "I am going to look at them." Taking off my boots would be a lengthy process as the boots, including the laces, were frozen. My near frozen hands struggled with the laces and as soon as I took off my boots, I realized that my socks were wet. I took out one of my spare pair that I kept inside my coat and changed my wet ones for much needed dry ones. After completing this, I looked around and could see other men checking their feet and changing socks if they had spare ones to put on.

Sergeant Pettit was going down the line telling the guys that if they couldn't feel their toes, to take their boots off and massage their feet or jump up and down to get the circulation going to them. This would hopefully prevent frostbite. Twenty minutes wasn't much time, but whatever we could do would help in the march to wherever our captors were taking us.

Sergeant Pettit and other NCOs were taking care of their feet along with repeatedly reminding us the importance of keeping our feet warm. They were a lot of help to us young guys who had never experienced war, let alone the sub-zero weather conditions. A whistle blew so it was time to move on. The weaker guys were again helped by those that were able, as we were not going to leave anyone behind if we could possibly help it.

At this point of the march, it didn't seem to matter. As I walked, I glanced towards the back of the column and saw the faces of once fighting men, now facing the biggest fight of all – survival. They were walking like mummies, appearing not to care where they were going. The most frequent words were, "I've got to make it. I've got to make it." This was enough to unnerve the strongest of man.

Most of us, at one time or another, didn't care where we were going either, as long as we could rest, eat and sleep. I found it a God-send that more men were not lost to this hard-to-endure treatment. Word spread throughout the column that we would be stopping at the last temporary camp in just a short while. About forty minutes later, we reached that destination. Most of us just dropped to the ground, some groaning, some expressing a sigh of relief and then some that didn't seem to care one way or the other.

My mind quickly drifted back to the start of the journey. I thought about the POWs that had died and those that had been shot because they were unable to walk for one reason or another. Here I was, only nineteen and had seen enough death to last me a lifetime.

The stay was brief, a few days, at the last temporary camp. The column was again on its way to the final camp. Excitement was in the air but also the nagging question of what was ahead for us for the duration of the war.

The weather was cold, brisk and there was still ice on the paths and roads that we traveled. After the Chinese had told us that it was another fifteen to twenty miles to Camp 1, the energy level and morale increased within the POWs. Our feet somehow kept us moving forward. I started noticing rice paddies, some North Korean farmers walking along the road, and once in a while, we were stopped to let trucks go by. This was an indication, we thought, that Camp 1 was very close.

One of our senior officers, directed to do so by the commander of the column, approached us and said, "I have been informed that we are within two miles from where we are going to make our home. There will be North Koreans along the side of the road, and we are not to challenge them or make any signs of hate. The Chinese will handle the North Koreans. You must understand that they hate us for this war in their homeland." He then assured the Chinese officer that he didn't have to worry about the POWs. They would cause no problems.

During this encouragement talk, I started to see people lining up on both sides of the road that entered into town. Koreans were all over the streets making faces at us, lifting up fists, making hateful gestures and saying in Korean that they hated us.

It is 1000 hours, the first part of spring 1951. The weather still gloomy with overcast skies. After finally making our way through town we reached the outskirts where the huts stood and here is where we would spend the duration of our imprisonment. The column had made its way to a cluster of huts and a playground when we came to an abrupt stop. A Chinese officer told us to get in lines of four, which we promptly did. I thought no more walking and at least some sleep could be in our immediate future.

As we finished lining up, the Chinese said, "There will be groups of twelve to fifteen men. We will assign you accordingly." They started counting and then we were escorted to the huts. The group that I was with had twelve men. Entering the hut one by one, again you could hear the sighs of relief. We were all so cold, tired and hungry that we just flopped on the floor and tried to get some sleep or at best, some rest.

Day one at Camp 1. The Chinese blew their whistle for everything we did; assembly, wood detail, chow and exercise. We were tired and hungry, but never surprised by what the Chinese would do next. We thought our diet would be better than boiled potatoes, but it was worse! It was boiled sorghum seed and some of the men refused to eat it.

After the commander welcomed us to Camp 1 and finished his speech, he suggested to the Chinese officer that he tell us what was to happen next. This officer introduced himself as Lieutenant Chang, second-in-command of the camp. He then told us that we would be eating within the hour. Lieutenant Chang continued by telling us that we must select one man from each hut to go to the kitchen to get the food for his group. Also there is firewood at the end of the playground that may be used for heating the huts. He suggested that this be done soon, as it would take about an hour to heat the floor so we would be warm.

One of the men in our group volunteered to get the food, so the rest of us that were able went to gather the wood. With the wood gathered and us back in the hut our food was brought in. Each man was given a small bowl of sorghum seed or millet seed, and that was the menu for that evening. When all of us had finished dinner, it was the person's job who brought the food to return the bowls to the kitchen.

With dinner out of the way we started to get acquainted with the guys who we would be spending the duration of the war with. We decided to build a fire so the hut would be warm. By this time it was getting dark outside and we also needed to find a spot where each one was going to call his sleeping area. Whatever spot that you chose would remain yours unless you became assigned to another hut. I chose to be close to the door, in the corner and against the wall. That way if it got cold I could get up and put more wood on the fire.

It seemed that just a few minutes had passed since our area was picked and a few had fallen asleep. Darkness has descended in our hut and you could hear the moaning and crying in the hut. A few of us were attending to the wounded trying to make them comfortable. When we could do no more for them I went to bed and it did not take long for me to go to sleep. As I was close to sleep I thought this would be the first night that all of us could lay down to sleep without dreading the morning and marching in the cold. This was very comforting. I quickly said my prayers, thanking God for getting us here, then I rolled over and fell asleep.

I was just opening my eyes to a new day when I heard a knock on the door. I looked around and saw that most of the guys were still asleep so I got on my knees and scooted over to the door. When I opened the door I saw Sergeant Pettit. He informed me that there would be an assembly in a little while then asked me if everything was okay. To this I replied that yes everything was alright. During this time I noticed the sun was just ready to appear from behind the mountains.

When I stood up, I realized just how tired, hungry and cold I had been when we arrived at camp. Having only one meal a day during the march did nothing to build ones strength and endurance. This would take some-time to regain.

After Sergeant Pettit left I stepped outside, looked around at the camp noticing smoke coming from the several chimneys. I hoped that everyone was staying warm. The weather was still cold; ice remained on the ground and the wind was blowing about fifteen miles per hour.

The sound of a whistle interrupted my thoughts. I ran into the hut then tried to wake up the sleeping men as I knew the commander would be expecting all able bodied persons to attend the speech. Some got up quickly, putting their boots and jackets on, while others let it be known that they were not ready to get up yet. Finally, all were ready so we left the hut and walked to the playground where we mingled with the other POWs.

The sound of a whistle brought our attention to Lieutenant Chang, who started telling us that the commander wanted to say a few words about our stay at Camp 1, and he, Lieutenant Chang, would translate the commander's speech. The commander began to speak then Lieutenant Chang, in English, told us, "The Camp is not suitable as we would like it to be but things will improve as days go by. We will try to make you as comfortable as we can. We will get medical help for the sick and wounded. We will get your daily essentials like toothpaste, tobacco, new clothes, better food and also dishes for you to eat from and pans so you can wash up in the morning. We will do this as soon as possible. We plan to change the menu as soon as the food supplies get here."

That concluded the commander's speech. Now Lieutenant Chang had his own words to pass along to all of us. He informed us that we would be doing everything by the sound of a whistle. In the morning we will get up with a whistle, then get in line for food with the sound of a whistle. We would be going on wood detail in the morning, after eating, so wood could be gathered for the kitchen. We would also be told at a later date when we would start studying Communism. I myself, as well as most of the other guys, didn't want any part in learning about Communism.

Almost everything we heard had lifted our spirits except the Communism stuff. It wasn't long before the interest of what the commander had said was lost. It was after this assembly that the men in our hut decided that one man would get our food from the kitchen for a week, and then we would trade off every week.

A few days went by when we were told that we would be able to celebrate Easter. The chaplain had talked to the commander and received permission to hold the services at the playground. Easter Sunday was now here and when we attended the services, we were to bring the sick and wounded if they could be moved. If not, leave them in their huts and the chaplain would see that they were given a service. The chaplain read passages from the New Testament and said a prayer for all of us. After we were dismissed several people socialized before returning to the huts.

During the next few weeks more POWs died from malnutrition and others succumbed to their wounds. The NCO and officers decided to have a pow-wow with the commander of the camp in which they would let the Chinese know that the food that was given to the POWs was not fit for consumption and as a result, men were dying, getting sick, and if at all possible, the menu must be changed.

The next day Lieutenant Chang told the American officers that they would change the menu. They changed it alright! Now we would be served boiled chopped corn. This so-called food was just like eating crushed glass. It didn't take long before we showed signs of what the chopped corn was doing to our insides. Guys started vomiting, coughing up blood and blood was showing up in their feces. This corn that was being given to us was the worst thing the Chinese had done to us since arriving at Camp 1.

We found out later that the corn had come from China and the U.S. had given it to Chiang-Kai-Shek during the occupation by American troops. The sacks of chopped corn were labeled 'Old Glory' with the American flag on it.

As the days passed, more and more men were hurting and laying in their huts just waiting to die. Some had flies all over them and had gone to the bathroom in their pants. Some of the healthier men tried to help them but it was futile. Whenever we attempted to help they would tell us to leave them alone and just let them die. Unfortunately, the chopped corn for our meals continued for ten days to two weeks. Without medication there was nothing to help these ailing men. Some of them had gotten to the point that it didn't matter how sick they got, nor did they care if they lived or died.

By this time we were losing four to five men a day. When you reach the point of no return, as some had, all some of us could do was pray that God would guide them back to the right path. Sometimes I wondered if God let them live long enough to die in camp and not in a ditch or somewhere along side of a mountain all alone. What I did know was that it was devastating to me watching buddies die one after the other. I talked to Sergeant Pettit and asked him, "What are we going to do about all these POWs that are dying?"

With no medical treatment available, prisoners were left to lay down and die. (Sketch by Nick A. Flores)

He answered, "I wish I had an answer for it, Nick." This problem was a concern for all of the officers.

After seeing all this, we decided to talk to our own superior officer to get some of the NCOs together and have a meeting to decide what we should do about the problem at hand. When Sergeant Pettit left with the officers to talk more, I then took it upon myself to tell these suffering men that were giving up, that they would get medical help. Maybe they would hang on and try to eat. The problem was that a lot of them didn't want to eat because they already knew what the corn would do to their stomachs.

When I was through with my pep talk I went to my hut. I felt so helpless when I saw these men suffering. As I was walking to my hut, I saw these guys that were skin and bones. They were just laying there accepting death, and I yelled out loud, "Why must it be this way?"

I started crying and Sergeant Pettit walked up to me and asked, "Why are you crying, Nick?"

I said, "Look around you, sergeant. These men are dying and there is nothing I can do for them except pray for them."

To this Sergeant Pettit relied, "That's all we can do, " and then he left.

I asked myself what kind of hell is this that we have to die like this? It doesn't seem fair.

The more knowledgeable prisoners were aware from the beginning that the wounded had died from not having medical supplies available. At the time of our arrival to Camp 1, March 1951, we had lost a few men to the cold and their wounds. The Chinese had stripped us of all medical supplies we had and used them for their own, as they were lacking medical supplies. On the other hand, the North Korean Army did not care whether you lived or died from starvation or wounds. We heard stories of how brutal the North Koreans were with the captives.

We were "lucky" to have been captured by the Chinese. From the beginning of our march north, the Chinese had told us that we were going to be educated about what was right and wrong.

We had been used to eating good food, but here, we were having to eat sorghum seed, corn and dried fish made into soup. Even the few packages of crackers that we were given did nothing for our torn up stomachs. Our stomachs were in no condition for this corn due to the months of starvation and the lack of vitamins and protein. When we ate, it tore up our insides.

There was never the problem of anyone pulling rank on us. Most of us respected the officers and NCOs in our camp. They even asked us not to call them "sir." The struggle to survive was indeed present but not to the point where you would kill or scuffle with someone to take his food – at least not to my knowledge.

You felt so helpless to try and force someone to eat when you, yourself were weak and didn't want to eat. The first few months after arriving at Camp 1, we had lost from five to seven men a day. It was evident that the majority of the POWs who were dying at camp was due to lack of medical treatment and, refusing to eat the slop the Chinese were giving us. Some had arrived at camp very weak and not eating did not help them to recover. The men that were a little stronger would help those who were giving up, even though some still refused to eat and just laid there and died. They apparently could not handle what life was handing them.

Sergeant Pettit was very helpful to us as he had been a POW during World War II. He was always giving advice on how to cope and expressed the importance of eating whatever they gave us because eating was essential if we were to survive and make it home at the end of the war.

I tried not to let all of what was happening, seeing these POWs so helpless and just giving up, get to me. As I walked to one of the huts, I glanced towards Sergeant Pettit's hut and he was coming out, hobbling because of his toes that had been frostbitten. I said to myself as I made my way across the playground, there must be something I can do for Sergeant Pettit so he can walk without hurting.

We met at the playground and started talking. He said, "Hi, Nick."

I replied, "Hi, Sarge. How you doing?"

He answered, "I wish I could get around better, but I can't get my shoes on with these toes the way they are."

I asked, "Is that why I don't see you around the camp?"

He added, " It hurts to walk without shoes."

"Sergeant Pettit, you know what I am going to do for you? I am going to make a pair of moccasins so you can walk around without hurting."

I went around collecting leather boots that the men weren't using or were not able to be repaired. I cut the tops off, using these pieces of leather for the bottom and used the leather tongue for the tops then made holes in both pieces so I could sew them with the bootlaces that were made of leather. Making these moccasins turned out to be a time-consuming task. After I finished Sergeant Petitts' moccasins, he told everyone what I had done for him. He was so proud of his "shoes" that enabled him to get out of his hut more often and some of the guys came to me asking if I would make them a pair. When I saw these guys hobbling around, unable to put their boots on, I figured I had time to at least make them comfortable. By making them moccasins, they could get around and I took it upon myself to do this for them. I eventually made eight or nine pairs which took me approximately five weeks to complete.

After I had finished all the moccasins for the guys, I was walking across the playground to deliver the last pair when a few guys approached me. They asked if there was any way I could make a boot that would fit over the knees. I asked them, "Why?"

"Well, we are going to amputate Dale Smith's (Smitty) legs just above the knees. If we don't, gangrene will kill him, so we have to do it now."

I replied, "Sure I can make him a pair." The next morning they decided to do surgery on Smitty. This was going to be a painstaking ordeal for the men who were going to do the operation. I did not know Smitty very well, but I did know of him when his legs were amputated. He was in the Army, blond hair, five-foot-four, my guess on his age would be 18 or 19, and such a happy-go-lucky guy. He was very thankful for being alive – and in my books, a courageous and brave guy.

Smitty's legs had been shot during our capture. He had been one of the POWs on a stretcher who made it to camp. The corpsman that had been treating Smitty on the march said that his legs would have to be amputated or he would die. Volunteers had been asked to help. The corpsman was going to perform the surgery. At the same time, there were guys boiling water for soaking and sterilizing the pig-skin thread that would be used for sewing the skin to overlap the leg. In a few hours it was over. Smitty had gone into shock but fortunately came out of it. By the end of two months, he was well on the way to recovery.

All this time I had been working on the "boots" for Smitty's knees. We were soon to learn that Smitty was not going to give up, as he had the determination not to miss out on what life had to offer. Also, he was not going to just lay there as life slipped on by feeling sorry for not having legs.

A few months went by and I took Smitty his leg "boots." I had padded them inside, then put straps on so he could fasten them to his belt. It was a slow, gradual recovery for Smitty's legs to toughen up enough to where he could walk.

Smitty continued to make progress. Some of the guys went by often to see how he was doing. About six months had passed since Smitty had his surgery and they told us he was out of danger.

After going by Smitty's hut and finding out he was okay, I went to check on the sick and wounded. They seemed to be doing alright considering they had no doctors or medicine as of yet. I asked them if there was anything I could do for them. One fellow prisoner asked, "Nick. How about a donut and a cup of coffee?"

Then he chuckled. I told him that if I could get some coffee and donuts, they would be the first to get them.

As I walked out, someone yelled, "Thanks for everything, Nick. Don't forget to pray for me."

I turned around while I was at the door and said, "I do that for you and all the guys every night."

Toward the end of July, the Chinese selected seven POWs to work in the kitchen, helping the Chinese cooks. I quickly volunteered, hoping that by working in the kitchen that would facilitate my departure from the camp. I had never stopped thinking about escaping. I just had to wait for the right time. The next morning, all seven of us reported to the kitchen. Lieutenant Chang was there to instruct us on our duties. While he was interpreting what the cooks wanted us to do, I looked to my right and there I noticed there was another Hispanic POW in the group.

After Lieutenant Chang left, the seven of us introduced ourselves to one another. I soon found myself walking over to the other Hispanic, telling him, "Hi. My name is Nick."

In return, he told me, "My name is Tom Cabello."

Tom was husky, had a round face, very dark hair and stood about five-foot-eight. He was not what you would call a talker; said few words which usually were followed with a shrug of his shoulders. None of this mattered to me, for we got along. After shaking hands, we started working together and became very good friends. On our time off from the kitchen duty, Tom and I would talk about where we were from, what outfit we were with, and so many other things. We had started talking in Spanish for no particular reason. It was probably better that way. At least if we said something that might get us in trouble, no one around us would be able to understand.

One evening, not long after we had met, we were talking about our kitchen duties, and then went by Tom's hut where we sat down outside. We looked across the playground, talking about the problems at camp and then out of the blue, Tom said, "I wish I could get out of here."

I replied with reservation, "You do, Tom?" I then continued telling him about my escape from the column, several days after we were captured. As I was sitting there, I thought to myself that maybe I could tell Tom about my escape plans. Maybe he would want to escape with me.

As it turned out, I did mention my escape plans to Tom and asked, "Do you want to get out of here? Think about it, and we'll discuss it later."

A few weeks had passed, but Tom and I still thought and talked about our plans to escape. We talked in Spanish so no one else could understand. It was something you had to think about, because our captors had told us that no one escapes from the Chinese. At that time we did not know if they would shoot us or just what they would do if we were caught.

All we had to figure out is when and where. One consideration was that since we went in every direction for wood on our wood detail, the guards sometimes couldn't keep us in sight, so maybe this would be the proper time. Another was that we could do it at night, as there were fewer guards because they were split farther apart from each other than during the day. Since food had not even been considered, we would just take a few things from the kitchen and let it go at that.

After we decided to escape at night, we had to decide when. One evening around 2100 or 2200 hours, we heard a plane's engine. As I got up to try and find out where it was coming from, I looked northeast and could hear the sound more loudly. Just as the plane was over the camp, flying low, we saw flashes from the plane. It appeared to be taking pictures. Little did I know, he was going to be coming once or twice a week. It always came between 2130 or 2200 hours, just before we bedded down. Some of us started calling him "Bed Check Charlie." It was nice to have him coming around. He would take two or three pictures of the camp, so Tom and I decided one evening that we would wait around for him, wave and maybe they would know we were there, that we were okay. It was a great feeling to most of us that the Air Force knew we were there and cared about us.

We had seen so many Chinese truck convoys pass through but we never paid attention to where they were going or what they were carrying. Later we found out that the Chinese had put all the POW camps on the main supply route. We put together "Bed Check Charlie," the truck convoys passing through, and realized why they were taking pictures of the camp. That is to say that all of this was being done so the POW camps, main supply routes and movement of the enemy could be monitored.

Chapter Five

A Few Good Men

During several days following, Tom and I tackled the task of finalizing our escape plans. As Tom and I were walking towards the huts, I happened to look down at the entrance to the camp where I saw a group of POWs being escorted by guards. As I walked through the playground, heading to the group of POWs, I said to Tom, "Look. More POWs." I could not believe my eyes. They were in bad condition and as I got close to them, other POWs came in my direction to see if they knew any of them.

They looked like death warmed over; their eyes were sunken-in, dirty, and most of them were being helped by other fellow POWs in the column. Some were limping, some were using crutches made out of tree branches while some were carried on stretchers. Most of them didn't weigh over seventy-five pounds. It was a horrible sight. After the shock of seeing them, we went over to them and the guards immediately motioned us to stay away. When one of the Chinese officers approached the guards that had brought in the men, they instructed us to help them take them outside a hut and sit them down. We stood there looking at them thinking most of them had barely made it to camp, and they would not last long.

We started asking some of the men where they had been and we came to find out they had been with the North Koreans. It explained why they were in that condition. They had been cut off from food, and had been beaten by the Korean Peoples' Army. The time now was about 1030 hours and after a few more minutes standing there in shock, I tried to figure out what we could do for them.

Tom said, "They sure look bad. I am glad I'm not in that group." The sight of those men must have bothered Tom because he quickly added, "I'll see you later."

I just could not get over the appearance of these men. By this time almost everyone had left except me. I could not let them just lay there and not do anything for them. As I am standing there, looking at them trying to figure just what I was to do for them, someone came and told me, "There is a Marine laying over by the corner of the hut and his name is Nick, from San Francisco."

I went to him to find out what I could do for him. His name was Nick Antonis. His health was so bad that all he could manage was to mumble.

I stayed long enough to assure him that I would do whatever I could to help him. At this point I didn't know how many Marines were in this group but it also didn't matter to me as I was going to try and help them all, if I could.

An hour must have passed while I was trying to find out who needed help the most and that was tough because they all needed help. As I was the only person left amongst these men, I wondered where to start. Soon one of the POWs that came over to look, asked me, "What are they going to do with them?"

I responded by saying, "I, and anyone else that will help, are going to take care of them and nurse them back to health."

I stayed to see what I could do for them. Someone approached me and said, "You're crazy! There's nothing you can do for them, they're too far gone. Look at them, there's worms coming out of their ears and noses. I don't think there is much hope for them." I knew that it was going to be a lengthy task but I was going to try and save some of them even though I didn't know what or how I was going to do it. They were so weak and pale from the lice sucking their blood. I stood above them looking to the sky and I prayed, asking God to give me strength, wisdom and fortitude to help these men who need it so desperately.

I asked a couple of men that were close by if they would help me and their response was "Hell no, man! I don't know what's wrong with them and I'm having a tough time surviving myself." I didn't ask anybody for help from then on as I felt I would get the same reaction.

It was still early, so I knew I had some time to help these men. I went to the kitchen and got a pan of warm water, then I washed their faces. When I got close to them I knew right then and there that I had to bathe them and boil their clothes because they were full of lice. Realizing this, I went to the camp commander to ask if he could get some pots over to where the POWs were laying so we could boil their clothes and bathe them. I also asked if the cooks could make some rice in soup form so I could feed the men. I would have to spoon feed them, for they were so weak they couldn't even open their mouths.

A couple of guards and two Chinese from the kitchen brought three big pots, six feet in diameter and a foot deep. They put rocks under the pots to stabilize them and also made them high enough to build a fire underneath. A few POWs came to help bring wood and water. I, taking a chance, asked them if they would start the fire for me and their response was, "sure." After lighting the fire, they left me with the wounded. I started stripping off their clothes, noticing again that they were skin and bones. There is no other way to put it. I knew I had a job ahead of me as these men were very close to death.

After removing their clothing, I put the clothes in the pots of boiling water. I kept moving them around with a stick, trying to get all the lice out. While doing this, a fellow prisoner approached and asked, "Do you need help?"

I replied, "I sure do." He volunteered to bring more wood and stir the clothes. I told him, "I'm very grateful for your help. I can't be in three places at once." He told me his name was Ken but I never knew his last name.

Approximately an hour and a half had passed when I was called to the kitchen. I was informed that the rice soup, which was only water, was ready. That was certainly good news to me, so I returned to the mission at hand. One of the cooks brought the rice water, some bowls and spoons to me.

I started to give the liquid to Nick Antonis first, giving him only about four ounces. I then continued on down the line. When I reached the seventh man, I discovered that two had died.

I looked up, then started crying. I said, "Lord, please don't let anymore die. At least let me try to help them. I can't do it any faster." I knew more would die before I could get help but also that I was doing it as fast as I could. A few minutes went by when I continued feeding them the rice water and then started bathing them, one by one.

About three hours after I had boiled the clothes, the camp commander came and asked how I was doing. I said, "I wish I could get some help."

He then pointed to two POWs that were standing by the building, and ordered, "You two men help him get these men up so we can put some clothes on them." I looked at them, then they started to walk towards the commander and me, asking what we wanted them to do. I asked them to give me a few minutes of their time so I could sit these guys up and get them ready for their clothes. They didn't like it but did it anyway. I didn't ask their names as it wasn't important, but what was important is the fact they were going to help. By the time the clothing was ready, three more had died. I was going to have to accept the fact that more would probably not make it, considering their condition. This did not make the reality any easier for me. I wanted to see that they all made it, but unfortunately, that was not to be.

One of the guys that was helping me said, "Nick, you look worn out. Why don't you go rest a bit while I watch them?"

I said, "I sure need it, thanks." I went behind a hut where I sat down, back leaning against the wall, and closed my eyes. I must have dozed off for when I woke up, two hours had passed.

I returned to the sick only to learn that two more had died. We went to the cemetery where we buried them, just like we had with the others. When I came back, I began spoon feeding the remaining ones and by this time, it was late evening. The weather was warm enough to let them sit or lay there until we got clothes on them.

The commander of the camp sent an officer to let us know that a hut had been cleaned for the sick and wounded. I started at one end then down the line, putting their clothes on. After finishing, we told them we were going to put them in their own hut. They weren't saying much, but I knew when I looked in their eyes, they were grateful for what was being done for them. We took them, one by one, into the hut where we laid them down, telling them that they would get a blanket in a few minutes in case they got cold. I told them I would come in the morning to check on them and also feed them. This way they wouldn't have to worry about getting up.

The next day a Chinese officer had chosen someone to watch them which gave me a break from all the work that I had done when no one else had seemed interested in doing it. The Marine Corps had taught us to take care of our own, you don't leave anyone behind, and they taught me well. When some of the fellow POWs saw me walking around camp, they asked me, "Why are you doing it?"

"Doing what?" I asked, followed by, "No one else wanted to do it, so what do you do, let them die because no one wants to help them? I took the job and I am going to see it through."

By weeks end, thirteen of the severely sick had made it. They were walking around and sitting in the sun. Six who had small wounds also made it. It had been too late to do anything for the others, but nineteen out of the thirty had survived.

Two weeks had gone by and they were well on their way to recovering, gaining a little more strength and acting more lively. I went to my hut, prayed and thanked God for his divine love, watching over us, and giving me the strength and health to make it. I was just as weak as the rest but stronger in faith. I was young and had turned twenty but I looked back at what I had done for the POWs, and it gave me a good feeling. I felt that if I didn't do anything else with my life, I had accomplished a mission that

God had put me there to help those men. I felt I had a purpose in life and this had been it. Because my mother had taught me well; I accomplished what I did the best I could.

After nursing the POWs back to health, I realized that Tom and I hadn't seen much of each other. It had been about ten days since I had spoken to him about our plans to escape. I went to the kitchen the next morning and was told I had been replaced because I had been too busy with the sick men. I figured it was just as well although I wouldn't be able to talk to Tom on a daily basis about our plans. I had drained myself, mentally and physically, helping those sick men and had been under a lot of stress. Before I left the kitchen, I helped with a few things just to be around Tom. I spoke to him and told him that after he got off kitchen duty we would talk about what we had planned.

We started getting together after his shift to discuss our plans to escape and what we had to look forward to, as far as consequences, if we didn't make it. We didn't know what they (the Chinese) would do to us but all in all, it would be a challenge to try and see if we could be free, and get to our front line even though we knew we were far north from that; or maybe we would be rescued.

One day, after talking to Tom, I went to my hut and thought of all the events that had occurred during the last three weeks. I then started thinking about our escape. I, for one, wanted to get out of the POW camp but I had to find out if Tom was serious enough to go, and if so, had he considered the consequences if we got caught. Being that we were so far north, almost in Manchuria, the escape was going to involve a lot of planning and a whole lot of guts.

After resting and thinking about our venture I went to the playground to talk to Tom and find out one way or the other about our escape. I saw Tom as he was leaving the kitchen, so we met at the playground.

"Hi, Tom," I said. "Let's go by your hut and sit down and talk."

He said, "Okay." We walked to his hut and found that no one was there so we entered and then sat down. I started by saying, "Tom, are you serious about getting out of here?"

"Yes, Nick, but all the planning is going to take a few more days."

"I know, Tom, but if we know what we are taking and what we need for the escape, it won't take that long. Also, have you considered the consequences if we get caught?"

He answered, "No, but I think we ought to wait and see if the war is over any time soon and then we won't have to escape."

All of us had gone through a lot of hell in the last seven months. We had seen many men die from hunger, sickness, wounds and especially from lack of medical treatment; and our diet was killing us a few men at a time. As Tom finished what he was thinking, I replied by saying, "Maybe if we wait till next year we may be a little stronger and maybe do it in June or July, it would be warmer weather."

Tom looked at me and he said, "I think that is very wise, not only that, Nick, but after all you did for the POWs, you seem tired and worn out."

So I said, "Why don't we do that and save it for next year?" With that thought we shook hands and I said, "I'll see you later" and I left his hut.

Walking to my hut, I was kind of glad that we had postponed the escape till next year because I was tired and worn out from the previous six weeks trying to nurse the men back to health. On the other hand, I felt cheated and let down because so much had been said about being free and getting out of Camp 1. When I got to my hut, I laid down, and my thoughts were on the postponed escape. Yes, we would be stronger and healthier next year so all in all, a very wise decision. I decided to let the subject rest and I went to sleep.

That evening I was awakened by Sergeant Pettit knocking on the door. He asked me to come outside because he wanted to say something to me. Following him outside, we sat down, leaning against the wall of the hut. "Nick," he said, "What you did for those POWs was very commendable."

"I did it because someone had to and it didn't seem like anyone else wanted to," I answered.

"I wish that I could have helped you but I barely could walk around."

"I know, Sarge. Thank God that I was able to do it."

The Sarge was always around to give us encouragement, especially to those that needed it. When he started to get up, with his hands holding him up, I asked how he was doing. He replied, "Since you made the moccasins for me, I walk a lot better and my feet don't hurt as much." As he was starting to leave, he said, "I just wanted to let you know how I felt about you taking to the job of helping all the POWs here at camp, including me." Then he turned around and started limping away when he said, "Semper Fi," and gave me a salute.

A few days went by and things around camp stayed the same, including the routine. The menu had not changed as yet. Men were still getting weaker and unfortunately, more were dying. The following day some of our officers and non-commissioned officers were summoned to the Chinese commanders' office. Along with them, we saw eight POWs go into the office as well. When the officers came out of the office, they had a grin on their faces. Our first thought was it must be good news. We approached them and were told to gather around, so there we stood waiting for what we thought would be good news.

The senior officer said, "Men, the Chinese are going to let us write letters tomorrow so you think of what you are going to say to whoever you write to. Also, make sure you write a nice letter because I know that if you write and say we are being treated badly, a lot of men are dying, they will not send the letters to the U.S. They are going to give us a return address so your loved ones can write to you. Remember, keep it simple and just let them know you are ok and well."

We all scrambled to pass the word around to fellow prisoners. With a return address, we would certainly hear from our family and this was a blessing at this point in time. This would help the ones that were homesick, like a shot in the arm, and maybe they would perk up. Being able to write home put tears in many a man's eyes, as well as the officers. Soon our loved ones would know we were okay.

In that instant, I thought about mom and dad having received a telegram from Washington informing them that I was missing in action. With me writing a letter, they would know that I was alive, even if I were a prisoner.

That evening it had been very difficult to keep our mouths shut. Everyone was talking about what they were going to say in their letters. We could not wait until morning when we would get our hands on some paper and pencils.

Before we bedded down for the night, I went and told the sick and wounded about our letter writing. They were so happy and the news brought tears to their eyes. I let it be known to them that if they needed help with the letters, one of us would write it for them. They started telling each other what they would like to write. All night whispering could be heard but eventually, I went to sleep. The next morning I went to the creek and washed up, as was the usual routine. The Chinese came around and issued the paper and pencils for our letter writing. With these letters, hopefully, it would let our families know that we were alive and put renewed optimism in their thoughts.

We were told that the Chinese Peoples' Volunteers and Americans were meeting at Kaesong to discuss a truce and hopefully an end to the war. This gave us hope and we were looking forward to hearing more about the talks. A couple days later, the Chinese had indicated to us that it was the

Americans that did not want the war to end because they would not give in to the demands of the North Koreans. The U.N. troops would rather keep on killing women, innocent children and peace-loving people of North Korea. Most of us know that this was hogwash, yet some POWs went along with what the Chinese said.

It was mid-August 1951, and the Chinese informed us that we would be getting winter clothing in a couple of months. We were happy about this because our GI issued clothes were not sufficient to get us through the cold, blistering winter. Also, after wearing the same clothes for a year, different ones would sure be welcomed.

It is beyond comprehension what we went through, day in and day out, wearing filthy clothes that were infested with lice. They were constantly biting, and sucking on our bodies looking for their life sustaining nourishment – blood. Unfortunately, as weak as we were, blood was one thing we could not afford to supply these little critters. Battling them was an every hour, every day job and put us on the edge of endurance. The lice had over taken the huts, so no matter how many you were able to remove, there were numerous others to take their place. The men that had it the worst was the sick and wounded. Lice were on every inch of their bodies and that included their wounds. This was a mental picture that you would give just about anything to erase but couldn't. It was just horrifying.

Winter was setting in. The days were getting colder, shorter and the trees around camp were losing their leaves. One day, while waiting for chow, Lieutenant Chang told us that due to the colder weather, we would be making two trips to the mountains because both the kitchen and the huts would now need more wood.

Some more talk was going around camp that we would be told to clean the huts, inside and out, yet no one knew when. After returning from wood detail a couple days later, the whistle blew for an assembly so we gathered at the playground. The commander of the camp told us that we must clean the huts, including the outside. He told us again that we would be getting new clothes but he had not heard from headquarters as to when. When he finished, someone yelled, "You've been telling us that for months and we haven't seen anything yet. Not even better food." That challenge went unanswered.

After the assembly, a group of us stayed at the playground and were talking about what we had just been told. We questioned the new clothes, and the need to clean the huts. Did this mean that the war would soon be over? Was the Red Cross coming?

Was that the reason for trying to make a good impression? The thought of the war being over was ever present in our minds. Knowing that talks were going on to end the war gave us incentive to look ahead with a positive attitude.

With Thanksgiving only a month away, we were told to assemble at the playground for yet another speech. The commander told us again that they, the Chinese Peoples' Volunteers, were going to make our stay as pleasant as possible as long as we followed the rules. They must be followed to the letter or we would suffer the consequences. The rules would be posted at the officers' hut and would be given to each squad leader. After the commander was through, we scrambled to our huts and discussed what this was all about. We decided that maybe we should have our officers talk to the Chinese, asking them to change the food, and issuing us tobacco and getting medical help.

These are the rules that we were to obey ... or else:
1. We were to go to bed when the whistle blew.
2. There will be no wandering around camp at night. Guards have been given instructions to shoot anyone going outside the camp area.
3. We must obey all Chinese officers.
4. There will be no fighting while at Camp 1.
5. There will be no fires at night, due to the aircraft flying over.
6. No food will be taken from the kitchen unless it is mealtime.

The list of duties we were to perform included:
1. You will be getting up at 0500 hours and do exercises.
2. Those who are able to walk will go up to the mountains on wood detail.
3. You will select one man a week to clean the hut and another to clean outside.
4. You will be told to participate in lectures and read books about the Chinese people so you can understand them better.
5. You will learn about Communism and Lenin in Russia.

And the two things we were told about our meals:
1. After your exercises, you will have hot soybean milk. After you have your milk, you will go on wood detail.
2. After you come back from wood detail, you will have rice and a side dish.

Once we were told about our duties and what to expect from them, we settled down and accepted the fact that we were going to be here awhile; so rest and get well. When the men talked about the rules, the biggest dislike was the rule about learning Communism.

I continued checking on the sick and wounded, making sure they were warm and comfortable. A few of us tried to talk to them about eating but to no avail as they just wanted to be left alone. Death was still part of Camp 1.

Camp 1 had never consisted of "model" prisoners that the Chinese expected. We did not accept the propaganda, did not read their books on Communism nor attend the lectures. Camp 5 was different, so we were told, by other prisoners who had been transferred from there. I didn't attend all the lectures for the simple fact that there were too many men dying needlessly and the food was not adequate to sustain the human body. There were more important things to do, in my opinion, like taking care of those who couldn't take care of themselves. Words of encouragement, and knowing they were not alone seemed very important to me.

The struggle for survival was always present in camp. This showed on the faces of the prisoners as well as the officers. There were so many obstacles that faced us that most men weren't able to handle in their condition. Our morale was down to nothing, the guys walking around like zombies, not talking or eating. With the lack of medical care, we found ourselves with insufficient nutrition therefore, unable to do what the Chinese expected of us.

The deadliest destroyer of life in camp was the men giving up, unable to cope or not wanting to live; their alternative was to starve. The mental anguish must have justified the decision to die rather than to live the nightmare. Those of us who were stronger looked after the weak. We tried to coax them to eat but sometimes it just didn't seem to matter as they had already given up the fight to go on.

1951 at Camp 1 had taken its toll, with almost two hundred and fifty dead and still counting. From the first day at Camp 1, our diet had been sorghum seed, millet seed, fish heads put in soup, and the chopped corn. The corn tearing up our stomachs with the end result, on some men, bleeding to death.

The attitude of the Chinese toward us had changed. They were being more tolerant and friendly. There were occasions when they would visit our huts and ask how things were going, want to talk about where we were from and talk about their families. It was difficult to understand what was happening. Why was their policy changing?

Late in 1951 we had our winter clothes issued. The sun was shining but it was cold that day as everyone lined up at the playground. As we stood there in line, you could still feel the presence of our first snow fall the first part of October. It definitely put crispness in the air.

Each man was issued a coat, pair of pants, cap and shoes, all cotton padded. The clothes were similar to the Chinese Army issue except theirs was khaki color and ours were dark blue. The excitement on the playground was overwhelming. Between the new found attitude by the Chinese and our new clothes, I thought that at last, things were going to continue to get better. And they did!

A few days down the road, we found out that the menu was going to change. Instead of sorghum and millet seed, we were going to be getting rice and pork. We didn't know at this time what was happening to cause all these changes, but we did not question any of it. One of our officers and a couple NCOs summoned those interested to the sick room to help put the new clothes on them and let them know what was happening around camp.

It did not take long, maybe two weeks, before we heard unwelcome news. All of our officers were going to be moved to another camp. To most of these officers, this change didn't bother them but it sure troubled us that would be left. We would miss them because they were always there with words of encouragement.

Thanksgiving and Christmas were celebrated just like any other day, with the exception that we were going to be able to write a letter to our loved ones. During this time, due to the weather being thirty below zero, we stayed inside the huts. For New Year's, we went to other huts to wish them a happy New Year and express our thanks to God that we were still alive and surviving this ordeal.

The winter months were agonizing for the most part because of spending it inside our huts. I laid there thinking of home and mom and dad, and wondered what they were thinking and doing. More often than not, you could hear the sobs of your fellow hut mates as their thoughts too, more than likely were on home and family. We had nothing to take up our idle time with, so thinking about camp was the end result for most.

By spring of '52, all the POWs knew each other by their first names. The morale was high and the food had improved immensely. The soybean milk was a treat, so even when the temperature dropped to thirty below with snow on the ground, men would line up outside in order not to miss the 0600-hour issue of the milk. Even the relations between the men had improved. We treated each other like family and looked after each other.

A list, requesting essentials that were needed, was put together and presented to the commander of Camp 1:
1. The sick and wounded would not be forced to go on wood detail
2. Toothpaste every three months
3. Towels and soap to bathe, as often as necessary
4. Improve medical treatment
5. Issue writing material at least every three months
6. Designate one Chinese officer to listen to our complaints
7. Select one man to represent us on all decisions made by the commander
8. Do not force any POW to sit in communistic lectures or read communistic newspapers

Things around camp were changing and the Chinese Peoples' Volunteers were helping with that. Someone had come up with the idea of bunk beds to sleep on instead of on the floor. A committee had been selected to approach our ideas and grievances to the Chinese. To our amazement, they were cooperative with the bunk bed idea.

Just a few days went by when we were assembled at the playground. The commander told us that he had approved the bunk beds and that we would be receiving toothbrushes, toothpaste and more tobacco per man. Also we would be celebrating Easter Sunday. He continued with telling us that we were to go on wood detail and get the proper logs needed to make our bunk beds. The best news of all came when he mentioned that a clinic would be set up, but in order to achieve that, we needed to clean some empty huts. There was never a thought in my mind that this would be a problem for the prisoners to quickly take care of. His last bit of information was that a doctor and nurse were on their way to camp.

We had just heard news that we never thought we would be hearing, yet we were skeptical. In 1951, we were promised a lot of things that did not materialize and the end result was death for some. Our views were, we'll have to see it to believe it. The day finally arrived when the commander of camp told us that we would have bunk beds. We would be making them for ourselves, and they would supply the rope. We would be showed how and go from there. The thought of a bed instead of the floor was a great relief to us all. The Chinese suggested we find logs about six inches in diameter and six foot long. The cross pieces were to be four foot long. We notched the legs two foot from the ground and one foot from the top. Then we notched the cross piece six inches from each end, which enabled us to put the notches together, tied with rope. The same procedure was then used for the six foot rails. After this was completed, we would then weave the rope length wise and then crosswise, making a net. Making the bunk beds kept us all busy for a few months. Finally getting a good night sleep was the talk of the camp. Our bunk beds became reality in the summer and what a difference they made. No more sleeping on the floor!

While we had been going on wood detail, I noticed that more and more guys were volunteering for this outing. Some Mexican Americans had discovered marijuana growing wild in the mountains where we went on wood detail. As the word got around that this stuff was up for grabs, it was brought back to the camp. I noticed, one day after wood detail, that there were weeds covering the roof tops of some of the POWs huts. To me it was strange but never paid much attention to it. I later found out that this was the way to dry the marijuana.

It did not take very long before a new Chinese officer noticed the weeds and approached a group of prisoners. He wanted to know why they were covering the roofs. A quick thinking POW told him that it was to camouflage the huts so we didn't get bombed. Luckily, the officer bought the story and nothing was mentioned thereafter. This marijuana, for some, became the only way to survive and endure the way of life that we had.

The Chinese introduced a new food to us. It was called pork dumplings. They tasted like stew pot pie. The way the Chinese showed the cooks to prepare these was as follows: roll a ball of dough out like a flat tortilla, put stew inside then bring the dough around the meat and crimp on top (like a giant Hershey's chocolate kiss). After that, put cheese cloth on a round tray which looked like it was made of bamboo and had squares on the bottom. These trays were four feet in diameter. Then place the dumplings one and a half inches apart on the cheese cloth. These trays would then be set on top of pots of boiling water. The lid was put on and left to steam for two to three hours. The cooks had three of these pots boiling which held approximately eighty dumplings per pot.

After eating this new item on our menu, most everyone made remarks that the cooks should make it more often. They were so delicious and different from our regular meals that it was decided to approach the commander to request them more often. He agreed which gave us something to look forward to. The biggest concern was whether or not the cooks really make them more often.

A few weeks had passed when the commander announced the sports equipment had arrived. This consisted of volleyball and basketball equipment plus a ping-pong table. This was an enormous lift to the morale around camp. Being able to play basketball or volleyball would help pass all the idle time. The Chinese had given us a hut to convert into a recreation room. The guys could hardly wait to get these things set up and put to use.

Not too many days had passed when I decided to go see Sergeant Pettit. While on my way to his hut, I saw a lot of guys involved with sports. Some were playing volleyball and some were playing basketball. While looking at the basketball court, to my amazement I saw Smitty playing basketball with the "big guys." Even after the painstaking episode he went through, there he was – standing tall.

As weeks went by, we still had a few men that could not handle the stress of being captive. For instance, I saw a young kid pretending he was home and would say, "Hey mom, may I have a Coke?" As he was saying this, he would go through the motions of going to the refrigerator, opening the door and reaching in for a coke. He would then yell, "Thanks, mom."

Another time, a POW passed by and said, "Hey, dad gave me some money. Let's go to the movies downtown." It was very disheartening to see this, yet there was nothing you could do.

A few older men had given up as well. One day I walked passed a sergeant's hut where he was leaning up against the side and said to me, "You know, Nick, I'm not going to make it."

I leaned down and told him, "Of course you're going to make it. You have kids waiting for you at home. You know something, Sarge, God doesn't give you anything you can't handle. You have to believe that you're going home, Sarge." I also added, "I believe God hears those that speak to him." He was tired, weary and he didn't want to eat. I tried to reach out to him by talking to him as often as I could. Two months later, I was one of the POWs that had to bury him. It was hard for me but for some it was just another dead POW.

One day I was walking across the playground when I saw Sergeant Pettit. I yelled at him and as we met he asked if I wanted to take a look at the market place. I told him that I did, so we walked over to the edge of the camp and took a look at what was going on. This market place idea was started with the idea of trading your stuff for some of the stuff that the other guys had or didn't need. As we moved toward the market, I said, "This is essential. These guys are to busy thinking about their problems and this gives them something else to think about. Look at their happy faces."

Sergeant Pettit asked, "Are you going to trade your tobacco ration?"

I told him, "I already gave it to the guys at the clinic who had run out."

As we were walking away from the market, we were talking about what was being traded. Sarge mentioned the fish heads that one of the traders had and I told Sergeant Pettit that they looked like the ones that were given to us last summer right after we got to camp. Some of the other items that were traded were tobacco for three teaspoons of sugar or rice crust. Some things were purchased with script or greenbacks, and in camp that was rare.

We were almost to Sarge's hut when he said, "Nick, I'm going in to rest my poor aching feet. Thanks for the moccasins, Nick." After leaving there, I headed over to check in on the sick, only to learn that more had died of yellow jaundice. This was something that I never got used to. It affected me in such a depressing way each time.

With each day passing, more and more guys were playing volleyball, baseball and basketball. This was a positive feeling and knowing it was due to the Chinese treating us better. The clinic was doing great. We had sick call from 0900 to 1200 hours every day. There was usually a long line for this clinic.

As Danny Arellano and I were walking around the playground, we noticed that the Chinese were laying wire around the huts that were surrounding the playground. We wondered what it was for. Two days later, we realized they were installing a public announcement system. We asked Lieutenant Chang what the p.a. system was for. He told us that with the p.a., we could receive news about the peace talks. Also, any assemblies, meetings or such would be announced over the speakers. He added that music would be played for us during our stay at Camp 1.

A few days had passed when we heard, over the speakers, the Chinese National Anthem and a few Chinese songs. One particular day that stands out in my mind was a song the Chinese played over the speakers. The title, *I've Been Away From Home Too Long*, by Perry Como. Another was *Danny Boy*. It was mental torture, to most, to hear these songs, yet welcomed by a few.

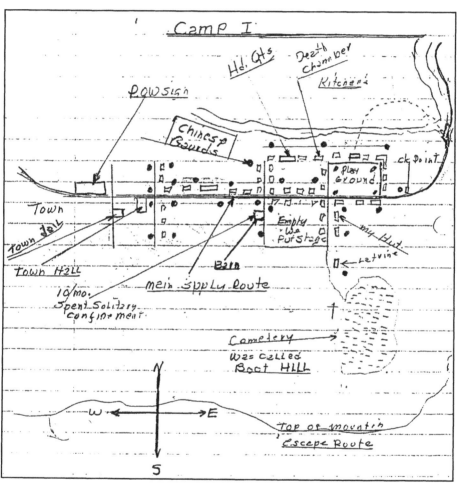

A map of Camp One and surrounding area as I remember it. (Sketch by Nick A. Flores)

We heard, over Radio Peking, that the Americans were ready to deal with the Koreans and Chinese about a truce and to decide the fate of all the POWs. This was good news but it seemed that we had heard this before, so most of us weren't very interested. This had happened before, getting us excited and then we would hear that the talks had ceased, due to the Americans not wanting peace.

Around this time, we were surprised by the arrival of British POWs. Watching them enter Camp 1, the question was where would all of these men be put. All the POWs greeted and welcomed them. After a few weeks, however, confrontations began between the British and the Americans. One reason for this was the British were blaming the "American yanks," as we were being called, for being in war because every time we were involved in war, they had to be involved. Therefore, they felt their men were dying for something they didn't believe in. Fighting and disagreements continued.

Both the Americans and British were using name-calling, the Americans called the British "Limies" and the British called the Americans "Yanks." These actions just refueled the tension that already existed. Finally, two NCOs decided enough was enough. They gathered everyone involved and told them that everyone was at Camp 1 because we were sent to the war by our respective countries. We are going to make the best of our stay at Camp 1. We were sent to fight for our freedom. We must all get along and that will start by the British referring to the Americans as such and the Americans will refer to the British as such. Is that understood? After that talk, most everyone got along, outside of a few that were still upset over what had been said.

We eventually found out that in the group of recent arrivals, there were Royal Marines and the rest were from the twenty-ninth Glochestershire (The Glosters) Brigade. They, too, had lost men on the march to Camp 1. Eventually, things at the camp mellowed, with people doing their own thing and leaving others alone.

Prior to our new arrivals, we had asked the Chinese about damming the creek behind the camp, creating a swimming hole and a place to wash clothes. To our astonishment, Lieutenant Chang informed us that the commander had given his okay and we could start whenever we were ready. After that news, volunteers were asked for, ending up with approximately three-hundred, and work began on the dam.

The creek was full of cobblestones and by the third week of construction, we had succeeded in our venture and had the swimming hole finished. We later came up with an idea for a diving board. Those involved in creating the dam were very proud of themselves and it goes without saying, this new play area was extremely busy.

One day I was crossing the playground, heading for the kitchen, and I heard jets coming over the camp. There were ten to fifteen of them. They were engaging in dog-fights with other jets that came from the north. The men that witnessed this figured they were F-86s and MIGs. Before long, a large group of fellow prisoners were on the playground to watch this entertainment. Even Lieutenant Chang and other Chinese officers rushed outside. One of these officers stated that their MIGs were better than our F-86s. Then I heard someone say, "Let's see who goes down first." We never did find out but we knew that the American F-86s were far superior to anything the Chinese had. These dog-fights continued two to three times a month and they were always a source of excitement.

As time continued to go by, I got to know some of the British POWs and became friends with some. My fond memories are of one in particular, Clarence Dawson, from Saskatchewan, Canada. He stood about five-foot-eight, reddish hair, and medium build. Meeting Clarence for the first time, you walked away feeling as if you had known him for years. He was very outgoing, went around camp talking with the guys and always doing something for someone – just an all around wonderful human being. I found them to be very jolly people and some of them would get together with others and sing. They worked as hard as we did and took care of their wounded.

I had not seen much of Tom and when I did, it was usually on wood detail. I spent a lot of my time helping out in the clinic so I hadn't been able to sit down with Tom and discuss our escape plans.

Chapter Six
A Genuine Escape

By the end of April '52, life at camp had improved. Not to our standards but enough that morale was higher and we were better able to cope. The food was better and more plentiful, in return, we were looking healthier. Most of the men were busy with their own lives. The POWs had established a pattern how they would live, day by day, in the camp.

The guards were farther apart. We went everywhere without seeing guards. We went swimming without looking over our shoulder to see if someone was keeping an eye on us. Some POWs were playing basketball at the playground while some were just sitting around talking about home or just telling jokes. A few had fashioned weights to build the body muscles and others played cards. The morale of the men was good and that was including the British that had arrived. At this point we were not losing too many men to "boot hill" so things had changed for the better.

Tom and I had talked about my idea and plans for escaping; but it was just talk, as Tom would not commit himself in saying yes or no. It was then that we would get together and talk about the escape. We had talked at various times about this escape but neither one of us made a commitment to each other. I had made up my mind, quite sometime ago, that I was going to escape even it I had to go alone. I asked Tom to give me an answer as soon as possible. I, with or without him, was ready to go.

Though some people who had heard about it had suggested that it was the wrong time; it was too far from the front lines, and that if we did escape and got caught, the Chinese would probably kill us. Everything we heard was negative, so I told Tom that if he decided not to go, there would be no hard feelings. Both of us decided at this time that if we decided to plan the escape, we would not tell anyone. Once we agreed on that we let it rest for the time being.

A week or so later I saw Tom on the wood detail. I walked up to him and asked, "Are you ready to escape or not?"

He thought a few seconds then said, "I've been thinking a lot about it. Let's do it. Why not?"

I asked, "Are you sure?"

"All they can do is kill us," and then he shrugged his shoulders and let out a small sigh and grin. As we were carrying a log on our shoulders, he got close to me and told me to meet him at the latrine that evening.

It was late evening when I went to the latrine to meet Tom. The latrines were about ten feet long, twenty-four inches wide and four to five feet deep. There were slates built across so we were able to squat. The latrine was about three hundred feet from our huts and the reason for late evening was that there was not very much traffic of men coming and going. Our main concern were the guards who were stationed near the latrine and at the cemetery.

When Tom and I had these meetings, we always spoke in Spanish. A mutual promise had been made that we would not talk to anyone, not even our friends or buddies. That included the Mexican-American POWs that were close to us.

One night, as we were both heading to the latrine, we heard the Chinese blow a whistle and then the guards got all excited about something. Tom and I continued walking and when we approached the latrine, the guard told us to get back to our hut. Then, out of nowhere, came a Navy "Black Widow" strafing close to camp. He came about one to two hundred feet above us. As we ran for cover, I fell in the latrine and Tom sat there laughing. After all the excitement, I went to the creek and washed off, but was not able to get the stink off. Tom brought me my GI clothes so I could change. When I went to bed that night, a few minutes later someone commented that someone had gone to the bathroom in his pants. The guys were unaware that I had fallen into the "honey pit." The next morning they had found out what had happened. That morning I went to the creek to bathe and wash my clothes. I put on my wet clothes but at least they smelled better.

That afternoon we found out why the Navy plane had strafed the camp. The Chinese and North Korean Armies had put every POW camp on the supply route for the convoys to go through to take supplies down south. They had posted large POW signs outside the camp so our planes would see them and hopefully not bomb the camps. We learned that a big convoy of about twenty trucks had stopped outside the camp. "Bed Check Charlie" apparently had known of this. Occasionally the Black Widow would come by, never shooting, just waving his wings as he passed, not making a second run.

The only few exciting happenings at the camp were the dog-fights between the F-86s and the Migs, "Bed Check Charlie" at night and the Black Widow appearing occasionally.

It was now the spring of 1952. Tom and I decided to put our plans into action. We went over all the things we had to do and things needed to take with us, such as an extra shirt and socks plus a few crackers to eat on the way. We were ready. Up to this point, no one had learned of this escape that we had planned for a long time. Both of us were feeling healthy and strong enough to undertake this task. Maybe, just maybe, one of us would make it. That night we went to bed just like the others so no one would become suspicious. About 2245 hours, we got up, gathered the things that were to be taken and left. First, we looked around for the guard, and noticed that he had gone down the street, so we headed for the kitchen. The creek that we had to cross was behind the kitchen. It would be easy just to walk; therefore, the guard would not suspect an escape.

Tom and I had on dark GI clothing. Spotting us would be hard for the guard. He was at the other end of the creek that was about a hundred feet away. We went to a bush near the creek and waited there a few minutes. When we spotted the guard heading back, we both sweated a little. I told Tom not to move so the guard would just pass by and then we could see where he was going. By this time it was around 2430 or 0100 hours. We could hear voices around the camp. The Chinese were laughing and talking to each other. There were rocks in the creek, which meant the sound of trickling water to help muffle our noise when walking.

I asked Tom if he was ready, to which he responded with a nod and said yes. We then crawled to the creek, about one hundred to one hundred and fifty feet away, and picked a shallow spot that we had decided on sometime before the escape, so we could cross it on our hands and knees. Just then a Chinese guard yelled and we immediately froze in our tracks. Looking around, we could vaguely hear the guard talking to someone but could not tell who it was due to the darkness, but the figure moved toward us. We both feared they had spotted us, but then I said, "Don't move, Tom." The person walking was thirty feet from the creek, then continued past us, then was gone from sight. It is a good thing we stayed still. We assumed that the Chinese guard had challenged a North Korean man who was not supposed to be anywhere near the camp or creek.

After making sure the way was clear, we went ahead and crossed the creek. All this time had been a terrifying fifteen minutes as I knew the guard would shoot first then ask questions later. On the other side of the creek we rested, thinking how lucky we were. The long journey was still ahead of us. We had to go under the bridge not knowing if they stationed any guards there. Close by, there were a few bushes within thirty feet of the bridge, so we decided to take a break before going on, hoping to detect any human movement.

All this time, we made hand signals just as a squad leader does when the enemy is close by. I made a sign to Tom that I would go first, checking the bridge, and if clear, I would motion him to follow. If they spotted me, I would say that I was alone as there was no use both of us getting caught, or worse, shot.

I started crawling slowly, making sure my hands did not hit anything that would cause sounds of any kind. Well, so far so good. Just about the time I was going to signal Tom to move ahead, we saw headlights coming toward the bridge. As it got closer, we laid down on our bellies and waited for the vehicle to stop or go by. It traveled really slow and once it was a hundred feet past the bridge, I decided to move. I made the sign for Tom to join me, then we got to the bridge. We had sore hands and knees from crawling so we rested, trying to rub the soreness away.

Once past the bridge we knew we were free because about seventy five feet away was the path that led up to the mountain. Once on top we would be standing, looking down at the camp and on our way. It was a great feeling to be free, enjoying every minute and not even knowing what was ahead for us.

We had been to these mountains before but never on the peak. Being unfamiliar with the trail, we were careful watching every step of the way. We pushed on, and by 0500 hours, we were about one half mile past the camp. We heard a whistle blowing for the men to get up for exercises. Tom mentioned that he was glad to be up there and not down in camp. He then took a deep breath, stretched his arms outward and exhaled with a sound of relief. I followed suit and I said to Tom, "It is good to be free and yet we take it for granted. When it is taken way, it is nothing but hell." After rejoicing, we rested then went on our way, keeping our eyes and ears open and ready for any surprises.

The pace was slow because in a couple of hours the sun would be coming over the mountain and we could be spotted. The mountain trail may not be used much. Nevertheless, we were aware that the Korean farmers used the trails on top of the mountains to travel from village to village so they did not have to use the road and go all the way around the mountain.

As the sun came over the mountain we looked for a place to hide, away from the trail and far enough that if someone was on the trail, we would not be seen. Going a few yards, we found a perfect place. A huge rock with a lot of vegetation. I told Tom, "This is it," so we sat down to rest. I took the first watch for two to three hours, then Tom woke up and it was my turn. I slept for three hours, then we got ready to go. Just as we were getting up, Tom put his hand on my shoulder and then a sign to be quiet. We heard voices coming from the trail, so we did not move a muscle. These people moved slowly, so the first thing that entered our minds was that they were looking for us. As we waited, the voices diminished little by little. After waiting another hour, very cautiously we got up, looked around and walked to the trail. The time was close to 1900 hours. We walked very slowly and did not encounter any more unwanted surprises.

In the morning of day two, we were able to see villages from the top of the mountain. Being still dark outside, we could not see if anyone was around. The only things we could see were a few dwellings and rice paddies.

From our standpoint, you were able to see for miles down the valley, venturing to say that the road that went along the foot of the mountain was about three quarters of a mile from where we were. At this time we evaluated the area to see which direction we should go. With this in mind, we were on our way and found a place to rest near the trail, which had a clump of bushes and some big rocks. This seemed perfect for our needs as we would be able to see either end of the trail and still not be seen by anyone who happened to be walking the trail. Both of us seemed satisfied this was the right location, so we decided to eat a few crackers and get some sleep. After resting, we checked the supplies and felt we had enough for a few more days. Tom told me that he was glad he had come with me and it sure felt good to be free. Also, people do not realize what freedom is until it is taken away from them. We sat there most of the day watching for any activity on the trail and listening for voices from the villages.

I was looking south, Tom looking toward the west. Being able to see all directions, we began talking about where we were from and our families. A little bit later we decided that one would take watch while the other slept.

In the beginning of day three, we realized that a lot of ground had been covered since we left. It was starting to get dusk and we would soon be getting on our way. We decided to follow the top of the mountain range for another night, then cross over the valley and road to the other mountain range.

When the time came to cross the road, we had to be very careful as it was a supply route. During the day there was not much traffic on the road. We stood looking to find a good location to cross so the Koreans would not see us. We more or less designated what route to go down so we could cross the road. There was not enough vegetation to cover us from being seen from the road, so we had to wait till we got farther down to decide how to cross. We walked slowly about one hundred and fifty yards and saw the only way was going to be crawling a few hundred feet, then stopping at the edge of the road.

We went in the direction of some bushes waist high and crawled to the edge. We then laid down approximately twenty feet away from the edge before crossing. We heard trucks coming so we waited for close to an hour before attempting to cross. I was to go first, so I told Tom to wait a few minutes before crossing in case someone saw me. When I knew it was clear, I would give him a short whistle. Looking to see if it was indeed clear, he walked slow as not to attract attention in the event someone was close. When both of us had gotten to the other side, we laid down on our stomachs for about half an hour, then crawled for fifty yards along a rice paddy.

Several minutes later, we reached the foot of the mountain and hid behind some rocks to catch our breath. We then proceeded to slowly climb the mountain hoping no one would see us. The Koreans had planted corn in the flat parts of the ground around the rocks because this was the only available location, as all the good flat land was for planting rice. We tried not to disturb the plants so no one would see that humans had trampled them. We had also been very careful not to leave any clues on the trail. About three to four hours later we were on top of the mountain where we would hopefully find a trail.

Once at this location, we rested for half an hour. It was going to be slow not knowing if there was even a trail to follow. The side we had already traveled had been familiar to us as we used it on our wood details. The darkness was going to be a disadvantage also.

We had noticed from across the valley that this mountain range was higher than the other, so being spotted on the top would be harder. As we were walking Tom suggested that since it would be dusk soon, why didn't we rest a while and in the morning we could look around for a trail or the best way to go. It became very difficult traveling because the mountains in Korea were nothing but rocks. We had to go around, sometimes over them and in some places there were cliffs next to the rocks that dropped down eighty feet. I agreed with Tom so we looked for a place to rest away from the top so they would not see us in case they were looking for us.

After all the crawling and walking, I was ready for a good sleep. We found a perfect spot where both of us could sleep and not worry about being found. The location had two huge rocks four feet apart, like a little alley. It was nine to ten feet long with the northern end blocked by scrubs. There is where we got our much needed sleep and when we woke, it was daylight. I told Tom that I would go look around to see what was out there. I came out of our little shelter very slowly, hoping no one was close by. After looking around in each direction, I could see a village down below. I started looking south, mountain after mountain, and then stood there wondering how far away our troops were and that it would be pleasing to get out of this mess. I knew we had a long way to go. Thoughts would come to my mind about; if we made it, we could get help for the sick and wounded, maybe they could drop medical supplies at each camp and send a team of doctors in with the International Red Cross. I knew the thought had been unrealistic, but it would help the POWs that were sick. After a bit, I went back to the shelter where Tom had been doing the same, thinking. We both thought about how long we had been gone on our escape when Tom asked whether this was our third or fourth day. I replied, "It's our fourth and I think we have gone eight or ten miles." Traveling just at night we were not able to make good time nor cover too many miles as the terrain was treacherous. Another thought came to mind so I said, "Tom, isn't it strange that we haven't encountered any animals like snails, owls or even squirrels? We haven't even seen or heard a wild cat." Of course we had enough to worry about other than the animals or the lack of them.

We waited for darkness to descend upon us. It was time again to get moving, as we had already picked the direction we were going to go. We traveled all night, doing quite well as we had found a trail and this one did not have a lot of rocks to keep running into. We were able to make good time due to the increase of our pace. After about six hours of walking we decided to rest a while. As we did, Tom asked if I was hungry and my reply was, "Yes, do we have any more food? His answer was no and I could see he was worried. I suggested that we move on, after resting, and then see if we could find something to eat or ask the Koreans to give us something.

We moved on for two or three more hours, then came to a valley where we saw a house close to the foot of the mountain. We got within a hundred yards of the house and by then it was almost morning. We were hiding behind trees and scrubs.

Tom thought we should watch the house for a few minutes to see who came or went, if anyone. Instead of a few minutes, we ended up watching for an hour and a half. Tom said he would sneak down to the house and find out if anyone lived there or at least get close enough maybe to hear voices. He went slowly, hiding behind shrubs one after another, till he was within fifteen feet. There had not been any movement so maybe this was a good time to hit the house for food. Tom walked closer to the house, hid behind the wall then got to the door. He entered and after five minutes he came out and motioned to me to come down the mountain. When I got to the door a little boy about eleven ran out the door and was gone.

Second Escape

Tom and I thought that maybe he was going to school or getting his father. We were eating rice that the women gave us when we were surprised, to put it mildly. The Korean Militia swarmed around us armed with steel bayonets attached to wooden rifles, so we put our hands up. Then they found some rope, tied our hands behind our backs and took us outside. With anger in their eyes, they started poking our backs with the bayonets, shoving us around and spitting in front of us, showing how much they hated Americans. As they did this, you could see in the distance a uniformed soldier approaching. They had Tom and me kneeling and the Korean soldier yelled at them. We did not know what they said but we were then stood up and they moved back away from us. There had to be nine or ten. Tom and I looked at each other as if to say "we tried."

The Korean officer approached, stopped three feet in front of us and said he was Captain-so-and so of the Korean Army. He spoke perfect English. He asked who we were and what we were doing there. Tom, in Spanish, suggested that I tell him. I said, "We escaped from Camp 1 and my name is Nick Flores, 1091431." He stated that we were very foolish for trying to escape and there were many mountains to cross before we could get to the front lines. There were too many Korean and Chinese troops for us to be able to reach American forces.

He looked at our hands, checking to see if they were well secured. He then told us that we would go with him to the Korean Headquarters and stay there until they decided what to do with us. We went along with him but were surprised no one else came. The Korean Militia stayed at the house where they had words with the officer, but they did not make a move. When we were leaving, they looked at us again and made a gesture of wanting to stick their bayonets in our bellies.

As we left the officer said that we would walk about a mile to the Korean Headquarters for interrogation. As we left the path along the rice paddies, we were now on the road. He put us in front of him about five paces, and he continued talking to us, telling us again how foolish it was for our attempt at escaping. We noticed he had taken a .45 caliber pistol out of his holster, then caught up to us and stopped us. He then put the pistol to my temple and asked me what would happen if he pulled the trigger? I answered, "I would fall deader than hell."

"You are very brave. You are a Marine, aren't you?"

I replied, "Yes." Then he placed the pistol at Tom's temple and repeated what he had asked me. All Tom did was shrug his shoulders while looking down. Then he walked over to my side and fired off his pistol right next to my ear. I crouched from the noise. It happened so fast that I did not react any other way. That incident scared the living daylights out of both Tom and me. The worst part was, my ears were hurting something fierce and it did not take many seconds before the ringing started. The officer then put his pistol back in the holster and we continued our walk as if nothing had happened.

He told us that he learned English at the University of California where he had attended for three years while living with some good friends in Oakland. Of course, my blood was getting warmer, maybe even boiling.

We finally reached the Korean Army Headquarters, where they put us in a cell, and left us waiting for a few hours. The Korean captain who had brought us there, told both Tom and me that we would be going back to Camp 1 in the morning by truck. Being late as it was, this would be the earliest time they could return us. He asked us if we were hungry to which we answered that we were. A Korean soldier brought us a bowl of rice and some water.

A guard was placed in front of our cell, armed with a submachine gun, motioning us not to get up or move. We ate our rice, drank the water, then set the glass on the bowl. When we started talking, the guard again motioned with his gun pointed at us not to move, so we did not move a muscle.

I was thinking of the tragic mistake we had made entering that house for food, but it was done and there was no looking back. I thought to myself, that next time; if there was a next time, we would bring enough food for at least ten to fifteen days of travel.

After being there overnight, we were woken up and told it was time to go. The guard opened the cell door and marched us to the outside where a truck was waiting. They cut and removed the ropes that tied our hands. Then we climbed into the truck where the guard who was to escort us retied them in front and very loose. When they had tied our hands in back, it had been very uncomfortable. Being tied in front made us feel more flexible. Once in the truck, the captain said something to the guard who turned around, looked at us and told us do not try it again. It will not be so easy next time.

The truck took off with us sitting on top of rice sacks and the truck was loaded to the hilt. Accompanying us was a man, woman and child, and the guard. I do not recall anyone riding with the driver. We were sitting toward the back with the guard five feet away. The others were behind the guard.

The truck was moving at a good clip on a straight away when he started to slow a bit. This was four or five miles from where we started. I looked around noticing we were moving on a slight downgrade, when I heard the driver put the truck in neutral, freewheeling down the slope. The truck was gaining momentum when the driver realized he was going too fast. He applied the brakes that slowed us a bit, but he had waited too long. As we are flying down the hill, I looked over at Tom and said, "He's not going to make it, Tom. We have to do something."

We both looked at the guard only to see fear on his face, and on the couple's faces. All this time we heard the driver grinding gears in hopes to stop the runaway truck. The curve was getting closer so I told Tom, "We jump when we get close to the curve. When I get to three, we jump." I was scared but knew if we did not jump off, we would be two dead POWs. This was all happening within seconds. I again yelled to Tom that when the driver puts on the brakes, I would count to three, then we jump. In the meantime, I told Tom to get the rope off his hand so he could break his fall. I did the same. Meanwhile the driver was frantically trying to gear down and when he did put on the brakes I yelled "one-two-three" and we jumped. We were very fortunate to have landed where we did because it was on a grassy part of the road. We laid there, dazed trying to figure out what had happened. We were both groaning from the fall. The pain was unbearable but during the next few minutes Tom and I checked ourselves over and to our great relief, discovered that neither one of us had any major injuries nor broken bones. We then knew, though as sore as we were, it was time to get out of there and go check on the passengers in the truck that had gone over the embankment.

Standing on the road looking toward the truck we were unable to see anyone moving so I said to Tom, "Let's go for help back at the headquarters." We had to get help and soon.

We started walking and after a few minutes a Korean Army truck came by so we tried to explain what had happened. Two of the soldiers ran over to where the truck went over the bank. A driver and Korean soldier took us both to the captain. I explained what had happened, that I was sorry about the people in the truck and that we jumped because we knew the truck would not make the curve. I also told him that the driver had taken the truck out of gear to try to save fuel but he waited too long to put it back

Second Escape

in gear. It gained momentum and was too late. The captain replied that there had been accidents there before, for the same reason – they went too fast.

We had scrapes and cuts on our arms and legs and were asked if we wanted medical aid to which we responded by saying no, it was not that bad. We were just sore but glad to be alive. They had sent a truck with a doctor aboard to the accident scene and then they took us to the Korean Headquarters. After going through all that, we were afraid and tired, looking forward to going home to Camp 1.

We were loaded up on a truck then driven back to Camp 1. As we arrived to Camp 1 headquarters, everyone was looking at us with praise for escaping, and glad that we were okay. Tom wondered what they were going to do with us. I told him that I did not know, but being back was somehow appealing. The commanding officer of camp came out and he asked what we had to say for ourselves. I answered that it is our duty to try to escape whenever possible and I thought that if he or any of his countrymen were in our position, they would do the same under the circumstances. The commander looked us up and down, then told Lieutenant Chang to take us somewhere. They took us to our huts where we would stay. Later they told us that we were going to an assembly and the commander would speak to all the POWs.

The next day everyone gathered at the playground; where some sat on the ground while others stood. The guards brought us with our hands tied and stood us alongside the commander, with two guards on each side.

The commander, through his interpreter, told everyone present that the two POWs standing before them had committed a crime against the Chinese Peoples' Volunteers; and they would not permit such action in this camp. They will confess and apologize to the Chinese Peoples' Volunteers and they will be punished. I was then asked to step up to the microphone. Moving up to the microphone, many fellow POWs clapped and praised Tom and me for escaping.

Standing with my hands tied behind my back, I said in Spanish, "If these Chinks think that I would not escape again, they're greatly mistaken. These suckers think I won't. They got another thing coming." Everyone started clapping and although most of them did not know what I was talking about, the Mexican guys were telling them what I had said.

The interpreter came to me and asked me what I had said and I answered that I had told them that I was sorry. Then they took me back to where I had been standing before with the guards and then they took Tom up to the microphone. Tom was not a talker, so he just said he was sorry that he did not make it. They pulled him back and the commander then spoke, still with Lieutenant Chang as the interpreter, sounding upset and embarrassed, to the POWs saying no one escapes from the Chinese Peoples' Volunteers or Camp 1. They will be punished and they lose their privileges for committing a crime against the Chinese Peoples' Volunteers.

They marched us to jail where we spent twenty days, sitting cross-legged for eighteen hours a day. I noticed other POWs sitting in cells, including Sergeant Pettit. We were not able to move, talk to each other, slouch our backs nor make any noise. We knew better than to disobey as a guard sat outside the door with an automatic rifle pointed at us during those long dreadful hours. That was not a pleasant time.

After serving our time, Tom and I were put into separate huts, with Tom in one corner of the camp and me in another. A few days later they took us to a hard labor camp located to the north. It was close to Manchuria, up in the mountains with snow on the ground and very cold. I cannot recall how long it took for us to get there. A Chinese officer that we had known at Camp 1 was in charge there. He was nothing but skin and bones, so we nicknamed him "Bones." The labor camp looked like a small fort having only one gate to pass through with two guards to open and close it. They told Tom and I that we would be there for thirty days. That seemed like a long time but just the same, worth every bit of it for our taste of freedom for those few days.

As we settled in our new home, we asked around to find out how many guys were there and what they did in hard labor camp. They stated that ten were there for fighting with the sympathizers; we haul wood, break up rocks, and shovel snow. That night I saw the camp mascot for the first time. One of the men had found a small dog wandering in camp. He then took possession, making it the mascot. When I asked what the puppy's name was, the reply was "Bones." Tom and I started laughing and knew that they had named him after the officer in charge. "Bones was a small man, short hair, very wrinkled face, sunken eyes and dark complected. He was wearing a padded cotton winter uniform so he appeared bigger than he really was.

That night after we had gone to bed, someone had yelled slang words, adding the name Bones, you s.o.b. That particular commander happened to be on the ground and had overheard what they had said. When this occurred the time was between 2200 and 2300 hours, and very cold outside. The commander arrived with six guards, ordered us to get up and go outside and to hurry up. We had not been allowed to put on our shoes or jackets so everyone had to stand in the cold with just socks on our feet. By that time the temperatures had dropped to twenty below.

He told us to line up, and demanded that whoever made the remark to step forward. No one moved. He then added that he would ask us one more time and if we did not confess to who it was, we would not go to bed. Since the temperature was so blistery cold, the commander felt so sure it would be so miserably uncomfortable for us, that whoever had made the remark would quickly say so, and then we would all return to our hut. Wrong! Even after this no one said a word, so we stood out there for quite a while, forty-five minutes to an hour. The guards standing with us were cold as their faces were showing displeasure. The commander returned from his office to ask us again if the person responsible would step forward. Still no one made a move so he left again. Another half hour passed, and by this time we were cold plus everyone's feet were frozen. The commander returned saying something to the guards and they made a motion for us to get in the hut. It was almost 2400 hours by the time we finally got in bed.

The next morning after we got up and completed our exercises, we headed for the mountains to gather logs for the kitchen, then shoveled snow in the "fort." Soon we realized that we had not seen our mascot, so started looking for him, searching every corner of the hut and even outside on the fort grounds, but useless. A terrible thought entered our minds. The commander had confiscated the dog because of the episode last night. All too soon the officer came to inform us he had taken the mascot.

For our dinner that night they told us it would be soup, so we settled back in our beds waiting, during which time we discussed the disappearance of our mascot. The whistle blew for dinner then the Chinese cooks came over to our hut and dished it out. After eating our soup and rice, we still had not figured out why they had taken our dog. One of the men went to the latrine then came running back to tell us that we had just eaten our mascot. The pelt was hanging by the latrine, put there purposely for us to see.

After all the commotion, the officer came out of his office, approached us and asked if we had enjoyed our soup. He grinned then left. Some wanted to vomit and a couple of men did, after the officer had told us what we had just had for dinner. All of us were sick at the thought that the commander had taken his anger out on the little dog. Tom and I thought the guy responsible for slurring the commander had been out of line but kept quiet so no trouble would start. That evening we were, by not admitting to it, all saddened and disgusted by the events that had occurred, so we just sat around thinking to ourselves. One man spoke up saying that he had never eaten a dog before. He wanted to know if he were going to die. Another yelled from across the room that he would not die, so do not worry about it. Being late and dark, some decided to hit the sack while others chose to sit in complete silence. Tom and I, being the only Mexican Americans, decided to stay to ourselves because some guys were real troublemakers; fighting with other POWs, stealing from men including the sick and wounded, and mouthing foul words to some Chinese officers. Tom and I were not liked because we did not mingle. We did what the Chinese told us to do, no more no less. In hard labor camp you lose the privileges that you had at the camp from which you came. You did not get tobacco, the food was not as good, and you slept on the floor. Believe me. Hard labor camp had its disadvantages. They, the Chinese, worked us every day with rest only after dinner, when we slept. After serving twenty days in jail and one month in hard labor camp, Tom and I were taken back to Camp 1, which sure felt good. We arrived about 1300 hours with all the guys whooping it up and very glad to see us back. Tom and I were shaking hands, some guys embracing us, saying, "Welcome back." After telling them where we had just arrived from, the commander of Camp 1 summoned us. Being escorted by two guards, we were taken to camp headquarters. We were told to sit, then the commander stated, once again with the help of the interpreter, that it had been a very unfortunate incident and he hoped we would not repeat it. No one escapes from here and we will make sure of that. He then looked down at his desk, straightened something and simultaneously looked at us saying, "If it did happen, we would suffer the consequences. Is that understood? We have tried to make you as comfortable as we can and treat you POWs as the Geneva Convention states."

He was quiet for a bit so I said, "May I say something, commander?"

He replied, "Yes," like not wanting me to say anything.

Tom nudged me with his elbow then said in Spanish, "Don't make any waves. It'll be worse for us."

I replied by nudging him and speaking to the commander while saying, "Why? Can you answer why did you let so many men die for lack of medical help, if you knew you had these many men as POWs? You should have been ready and had medical assistance, even a doctor and a nurse would have saved some of my friends. By the time you got medical help for us, almost one hundred and fifty had died for lack of food and medical assistance, so don't try to make us believe you have done everything according to the laws of the Geneva Convention. I won't buy that, commander."

A few seconds went by when he told us again that no one escapes from here and if you do, you will suffer the consequences. He then motioned the guards to take us out. Everyone outside wanted to know what the commander had said to us; and if we were going to escape again. Someone in the crowd yelled for the guys to give us a break, as we had been through a lot. With this, the crowd dispersed. Tom and I went back to our respective hut, sitting there thinking about what the commander said to us about escaping, when I said, "Let's do it again Tom!" He did not answer right away.

When he did, he said, "I'll think about it," as he looked at me grinning.

After we settled in the routine of Camp 1 again, we started thinking about the mistakes we had made. Still trying to avoid some guys because they wanted to know how far we had gotten and how we got caught. When they asked me, I would say, "Freedom was a good feeling and that it was our fault, not the elements that brought us back."

The same things were going on in camp as before: trading, wood detail, lectures, etc. I went to sickbay to visit the guys and see how they were doing. When I went there, some POWs felt bad that they had caught Tom and I, but glad we were back and safe. We went back to going on wood detail and other things around camp. One morning I was talking with Tom asking, "Have you noticed that the guards are keeping a closer watch on us? They seem to be concerned about us escaping again." Tom nodded his head as usual then agreed saying he had been watching them also.

Upon returning from wood detail we went to our hut when no sooner had we sat down, a guard called me to accompany him to the commander's office. Some guys at the square saw me heading toward the commander's office escorted by a guard and wanted to know what was wrong. I told them that I did not know.

When the guard and I got to the office I was told to come in and sit. The commander had been standing then he sat down. After sitting, he squirmed a little to get comfortable, then he leaned back in the chair, cleared his throat then wanted to know how I was doing in camp.

I said, "Fine."

"How is Cabello doing?"

I answered, "The same." He then told me that he would be separating me and Tom because he had a report that we were spending a lot of time together and talking. I knew right then who had ratted on us. It had to be one of the turncoats because he was the one who asked if we were planning another escape.

The commander continued, saying that if he were Tom and I, he would not even think of escaping again. Also he hoped that we had learned something from the punishment they had given us after being caught. I could see his beady eyes looking at me as to say, do not tarnish my record by escaping again. He then informed me that they would assign me to the hut on the left side of the playground. Cabello would be on the right side. That way I would not get in trouble and if I behaved, I might just make it home with the rest of the POWs when the war is over. While being at the office, I looked all around to see where everything was so if I needed something that we could use on our next escape, I knew where to get it.

The commander then said that I was dismissed. I said to him as I had before, "That as a Marine and POW it was my duty to try to escape whenever possible." Then I said, "Thanks for the talk" and as I am walking out the door I said, "Semper Fi" and not to worry about us escaping again.

I departed to my hut and went to pick up my gear so I could go to the hut to which they had transferred me. As I was walking through the playground, they asked me what the speech was about. "Nothing, they just wanted to tell me that I was being separated from Tom so as not to cause any more problems."

Chapter Eight

Scheme and Strategy

Tom got settled in his new hut and I in mine. Well, so be it, we would have to find a way to meet at a designated place so no one sees us together. This would be difficult for the reason being we did not know all the turncoats that were sympathizers and stoolies for the Chinese, since there were about three hundred to three hundred and seventy-five POWs in the camp. We had to be very careful not to be seen talking or even walking together on wood detail.

We went on wood detail the next morning and I came up with an idea while walking. It had been on my mind of how to hide the crackers and food for if, and when, we escaped. So it came to me. Why not pick a location or hiding place up in the hills where we could go on wood detail? We go there every day and Tom and I could hide our crackers and food at the hiding places.

That evening I motioned to Tom as he was walking to his hut to meet me at the latrine about 1930 hours. I got there about 1900 hours and it was dark. I knew the guard would not know who it was at the latrine. Tom showed up twenty minutes later. All this time Tom and I talked in Spanish, that way no one would understand if they showed up at the latrine. I said, "Tom, let's hide our ration of crackers at a hiding place in the hills where we go on wood detail. All we have to do is find a big rock on top of the hill and hide them there. What do you think?" He thought that might work, but would take too long to hide enough for two or three weeks supply. I suggested, "Why don't we ask all the Mexican guys that we can trust? Tell them of our plan and they can help us with their rations, take them to our hiding place. What do you think? In four or five days it would give us about fifteen to twenty packets each."

I told Tom we would have to do it soon so we could get out before the cold weather gets here. It was the middle of July and we had planned it for just a few weeks away. From the time they caught us, I was thinking that we had to escape again. After agreeing to what we had talked about to our Mexican friends in helping us with the food, we parted company. Before Tom left, I said, "Let's meet in two days and figure what we need besides food." Tom then left and I waited a few minutes so as not to let anyone see us together coming from the latrine.

The following day I talked to some of my Mexican friends about our plan and hopes that they would share their rations. They agreed one hundred percent to taking their rations on wood detail and hiding it where we had chosen. By this time I did not know who Tom had talked to, but we had everything in motion. It felt good to know we were going to be free again, very soon.

We had given the guys the location where we were hiding the food, which was a huge rock that we always passed by when we went on wood detail. It was not on the ridge, but on the way up to it and was surrounded by brush and dead trees. You could tell where it was because a dead tree resembled a big Y.

The next morning we got up to some sad news. They had taken some POWs during the night while they slept and we did not know where they had taken them. They told us that some soldiers with shiny boots came with a flashlight and took the guys out. Someone speculated and said that they looked like Russians, but he could not swear that they were as he only saw the boots. We were puzzled because we had not seen anyone that night and someone always is walking around the camp during the night. No one could come up with an answer. About fifteen POWs were missing and nowhere to be found. Someone suggested talking to one of the Chinese officers to find out where they took them and why.

Someone had gone and asked an officer while we were there close to the playground. They came back and told us that the Chinese had taken them to another camp. The question in everyone's mind was why did they take them in the middle of the night? This was something we did not buy from the Chinese. There was concern and reason for alarm because we started thinking who is going to be taken next and by whom.

The next day Tom and I were supposed to meet but everyone at the camp started worrying about what had happened. Some were saying that maybe they were taken to the salt mines in Manchuria or taken to Russia.

Many younger POWs were asking the older ones about what to do if they came after them during the night. Throughout the day this was the topic of conversation and it surely was reason to panic. You could do nothing but just hope that they would not take you. As the evening wore on and it was time to start getting ready to go to bed, guys said they were not going to sleep because they did not want to be taken. I went to bed and just prayed that it would not be me.

In the morning we heard the whistle to get up and the first thing we did was take count of the guys in the hut. They were all there and I looked up at the ceiling and said, "Thank you, Lord." We got up and as we were getting dressed someone asked how many guys are going to be gone from the other huts. We went outside, lined up at the playground for exercise. When we finished with that, we looked around and asked everyone, is anyone missing? It seemed like no one had been taken during the night. Everyone relaxed a little bit and there were comments from many men like, maybe they are getting fifteen from every camp or they had all they needed.

A few days later the same thing occurred. This time they came to my hut and it was dark so I did not know what time it was. I just happened to wake up, turned my body to lie on my other side, when I heard the door open and saw flashes outside, like coming from a flashlight. Whoever it was, they just walked in and I noticed that they were kicking the feet of the POWs. Then I noticed that they were kicking only certain guys. They came in my direction and kicked me but I did not move. When they passed me, about two feet from where I was laying, all I could see was that they were soldiers with shiny boots. They were the same as what the Russian Officers wear. When they took two of the guys from our hut, I knew that trouble was brewing. I later found out that my friend, Pat, had been taken. The next morning we found out that twenty more men from the camp were missing.

There were a lot of questions around camp and no answers. If they were going to be taken to another camp, why not just take them in daylight? Why at night? Why the Russian officers? Why were the Russian officers looking in our huts, and were the men that were being taken away picked at random?

I knew these soldiers that were wearing shiny boots were Russians. They wore boots that resembled the ones worn by the men that I saw in my hut at night, on a few occasions. Their uniforms, including their shoulder pads and cap, were dark drab olive in color. The caps had two red bands with a red star on it. The camp commander and Lieutenant Chun were escorting these Russians. I was so positive that these soldiers were Russian that I was not going to be told differently, and I was going to try my best to sleep with one eye open.

Sergeant Pettit told us not to make any accusations to the Chinese. He said we should just lay low and see what happens. The problems about the unanswered questions were brought up, and Sergeant Pettit said that he would look into it. Just to sit tight. We had no choice but to be patient. Sometime later, approximately a week, Sergeant Pettit went to the commander's office and was told that they transferred the men to other camps because this one was getting very full. That is where the subject closed for everyone.

About two hundred of us went on wood detail. While we were walking, I kept looking around to find Tom in front or behind me, as I had not seen him at the playground. I was hoping that he had come along because this was the day we had agreed to meet. While the column was moving, I passed the word to some guys to see if they could spot Tom. I did not want the guards to see me trying to find him because then they would suspect something and tell the commander. A few minutes passed when word came that Tom was about twenty men behind me.

There were not many guards to watch us, about fourteen guards for two hundred men, so I knew they probably could not keep an eye on all of us once we got to the top. After making it to the mountain, we went in search of logs and we then separated from the group. We covered an area of about one hundred yards in each direction, so it is a lot of area that the guards have to cover. Once we got up on the mountain, I avoided the group and the guards, as did Tom. As we are looking for wood, we are talking in Spanish so the guys that may be close to us did not understand what we were saying.

I told Tom that we had to move on, meaning the escape, because we may be pulled out some night never to be seen again. Tom agreed. Then I said, "Make a list of some things we should take and I'll write another, that way we may not miss something important." Tom suggested we should meet at the latrine that night, at the same time as before, after it gets dark. We then got away from each other, and strayed in different directions looking for wood, so the guards would not see us together or close to each other.

We got our logs and started down the mountain when the guards blew the whistle indicating we were leaving. We left the mountain and started back to camp. On the way a British POW asked me if I was the guy that escaped. I said, "Yes, why?" He then told me that I had a lot of guts. There's nothing but mountains in this bloody country. There's nothing but rocks and the people don't like Yanks. I simply replied by saying, "It's good to be free and I had to do something to notify our forces that many guys were dying here. Maybe they wouldn't have been able to do anything, but it would be worth a try."

He said, "Good show. It's all worth it."

I started laughing and said, "Someone has to try it." We moved along and finally got to camp after five or six hours of wood detail. We dropped the logs on the pile and headed to our huts.

The first thing I did when getting in my hut was to think of what we missed on our second escape. The few things that had come to my mind was a map, compass and flashlight. I went to look for a nice place where I could sit and think and write what we needed. I found a place near the creek by a hut and sat down. No one could see me except the guys who were bathing in the creek, but they were too far away to know what I was doing. There I tried to figure a way to get the essentials for our escape. I knew that the instructors at the camp who gave the lectures had maps. They also had flashlights because at night when they checked our huts, they used them. Before this, they had shown us a map of where the camp was. I knew that they were available somewhere in their head-quarters, but the task was to figure out how to get them. I knew we had to speed up our plans so we could leave in a few days as it was almost the end of July.

This was all I thought about day in and day out. I could not forget it. I tried to figure angles to make this escape a success. I prayed and asked God to give me the strength and courage to undertake this task, to guide us through all this and be triumphant in the end. We were putting our lives on a tightrope, and neither of us knew what lay ahead if they caught us.

After thinking of the things we needed, I got up and went to my hut. As I was almost to my hut, a POW in an Air Force uniform approached me and said that he understood that I was planning to escape, so he would like to contribute his uniform and boots. Because it was going to be cold out there it would protect me from the elements. I said, "Thank you, and what about you? It's going to be cold and you need it here at camp." He answered that since I was going to do something very courageous he wanted me to take it. I could not find words to thank him. I cannot even remember his name. All I said was, "Thanks. I'll take it two hours before I leave." He reminded me not to forget to pick it up and then he left. I entered my hut, went to my bunk and laid down. I was mentally exhausted from think-ing and trying not to forget anything we had to take.

After laying there for about an hour, the Chinese blew the whistle for us to pick up our dinner. The guy whose turn it was to pick up the food, rice and a side dish, went to get it and we all had our bowls ready by the time he came back. We got the cards ready. Whoever drew the highest card got his meal first and then the next, so on down the line. We drew cards as a way of making a routine a little more exciting and no one could say there was favoritism. We ate and it seemed like most of the men were more relaxed about the Chinese or whoever was taking the POWs at night not to be seen again. They did not discuss the subject so it seemed they had accepted it.

When dinner was over, we picked up the bowls and washed them at the creek. By that time it was dusk and soon it would be time to meet Tom at the latrine. I got my list containing the things we needed, waited till it got dark then went to the latrine, walking very slowly to give Tom time to get there.

I was on lookout for the guard because he was not where he usually stood. I could see someone coming, and by the way he was walking I knew it was Tom. We sat down comparing notes of what we needed to take when Tom looked at my list and saw I had a map, compass and flashlight on it. He asked, "Where in the hell are you going to get the stuff from?"

I replied, "From the Chinese Officers' Headquarters, where else? Don't worry. Leave it to me. I'll find a way."

We continued going down the list. I read the list to Tom because it was dark and you could hardly see. I had memorized it almost and I knew what I had written. After discussing all the things needed to take, Tom asked again, "How are you going to get the map, compass and flashlight before we leave?"

I told him, "I would find a way. Where there's a will, there's a way, Tom." I then emphasized to Tom the importance of going over everything in the next few days so we could get out of this camp. The days were warm but the nights were cool, sometimes dropping to forty at night. Since we would be traveling by night, we could not waste time. August was just around the corner and it would start getting cold.

We returned to our huts where I kept thinking – was there anything we were forgetting? At this point we had decided to escape and all we had to do was set a date. By this time everything had been thought out and we put the wheels in motion for the food to be hidden during wood detail. We spoke to our friends that had volunteered to give us their crackers and to hide them in the secret place that we had showed them. I also knew that I had to go to the kitchen to figure out what they did with the leftovers and where they put it. With all this taken care of, there was the map, compass and flashlight still left to get. Well, it came time to go to bed and in the morning go on wood detail and get the food hidden.

The next morning the whistle blew and we all did the exercises then drank the soybean milk. As we lined up to go on wood detail, something very irregular happened. Only fifty POWs were chosen to go and that had not happened before. This was very odd, because every time we went on wood detail since we were in Camp 1, every able-bodied POW would go along. This kind of threw our plans off because some guys that were going to take crackers and hide them were not among the group of fifty selected to go on wood detail. I was going but Tom was not in the group. Only three of us who had food were going. They blew the whistle to move so we left. We only had four guards; one in front, one on each side and one covering the rear of the column.

Four of us that were in the column spoke Spanish. We already knew where to hide the food so we walked and talked deciding that one at a time we would veer off to the hideout dropping off the food, with the rest following suit. This was accomplished and the guards never saw any of us near the dried up tree.

After two or three hours we started down the mountain, which took about forty-five minutes to get to the road. Carrying a log that weighs about thirty pounds on your shoulder, going down a mountain that is full of rocks, is hard work. You had to be careful where you stepped as one wrong step you could twist your ankle or break a leg. We rested at the bottom of the mountain waiting for the stragglers, which was customary. The guard counted us and they had the same number with which they had left camp. You could see their happy faces.

On this wood detail, we had a guard who was older than the others. He must have been about thirty or forty. It is hard to tell or guess the age of a Chinese person. The only reason that I knew this guard was older is because the regular guards that we had at the camp appeared and acted younger. I would venture to say that they were sixteen to eighteen years old because of the way they behaved and their skin; you could tell they were teenagers.

As this older guard was walking along to the left side of us, he was talking to the other guard. We did not know what he was saying, but the younger guards were listening. About a quarter of a mile from camp we asked the guard if we could take a breather, and he stopped in his tracks, faced us and with a loud voice said, "No!" We were amazed at his answer, especially with the loudness that he said it. We kept walking, the logs getting heavier and we could see the camp from where we were standing. As we were walking toward camp, about a hundred yards, he could see that we were tired. The older guard started smiling and made a statement to us that if we have a God, why doesn't he get us out of this?

We looked at him and just about that time we heard a roaring noise. We knew it was a plane as it was loud. I knew the plane had to be really low. As the plane came around the bend, we dropped our logs and hit the dirt away from the road. The pilot let go with his guns, and we saw dirt fly everywhere on the road. He had strafed just fifty yards before the entrance to camp, which was where we were. It happened in four or five seconds. It was so fast that some of us were not able to hide by the side of the road. After he made his pass, I saw him disappear. The guys and the guards were in disbelief of what had happened.

We started checking on everyone. I yelled, "Is everyone okay?" Some guys got up and asked what the hell was that? I replied, "That was a Black Widow from one of those bases down south." We looked around to see if anyone was hurt and on the other side of the road, we saw that they had hit the older guard through the heart and face. Of course, he was dead.

Standing there with the logs on the ground, we looked toward the camp and some officers were running with more guards. They were saying something to each other and the guards that were with us were telling them what happened. The guards that came sent a guard to get POWs to help us with the logs; we were still shaking from what had happened as it happened so fast. I presumed the Chinese officers were bewildered that no one else got a scratch except the older guard. The Chinese officer stayed there at the scene and the guards had taken the column into the camp.

They had asked us if anyone got hit. No, we answered. Someone said, that s.o.b. scared the daylights out of me. That guard got it right between the eyes – what a way to go.

The other POWs had brought the logs to camp and the strafing was something you did not get over in a few hours. We headed for our huts to try to get ourselves together as some of us were still shaking.

I went to my hut, located a quarter mile from where we dropped the logs, and tried to figure what had happened. Our planes had never strafed that close to our camp. They had flown by and waved their wings, but never that close. Some of us gathered around to try to put two and two together because "Bed Check Charlie" had been taking pictures the day before. Maybe a convoy of troops or supplies had been spotted by the entrance to the camp. Very frequently we had convoys from up north come through here. The Chinese use that route for supplying the troops in the south. Maybe the pilot thought we were Korean or Chinese troops moving to the south. Understanding what was on the pilot's mind is hard.

After discussing it we all went back to our huts. One of the guys came up to me and said that it must have been really scary out there, Nick. It happened so fast there was little time to be frightened. After it happened, it shook me up a bit. With the event that just occurred, the day went fast as it was already time to go to bed. The people at my hut were talking about the incident but I just went to bed. I was tired and needed to get some sleep. As I lay there, I thought maybe it was meant to be that way. If the usual column had gone on wood detail, for sure some POWs would have died, because about one hundred-and-fifty to two hundred go on a normal detail. After thinking for another few minutes I finally fell asleep.

The next morning at exercise I gave Tom a note telling him to meet me at the latrine that night, at the same time. With exercise over, we drank our milk and then went on wood detail. This was different as we were taking food to our hiding place. The normal group went and all our friends took food to our hiding place. There were about six guys taking food besides Tom and me. This gave us about twenty-four packs of crackers. I figured that two more wood details would bring the total to approximately sixty packs. We could not take too many for we did not have room in the sacks that we had made to carry our food. We also had to carry other things like clothes, matches, flashlight, map, compass and utensils. It was going to be a long haul because our front lines were way south and we were way up north. We went on wood detail and everything went according to plans, all of us took crackers. We got to our logs and came down the mountain and headed for camp. We got back to the camp, dropped the logs on the pile and headed for our huts. I got to my hut where I sat down and rested. I did not say anything, I was just thinking. Even during our meal, I was silent. Someone mentioned that I had been quiet. "What's wrong? I bet you're thinking about leaving this place, am I right?" I did not answer. I just shrugged my shoulders, laid down and went to sleep. The next morning we got up, did our exercises then lined up for milk. Today was the last time we would take crackers to hide. With this trip we would have enough for our escape. We headed for the mountains with about the same amount of guys. I was looking for Tom to see if he were in front or in the back of the column. At the same time Tom was looking to see where I was. Just then we saw each other and we nodded our heads in acknowledgment. He was in the very front so he got back in the column and kept walking. The guards did not seem to pay attention to the guys talking and had not noticed us out of the column. The guards were with us so long at the camp that they had picked up some English words and can carry on a conversation with some of the POWs and they would talk among themselves.

We reached the mountain and hid our crackers, one person at a time, and it went well. The guards had not suspected anything had been going on. We looked for our logs then went down the mountain. At the bottom I spotted Tom sitting on his log resting and as I was coming down, I dropped my log about twenty feet from his. We started talking about when to meet and execute the last phase of our escape. At this time, some of our Mexican friends were coming down when they also dropped their logs and started gathering around us saying that they were interested in going with us. I looked at Tom and he looked at me, then I said to them, "You have two days to get ready because we need to get out of here before it gets any colder." The guard blew the whistle so we started, with our logs, toward camp. Tom caught up to me and asked, "What do we do now?"

I said, "Let's talk about it when we get to camp."

When I arrived at the hut, I tried to figure out a way that I could talk to Tom. We needed to discuss all those guys wanting to go with us. We had to do it some way, so the Chinese would not suspect anything was happening, or something going on between us and the other guys. As I sat there, I came up with an idea that Tom could talk to half of them while I talked to the remaining half. Talking to all the guys was dangerous for us as the Chinese would suspect something if they saw us together. It had to be within the next forty-eight hours because our plan was to leave in two days, which was the last day of July or August 1, 1952.

I finally gave a note to someone I could trust and told him to give it to Tom. The note said *nos veremos escusado* (meet at latrine). I wrote it in Spanish so no one could read it.

That evening I met Tom and told him of my idea – of him talking to half of the group and me talking to the other half, so as not to risk any suspicion by the Chinese that something was going on. Tom thought that was a good idea, but to make sure they would not tell anyone. There was too much at stake, plus it could be fatal if the wrong person found out our plan.

We sat there in the latrine and talked. "Tom, do you agree in taking these guys with us? They already know our plans and I don't think that if they decide not to go at the last minute they would say anything to the Chinese, in fear that they might be punished." We made a memory list of the men that were going: Danny Arellano, Ramirez, Marcos, Stanley Burke, Tom and myself. I said, "Okay, the day is the day after tomorrow, at 2430 hours. We're going to meet behind the kitchen at exactly that time, which gives us an hour to know who is going and who is not. I'll go there at 2300 hours and check around. I want you, Tom, to be there at 2345 hours. That way the Chinese and cooks will not suspect anything. Don't forget to let the guys know that they are to be there fifteen minutes apart. Then from there we'll walk to the creek."

Tom asked me about the map, compass and flashlight. "We are going to create a diversion tomorrow, to give me the time to get the stuff. When the officers get out of the office, I am going to hide around the building and by the time the fight is over, I will have gone in and gotten the compass and flashlight."

Tom wanted to know about the map. "I got that four days ago when I went to the office and asked if I could borrow a book on the way Russia runs Communism. When he went to the other room I knew where the map was and I stuck it inside my shirt. If the diversion goes okay I will have the compass and flashlight, but it will be just before we go, about 2130 or 2200 hours."

After we went over the plans and the time it was to be executed, we parted company and we went to our huts. As I was walking to my hut I remembered that my mother had told me when you are undertaking a task and you need help, go somewhere and talk to God. He will listen and he is there to help. I walked to the creek and sat there talking to God. I said, "This is a hazardous journey we are undertaking, too many lives involved. Please guide us and give us the strength to succeed in our escape."

Chapter Nine
Freedom ... Again

We were to leave the following night at 2400 hours. The word was passed to the POWs that were going with us. The next morning some guys that worked in the kitchen asked Tom if they could join us. Tom's response was that they talk to me and I would tell them yes or no. After Tom told me this I knew there was not enough food for twelve guys. I then headed toward the kitchen to talk to the additional men. Not knowing what I was going to tell them, I had hoped that on the way something would come to mind.

As I walked across the playground, I thought I don't even know who they are and I am not going to ask everyone. I then decided to talk to Tom and have him point out who it was that had asked him. There were at least twelve guys working in the kitchen and some I hadn't met yet.

It was very puzzling to me that someone had leaked information concerning the escape. I just prayed that it didn't get back to the Chinese, as that would be a catastrophe. I looked at my hands and they were shaking. I was worried. As I was walking to find Tom, I was thinking about which of the guys that decided to go had been overheard or took it upon himself to talk to other POWs about it. It was too late to even try and find out as we were less than eighteen hours from executing the plan.

Walking across the playground, Tom saw me then made a motion to follow him. Staying about a hundred feet behind, we stopped at one of the huts that shielded us from the Chinese Headquarters, hoping no one would see us. It was daylight so we stayed towards the back of the hut. Up until now, we had been very careful not to talk during the day because of all the people walking around camp.

Tom started by asking, "Well, what do you think? Can we do it with twelve guys going?"

"Tom, do you realize how easy it will be to spot that many men leaving the camp? Not only that, there will be twelve missing, not seven, and especially from the kitchen. They will find out early in the morning when they don't show up to cook for the POWs."

Tom interrupted by saying, "We should take them and hope for the best." This was hard to accept but there was nothing else we could do but take them and hope that the Chinese guards wouldn't spot us leaving. We parted company, going in different directions so as not to be seen together.

When I reached my hut I tried to figure out what to do about the present problem of twelve men going. I had planned the whole escape for only two of us – then six; and now twelve. I got a pencil and paper then proceeded to write down all the drawbacks of taking this many men on the escape: 1) We didn't have enough food for that many people; 2) They would miss the cooks early in the morning, then the rest of us; 3) We would be walking slower with that many; and 4) It was going to be easier to spot twelve men on the ridge versus two. Most important, now there were twelve lives that I had to worry about instead of two.

It was difficult to decide whether to go or wait for another time. I knew that we had to go because sooner or later someone would leak information. I was nervous and worried. It certainly was something to think about, cautiously. I went to the creek, sat down, prayed and asked God for his help. I said, "Lord, I am going to leave it in your hands. You let us know if it is your will for us to take them, then so be it. I just feel that I can't handle such a burden at the present time. Thank you Lord. I ask for your divine guidance and love so we can be successful on this escape. There are so many lives involved and I wouldn't want to be responsible for them if something happened."

By this time it was getting close to dinner. One of the guys from my hut came in to ask me if it was okay to go for the food at the kitchen. I suggested that he wait as all the guys weren't here and that way the food wouldn't get cold. It's still a little early and if they come in late, I would go and get it. He then left. My thought was that if I went when there weren't many people in the kitchen, I would be able to talk to the cook, if possible, hopefully with ample time and without interruptions.

The cooks didn't know me so my only concern was if one of the people who might walk in there would be one of the stoolies we had at camp. I got the dishpan for the food and crossed the playground, then walked into the kitchen. As I looked around, I thought that maybe I would know one of the men who was going. Still looking around, one of the cooks said "hi" to me and asked what he could do for me. I saw that a couple of Chinese cooks were stirring the rice pots causing a lot of steam in the kitchen. I realized they were steaming pork dumplings, so this would give me a chance to talk to at least one of the GIs. Before I could say anything, the guy that had hailed to me ended up being one of those going on the escape. I said "hi" to him and then asked how he was doing. I told him, "At night fall the river flows at 2330."

He answered, "All is okay in the home front. By his response I knew he had gotten the message that we were to leave at 2330 hours that night and would be crossing the creek behind the kitchen.

A few minutes went by before the cooks started dishing out the food. There must have been three hundred pork dumplings and three more racks were steaming over the pots. I went to the end of the food line and while I was standing there, someone comes behind, nudges me and asked if I was ready. This person was Marcos Martinez, so I said that I had been ready for several months for this. I asked, "Are you ready?" He replied that he was.

We were moving in the line for chow when I motioned him not to say any more in fear he might say something about the escape. He asked about Tom, to which I said, "I guess he is okay. I haven't seen him for a few days." While approaching the door to the kitchen, I noticed that Lieutenant Chang was standing by the door. He had been inside with the cooks. I started to get scared and lots of thoughts came to my mind. Did they find out about our escape? Did he come to talk to the cooks that were going with us, or did the cooks talk about the escape while cooking? I wondered what Lieutenant Chang was doing in there as this was very irregular. The Chinese had not sent an officer while the cooks were dishing out the food before. I thought to myself that no matter what, we were going through with the plan.

I took the dish of rice and dumplings to the hut. While I was eating, I remembered that I still needed the compass. Everything seemed to be falling in place for our departure out of the camp.

We only had five hours before we left and there was a lot to be done. I went to the creek to wash the bowl. There I was, going over everything in my mind so as not to forget anything. If you did forget something, it is not like you could say that you would be right back because you forgot something. I wasn't at the creek long when a POW walked up to me as I was bending over rinsing my dish.

I heard him ask, "Are you Nick?"

I then asked, "Why?" I was very cautious when someone walked up to me and asked if I was Nick – especially in this circumstances because there were too many lives involved plus too much at stake. One little mistake and everything would go up in smoke.

He continued, "A cook pointed you out and I wanted to know if you wanted to take a compass ?"

I asked, "Did someone tell you I needed one?"

"Yes," he replied with a grin, "I understand you're going on a trip."

I got up then told him that he came well informed. As I stood there shaking my bowl to get the excess water off, I said, "As a matter of fact, I do need one."

He then said, "I will go get it. I have it hidden in my hut."

I waited there for about fifteen minutes. When he returned, he handed the compass to me and said, "Best of luck. I hope it comes out the way you want it."

I told him, "Thanks. I need all the luck in the world for this venture." He shook my hand and left. I never asked his name but he was the answer to my prayers.

I walked from the creek to my hut, and as I was getting close, I saw a figure at the corner of the hut, hiding. Then I heard, "Psst. Nick?" It was said so softly that I knew it was Tom. We looked around to see if anyone would see us but didn't notice anyone close by. There were POWS walking around but not close enough to see that we were talking.

Tom started asking me if everything was ready. To that I answered, "Yes." There are twelve guys going and we will meet as planned, behind the kitchen at fifteen-minute intervals. We are going to do this at 2300 hours but I want you and myself there at 2245 hours so we knew exactly how many people were going." I added, "We picked a good day for this because it will only be a quarter moon. It will be difficult for the guards to see us." I thanked God for that.

Tom added, "We sure needed that in our favor."

As Tom was getting ready to leave he said, "I am going to talk to the guys to find out if they had gotten their instructions of when to go to the back of the kitchen and you check on the cooks."

I answered, "I will make sure they were still going. Also, don't forget to remind the guys to bring a change of pants. We are more than likely to get wet crossing the creek." We parted company to do our last minute inquiring of who was going and who wasn't.

Tom left very secretively, then disappeared into the darkness and I then entered my hut. Once inside, I sat down, thinking to myself about the mistakes that Tom and I had made the last escape. I did not want to repeat those. My mind drifted back to when I had run away from home at the age of fourteen and how very unprepared I had been. I had been gone two months when the police found me in a moving van in Gary, Indiana and called my parents with the information. I was returned home into the hands of two very angry parents.

As I was laughing about this, someone in the hut asked me why I was laughing. I told him, "I was thinking about the time I ran away with my girlfriend and her friend, then ended up in Indiana. We had been so unprepared that we didn't have money, jackets, much less food for the trip. When I had gotten back, I couldn't sit down because my blistered butt was swollen from the whipping' dad gave me with a razor strap." When I had finished they started laughing but after a few minutes they laid down, and some went to sleep.

I pretended to be going to sleep but after a few minutes I tiptoed out of the hut, closed the door softly, then looked around to see if there were any guards around the hut or kitchen. Not seeing anyone I went to the hut where the guy with the Air Force uniform was staying. I knocked twice then he came out, handed me the boots, jacket and flight overalls. As a way to say thanks for the uniform I saluted him. He responded in the same manner then closed the door. He knew that I had done this so not to wake anyone else up. I then went behind the hut where I took off my shoes and clothing. After putting on the Air Force uniform, boots and jacket, I rolled up the discarded clothing. I had put them into my backpack so I could use them sometime on the trail.

I again looked around, then very slowly walked to the rear of the kitchen. When I got there, I was ready to sit down, when I heard footsteps and asked who goes there?

The reply was, "Are you Tom or Nick?"

To this I said, "Nick."

He came within a foot of me then said, "The cooks aren't coming. Not that they were scared, but they had talked about it and felt that they may hamper the success of escape if there were too many guys going.

I told him, "I am sorry about that" and thanked him for the thought and at least they had thought about our success of making it.

He shook my hand and wished us luck. As he was leaving he said, "Don't worry about them saying anything to the Chinese."

Just when he left, Tom showed up, squatted down and I did the same. He started by saying, "The guys should be coming soon. Do you know what time it is?"

I said, "It is close to 2330 hours and the rest of the cooks would not be going along. It is just going to be the six of us."

I had an idea that it was close to that time because the Chinese blew the whistle at 2200 hours for us to go to bed. I knew at least an hour had gone by, possibly more. Just as I was telling Tom the time, Ramirez showed up, then a few minutes later Marcos and Burke showed up and squatted by us.

Tom said, "Nick, tell them the plan."

I asked, "Do you have something to put the crackers in?"

They replied, "Yes, we do."

I suggested that we wait for the rest of the guys and I'd explain the plan to all of them. After a few minutes Danny Arellano showed up saying his usual greeting of "Hi guys." He then informed the group that Bob wasn't going so this was it.

I said, "Okay, we are going towards the creek one at a time, at one-minute intervals, with no talking. Just motion with your hands if someone approaches or if something goes wrong. I will go first, then you. Tom will be last because he knows the trail. Let's say a prayer before we go." We then bowed our heads, then each of us in our way prayed. "Okay fellas, are you ready? One more thing, if anyone wants to come back to camp don't mention any names. Just keep the Chinese guessing. There won't be any hard feelings if you change your mind."

I went first as had been discussed. I hunched down so I wouldn't be seen then I prayed, "Lord, guide us in this venture as we need your help to make it a success." At this time there were only six of us going and I felt that God had a hand on this. There had been too many before but I wasn't the one to decide that.

I looked back and saw the guys coming one by one, and in a few minutes we reached the edge of the creek. The creek wasn't deep but the current was swift. There were a lot of rocks and the water was about knee high. Ramirez wanted to go first and he thought he could cross it standing up. Well, he was wrong because as soon as he got three feet into the creek, he was swept away by the current. Tom started running down the edge of the creek to try and stop Ramirez from going to far. We couldn't yell because the guard was only two or three hundred feet from the creek. At about a hundred and fifty feet, Ramirez finally got himself to where he was able to hang onto a big rock approximately five feet from the edge on the other side.

There were so many rocks in the creek that we knew he had banged his body and would be hurting. We looked in his direction, and Tom was motioning for him to stand fast and we would get to him.

During all this we were thinking about looking for another place to cross but it only got worse farther down. Tom returned and whispered, "What do we do now?"

I said, "When you cross something like this, especially with the current so swift, I will show you guys how to do it. You watch me." Stepping into the creek, I looked at Tom and said, "When I get across, throw me the sacks so they don't get wet. Put a small rock in the sacks to weight them. We can throw them farther and they won't land in the water."

As I was in the creek I laid down, then rolled with the current. It was hard but I got to the other side about twenty feet from where they were, but down the creek towards Ramirez. Just after reaching the other side, Tom threw the sacks across the creek and I left them where they landed. I immediately went to Ramirez, going slow so the guard wouldn't see me. I waded in the creek and got him out. After doing this I asked him how he was. He answered that it was stupid the way he fell into that one! Also he was hurting from his neck. Ramirez had a piece of shrapnel in his neck that had been hurting him since his capture and the tumbling in the water had aggravated his wound. The Chinese had wanted to remove it but he refused, so he just kept on hurting.

Ramirez got up with my help and I whispered, "Can you walk? If you can't, we'll get a couple of the guys to come help us get over there." I pointed to where the rest of the guys were. We were all wet but safe as we had made it across the creek. Ramirez and I made it to where the other guys were and rested a few minutes, then we left. When we were moving it was slow due to us being wet and cold.

We walked the same path as Tom and I had traveled on our last escape. We walked towards the bridge and every thirty feet we would try to spot the guard that was at the entrance to the camp. When I looked back I saw that everyone was moving along. We noticed that the guard had moved farther away from the bridge and if no one saw us, we would be home free and that was a welcome thought. We continued another hundred feet and we made it to the bridge. There we stopped for about ten to fifteen minutes to take a breather.

The only one in the group that didn't understand Spanish was Stanley Burke, a fellow Marine, so when we did speak Spanish we would translate for him. We weren't talking very much as we were mostly giving hand signals until we got to the ridge of the mountain. After taking our breather, we asked in a whisper if everyone was OK. I said, "Now, we are not stopping until we get to the ridge and get to the hiding place to pick up our crackers. We have to keep moving you guys, and in another four hours it will be dawn … so let's do it!" They followed me under the bridge where we veered away from the creek and got to the path where we usually went on for wood detail which was just at the bottom of the mountain.

When we arrived, we were all shivering due to our clothes being wet from crossing the creek. We had a change of clothes but didn't take the extra time to change as it was getting late. We had to be at the ridge by 0400 hours, not much later. I wanted to be at least one mile from camp before the Chinese blew their whistle for the POWS to get up.

We started climbing the mountain slower than when we went on wood detail because it was dark. It took us about an hour and a half to reach the ridge and we were glad we had made it with no incidents. We squatted down and then I said, "Let's change clothing and we'll rest for about twenty minutes and then start on the ridge trail. Tom and Marcos will pick up the crackers and we'll take turns carrying them. We will leave as soon as Tom and Marcos get the crackers." We changed clothes and waited for the guys to come with the food. After they returned, we rested about ten minutes more then decided we would start the journey to freedom.

We were moving faster traveling along the ridge, than when Tom and I had escaped the last time. I occasionally looked back to see how the guys were doing. They were three to four feet behind each other so they wouldn't get too far behind. I was in the lead with Tom bringing up the rear. Ramirez was complaining about his neck hurting so we slowed down a bit.

By this time I am about ten feet in front of the rest and as I am walking along, I suddenly fell into a deep hole. I had a strange feeling as I tried to figure out what had happened and where I was. I felt around me and there were two jagged rocks which I had fallen between. I couldn't see as it was pitch black but I looked up to see the hole above me. I could also see the sky from where I was sitting between the two rocks.

I heard voices but they were nowhere around me. Tom was asking where I was. "I am here, Tom," I responded. Being scared and disoriented by the fall, at first I forgot the flashlight I had. As Tom got closer to the hole, I remembered it. I took it out of the Air Force suit, turned it on and pointed the light to the top of the hole. I couldn't estimate the depth of the hole but when Tom saw the light, he came and looked down. He then asked me if I was alright. Thinking about the jagged rocks that I had fallen between, I knew the good Lord must have been watching over me. If I had hit one of those rocks when I fell, I would have suffered a very severe injury. The depth of the hole must have been six to seven feet because Tom had to use a pair of pants as a rope so he could get me out. After Tom and Stanley pulled me out, one of the guys commented that it was no time for me to take a nap. They had wanted to know where I got the flashlight but I replied that it was a long story and we needed to get out of there. We moved on still wanting at least a mile behind us so as not to be close to camp when daylight broke. I would say that we covered about three quarters of a mile by dawn. We had to find a place to rest during the daylight hours.

We scouted around and found a spot with lots of vegetation and rocks. This would hide us from anyone who passed by on the trail and it was far enough we would not be spotted by the guys on wood detail. It was located on a ridge opposite the camp. Before settling down we could see the camp behind us and we felt good being at least a mile away from there. As we moved towards the location we had selected to hide, Marcos Martinez came up to Tom and me telling us that he was having chills and wouldn't be going with us and that he was going back so he didn't hold us up. He also said that Burke was going back and he was sorry about getting sick. Burke walked up, then told us he would take Marcos back to make sure he made it to the camp.

We are huddled up listening to Marcos and Burke when Ramirez comes up and said that he was hurting and he couldn't decide whether to go on or go back since it was still close to camp. He mentioned that his wound was aggravated when he rolled down the creek and it had not stopped hurting.

Danny interrupted saying, "I'll go back with Ramirez and if all four of us go, we might not be punished so severely. Maybe the Chinese will be glad we didn't go after all. Maybe this is the way it's supposed to happen, that way you and Tom will have a better chance to make it a success. You guys take our portion of the crackers and maybe that will last you long enough to reach freedom."

I said, "I'm sorry that you're not able to go with us. One thing I ask of you guys; don't go back till around noon. That way it will give us a chance to get further away from camp. You can rest here then leave when you decide. Tom and I will go after we rest a few minutes. Thanks for the crackers."

I suggested to Tom, "Let's put all the crackers in our sacks and you carry half and I will carry the other half. After we do that we should take off. We still had a couple of hours of travel time on the top of the ridge and from there we know the trail fairly well from the previous escape." It was time to move on so we said goodbye. They wished us luck and hoped that we would make it. Tom and I waved at them and then I said to assure myself, "If they ask which way we went, you don't know. That way it will give us a chance to get a bit farther. Thanks." We then disappeared into the darkness.

Knowing it soon would be daybreak, we increased our pace to get as much distance as we could in the two hours we had left. We were trying to reach one of the places we had stopped before as it would be an ideal spot to rest until nightfall. After about an hour of walking, Tom said, "I think this is it." We then got off the trail and sure enough, it was the place.

We took off our sacks that had been made into backpacks, got comfortable by sitting on some weeds that looked like fern then just leaned back and rested. I looked to Tom and said, "I wonder if anyone travels this path early in the morning?" After watching a few moments to see if anyone was coming and there wasn't, we took off our boots. We massaged our feet as they along with our bodies were very tired. After soothing our feet we laid there reminiscing about our last trip through here and how good it felt to be free then, and here we are doing it again. It sure felt good.

We heard a noise that sounded like a convoy of trucks. Tom reached for his boots, put them on then sneaked over to the ridge to take a look. I was looking over in his direction when he motioned for me to come over. I hastily put on my boots without socks then hurried over, and sure enough there was a convoy of trucks with supplies for the front lines.

We tried to count the trucks while lying prone, and there must have been twenty to thirty. We were able to see pretty well as it was almost daylight, sometime around 0630 to 0700 hours.

Going back to our hideout we took off our boots, then put on our socks; leaned back and rested. Our legs were hurting from going over so many rocks. As we rested it was decided that one of us should sleep while the other stood guard. Tom suggested that I get some sleep and if things were quiet, he would also try to sleep. As I was trying to sleep, I was thinking what day of August it was but decided I needed rest more than I needed to know what day it was, so I went to sleep.

I woke up and saw that Tom was sleeping which was a good sign. I sat back, leaning on the rock behind me, then opened my sack of crackers and started munching on them. As I was eating, my thoughts went back to Camp 1, wondering what the commander was going to say when the guys returned from the escape. I just prayed that they wouldn't be too hard on them.

As I was wondering about the events at Camp 1, Tom woke up and stated, "It sure felt good to get some shuteye. I didn't realize how tired I was."

He sat up and I said to him, "Tom, we should have told the guys to walk to the location where we went on wood detail. They could wait there, hide and when the column comes on detail, mingle with those guys and the Chinese will never suspect anything."

Tom answered, "No one would have known that they had escaped because there are about two hundred guys that go on detail."

The ridge that we were on wasn't very high. The altitude must have been no more than three hundred feet but as we moved southwest, it kept getting steeper.

That was better because it would be harder to spot us on the ridge. The nice thing about it was we were in better health on this escape than the other. We had been eating better food. The soybean milk was nourishing; we had gained a few pounds and we felt better. Not only that, we had at least enough food for ten to fourteen days. We didn't know if there would be wild berries or some kind of fruit we could eat to supplement our crackers and water. We hadn't brought water because on our previous escape, we noticed a lot of streams on the route. Also, the added weight might have become a problem. One thing that was odd was we never saw deer, jackrabbits, or even a squirrel and they were usually up in the mountains. We had seen a few birds on wood detail but that was normal.

I was thinking out loud and said, "Well here we are again, alone and soon we'll be hitting the trail."

As we sat there talking about what was up ahead and trying to find shelter at the same locations where we had stopped before. Tom added, "At least we don't have to get off the ridge to find food for the next week to ten days."

Time was passing by fast and soon it would be dusk and then we could move on. By the time we got ourselves squared away, it would be time to go. We left our little rest stop and commented about hoping we never have to use it again. As we moved along the trail, we were always cautious of seeing someone coming or we would hear noises from below and if there was someone we hoped we would see him before he saw us. This would be our second night and we had to or would like to put some distance from Camp 1. Knowing the trail helped us to walk a little faster and cover more distance than the first time we came through here.

I was in the lead with Tom about four feet behind, trading the lead position every time we stopped to rest. We had been walking for about three to four hours when we heard a rumble. Tom said, "There's Bed Check Charlie, so it must be around 2100 or 2200 hours. He never misses." We saw the flashes somewhere close to the camp. As I saw the flashes, I mentioned that it would be nice if we could signal that plane and they could send a chopper to pick us up. Tom laughed then said, "That sure would save us some leg muscles."

We were walking when Tom suddenly asked, "Where in the hell did you get that flashlight?"

I answered, "I never told anyone, the group or you for that matter, because I was afraid that someone would find out and say something to the Chinese. I decided that I would tell no one until we were on the trail. It wasn't lack of trust, it was just to protect our success in the escape. There were too many lives at stake. Tom, remember when the Chinese commander split us up that night or should I say early evening? Lieutenant Chang, the officer who came around checking on us left the flashlight on the floor after talking to us, so I kicked it under one of the bunks after he left. When it got dark I hid it. He came back a few minutes later and asked if anyone had seen it. Our answer of course was no and that maybe he had left it in one of the other huts. He looked at us and said "maybe so," then left. That's how I came to have a flashlight."

Tom said, "When you had fallen in that hole, I couldn't believe what I was seeing. I had forgotten to ask how you came to have it."

We kept on walking, dodging limbs, rocks and what ever was on the trail. We were moving at a good pace and taking a lot of precautions. We both wondered how far we had gone and we thought about two or three miles. We had about six or seven hours of night travel ahead of us so we could take advantage of knowing the trail. Since we had traveled for a few hours we decided to rest a while. I grabbed a pack of crackers to munch on and then handed Tom a couple. We rested for about ten minutes then we hit the trail once again.

After traveling for three days we got to the end of the ridge and had to cross the road where we had to head down, as we did before. On our second escape, this was the location where we were out of food. It sure brought back memories of that escape. It was still dark but getting very close to daybreak so we decided to look for a place to wait out the daylight hours and wait to cross the road until night fall. This way we could see where to cross and then decide how to cross it.

We were looking for a place to hide when we heard a truck moving down below. With the morning still dark, we laid down close to some brush, then watched at the road. The truck had the headlights on, going southwest. We must have been high on the ridge for we could barely see the lights. We moved back, stood up and continued to look for a place to spend the day, get some rest, as we were bushed and hungry.

We found a place to hide about thirty feet off the trail. There were plenty of trees and rocks to hide behind so we sat there. Tom said, "You stay here and I will stand on the trail, and look back this way and see if I can spot where you are." He came back and said, "It would be hard for anyone to see us from that distance."

Knowing we had most of the day to wait till sundown, we sat there talking. As I am thinking out loud, I said, "I wonder what they will do to those guys that went back?"

Tom replied, "I don't know but if we make it we'll never find out. It is to bad they had to get sick and go back. I thought that Ramirez shouldn't have come because of his sore neck. It's been hurting him since his capture. I just hoped they didn't get punished too severely."

We had finished our conversation so I asked Tom, "Do you want to take the first watch and I'll get some sleep?"

Tom said, "I will," so I laid down, got comfortable then tried to sleep, or at least get some rest.

I woke up to see Tom sleeping so I tried not to wake him up. I was very quiet sitting up and then opening my food sack to get some crackers to eat. I sat there thinking about everything; the way things happened at Camp 1, the men that died for no reason whatsoever except for the lack of medical care, rotten food and poor diet. I had seen so much death at the age of twenty, that I knew I would never forget – it was so much at one time.

A few hours had passed when I looked towards Tom and he was waking up. While stretching his arms and legs, he said, "Getting some sleep sure felt good." The day was wearing on and soon it would be getting dark so I asked him, "Are you rested enough?"

He said, "Now I am ready for a long walk."

I mentioned to Tom, "While you were sleeping a thought had come to me about our last escape. We had both gotten caught and I thought that maybe by splitting up that maybe one of us would make it. Maybe both of us would with any luck. Why don't we think about it while we cross the road tonight and then when we get to the ridge of the mountain, you can let me know what you think."

It wasn't dark enough for us to attempt to cross the road. We were going to cross more or less at the same place where we had before, so that meant we would have to crawl some distance before we got to the ridge of the road. I told Tom, "Maybe we could go standing up and we'll stop every fifteen paces to make sure no one sees us."

He replied, "That sounds good. I don't feel like crawling on my belly for a hundred yards like we did before."

We sat there for a couple of hours. Finally, it was getting dark so we checked our food supply and by that time we were ready. Moving slowly down the mountain, we could notice that we were exactly on the same path we had been before. There was a lot of small brush and trees but nothing that would hide us from someone, plus the farther down we went there were less trees.

It was quite a ways down especially walking slow. We would go about twenty paces then squat down looking to see if anyone was on the road or in the rice paddies. When you're on the mountain with the valley sound traveling as it does, you try to make as little noise as possible. We kept stopping and going and after a couple of hours we got within fifty feet of the road. We decided to wait a few minutes to see if any trucks would come by, because it would take us another half an hour before we got to the edge of the road.

We got up from our rest, started moving towards the road and had just about took our fifteenth step, when we heard talking coming from the area of the road. We got down on our bellies, heard them laughing and talking in Korean, so we laid there about forty-five feet from the edge of the road. Watching them come parallel to where we were, we held very silent until they passed our location. After about fifteen minutes, I told Tom, "That was close! We had better wait for a few more minutes and see if we get any more surprises." We waited another twenty minutes and when we didn't see anyone else coming nor hear any voices, we started going down to the edge of the road. As we got there, looking both ways and still not seeing anyone, we crawled across the road to the other side. When we got there, we looked both ways again then laid on our backs near the rice paddies and rested for a few minutes.

I said to Tom, "It would be nice if a convoy came by real slow so we could jump on the last truck and hide on all those supplies they have then jump off before dawn and they would never know we were back there."

He said, "That only happens in the movies."

It was time to go, so we headed toward the mountain, along the rice paddies. Since there were clumps of brush along there we didn't have to crawl; we just walked and stopped, and squatted down, to listen for noise coming from the village up ahead. This had been where Tom and I had gone on our last escape, to get food, and were caught. We wanted to stay as far away as we could. Since this is as far as we had gotten last time, whatever was in front of us, as far as climbing the mountain, was going to be new to us. This mountain was higher than the one we had just climbed down so it was going to be a slower process getting to the top. We didn't know if there was a path on top, or what we would find once we got to the ridge. It must have been about 0300 or 0400 hours because it was cool, not cold, and we had to climb to the top, if we could, before dawn.

The higher we traveled on the mountain the more rugged it became and thus slowed our climbing down to a snail's pace. There were many jagged rocks. Other places were steep and we had to either walk around them or very carefully crawl over them. All the while it was dark and this hindered our traveling even more. At this point, it seemed that reaching the top was not going to be easy.

I whispered to Tom, "Watch your footing because if we miss one, it's good bye."

As I'm waiting for Tom to catch up with me, he was about four feet behind me, he again asked, "Why did you have to pick Mount Everest to climb?" We both chuckled then stopped to wipe the sweat from our forehead.

I told Tom, "Even though it was hard climbing, we'll be safer up here than on the road."

With our legs starting to cramp up, Tom said, "It better be soon and also we have to be to the top before the sun comes up." After Tom said that, I began wondering how much farther we had to go to reach the top. We kept going and it seemed like every time we looked up to see how much longer, it looked like the mountain was growing with no sight of the ridge top. Tom finally suggested, "We better take a breather. No one can see us in all the trees and furthermore, I am unable to take another step." I agreed. We took off our boots, took out some crackers to munch on, and rested.

We were sitting there looking up at the mountain but we couldn't see the top. The sun would be coming out soon and we needed to get to the top before then. Also, the sun would hit where we were because of the height of the mountain. We continued sitting, massaging our feet and giving our socks a breather so they would dry. They were wet with perspiration. We rested another twenty minutes then put our socks and boots back on. We got on our feet and started moving up the mountain.

After walking for another two hours, we finally saw the ridge top. We could see up through the trees and knew we had made it to the top of the world. Tom leaned on a big rock, gave a sigh and said, "That was one hell of a climb!" We walked about a hundred feet and we were there on top. After we took our backpacks off, we just threw ourselves on the leaf-covered ground with a sigh of relief. I thanked the Lord for getting us there without any problems, and we were safe; and asked that he please help us the rest of the way in however it may end up. In Jesus' name, Amen.

Chapter Ten

On My Own

After resting our tired bodies, we got up and decided to search the area where we were to spend the day. We did not anticipate any foot traffic, but we had to be very cautious because of not knowing what was ahead. The ridge gave us a good vantage point to where we could see the best way to go.

We continued looking for a suitable place close enough to the top of the ridge, but far enough away, so that someone walking on the ridge would not see us. Soon we found the place where we would spend the day and wait for dusk, so we could continue our adventure to freedom. We were standing behind some trees looking at the scenery, both of us in awe of what our eyes were taking in. It seemed like we were looking at Korea as far as the eyes could see – mountain after mountain, several roads and also what looked like a railroad track in the distance. It was a good feeling to be free, with the morning breeze hitting our faces. I said to Tom, "Isn't this great? We're free, no more wood detail, whistles or lectures!" I paused, thinking of how I felt but it is something difficult to put into words. It takes over your body and you can't describe that feeling – you just feel good inside.

Tom broke my train of thought by saying, "Isn't this worth paying a price for? Freedom, no matter if we get caught or not, will be worth every minute of every day we have been away from that camp."

We returned to our resting spot, sat down and decided to munch on some crackers. While doing this, I asked, "Tom, what do you think about the idea that I had mentioned before, about us separating and going in different directions? Maybe one of us would make it."

He replied, "If we had done that last time, maybe we wouldn't have been caught."

I said, "Yes, but that's the chance you take when you escape."

He then replied, "I like the idea, but more importantly, how do we know which way to go?"

I reached in my backpack and took out the map. When I opened it, Tom's eyes got big with surprise then he asked, "Where in the hell did you get the map of Korea?"

I told him, "I stole it, what else?"

Tom's response to that was, "Holy cow! You sure came prepared, not only that, you sure took a lot of risks with your life trying to get all these things for the escape."

I told him, "I wanted to make sure we had all these things and have a chance of making it. After all, I wanted to escape well equipped." We both laughed.

With the early morning sunlight, we laid out the map trying to find out where camp was and where we would go from there. I showed Tom more or less where it was, and followed the ridge where we had been for the last five days and approximately where we were now. The mountain where we were was at least three hundred and seventy feet above the other one that we had come from, so no wonder it seemed high. The other ridge was about two hundred feet, according to the map. Our map reading training on how to determine the height of a mountain had been in the Marine Corps manual. The mountain is calculated by lines every fifty feet or one hundred feet, depending on the height of the mountain. I was explaining this to Tom, about the mountains and terrain around the mountains. The map also showed roads, train tracks, airports and cities in that area.

"What we'll do, Tom, is you take the map and I'll take the compass. That way, just maybe one of us will get through."

Tom was going to run into more villages the way he was going but he said that he would stay on the ridge. I had studied the map and the way I would be going, there would be only one railroad track to cross. The only time I would run into anything would be in Sinun-Ju, which was the supply city for the Chinese Army. Then I remembered that it had been bombed and there wouldn't be too much activity in the town.

After giving this some thought, we decided that Tom would go south and I would go west. After this was agreed upon, we thought that maybe we should get some sleep. The spot we had chosen to spend the day was ideal because no one could see us. We were sheltered by trees and brush that would protect us from the cold wind on top of the mountain. We bedded down then got some sleep.

We woke up after about six or seven hours, and sat there for a few minutes to get ourselves oriented about which direction each of us would be going. To minimize the weight that we carried, we never had a container for water, so we always drank when we crossed a stream. They were few and far between, but it helped us to continue. We got out some crackers from our sacks and while we were eating, we talked about the life at Camp 1. We both wondered what happened to the guys after they got back to camp. We never talked about what they would do to us if we got caught. A positive attitude was what we held on to during our escape.

We knew that each of us would miss the other, but this was something we had to do, in hopes that getting out would materialize and one of us would be free – or better yet, both of us. It was going to be a very lonely journey.

I said to Tom, "I'm going to ration my crackers so they last."

Tom replied, "I will do the same," and with that we put our socks and boots back on and rested a while longer. Dusk was descending upon us, so we stood up and said our good-byes. After checking our gear, we wished each other good luck.

I said to Tom, "Vallia con Dios." Go with God. As we parted company, we waved as we got about twenty feet from each other. I stopped, then watched Tom disappear into the darkness and I then felt so alone and empty that I had tears in my eyes. Tom and I had been through so much that I considered him family. I trusted him and he trusted me. As I am standing there wiping the tears from my eyes, I looked up and said, "Lord, take care of him, and me also." I then turned and started to head down the mountain so I could pick up the trail on the way, always thinking forward to my destiny.

As I started heading in the direction of Sinun-Ju, it was difficult for me to stay on the ridge. I was crossing ravines and gullies but still high enough so that no one could see me. Was I scared? Of course. I was alone and it was dark, except for the moon. It wasn't full, but was close to it.

When you're alone, scared and thousands of miles from your home, you come head-to-head with your past, drifting back in time to what you did. I went back to when I was a boy of nine. I used to go to the movies at the school auditorium. I never paid to go in because I used to help the night watchman during the evening, pouring poison on the anthills. This enabled me to get in free. We watched horror pictures, and by the time the movie was over, it was dark. The wind would be blowing and it seemed like every tree was coming at me – it was scary. We lived two blocks from the school and my mother knew I would be scared. As I was walking I would yell, "Mom, are you there?" Sometimes she would not answer until I called her a second time, then she would say she was there; then I knew I was safe. She told me later that she was always there but she wouldn't answer so maybe I would quit going to see the horror movies.

My thoughts then jumped to when I was thirteen and ran away from home in San Jose, California. I was hitchhiking to Del Rio. A guy picked me up in Tucson, took me to a highway going to Globe, Arizona, and left me there. Again I was all alone on the highway, miles from nowhere. I started whistling, walking on the white center line of the road. I could hear the coyotes howling and the cactus looked like someone was coming after me. I would ask if there was anyone out there but thank goodness, no one answered! My heart was pounding but I kept walking, thinking that all that was out there were coyotes, cactus and little ol' me.

Returning from my childhood memory excursion, I found myself alone in a foreign land and far away from home, and scared once again. I didn't know what the consequences would be, but I figured I would leave it in the hands of the Lord and let him be my guide. I decided to take a break, so I sat down, and looked all around me to see where I was. The night was still young and I couldn't wait till daybreak.

It was scary not knowing what to expect so high up in the mountains. I thought there could be mountain lions or wild boar. I didn't have a weapon of any kind so what do I do if an animal attacks me? Just then I thought, why not look for a stick that was sharp, and carry it with me just in case? It wasn't much of a weapon but I felt better; at least I would have something to defend myself with. Of course there was the flashlight that I could use as a club. After that thought, I laughed to myself trying to put away my fears that sometimes get you in trouble. I decided that I had better be on my way.

I walked for another three to four hours then I rested. I was so thirsty, but had not passed any streams in the area. Then I remembered that one of the times I visited my grandfather in Mexico, I had met an Indian who took care of my grandfather's mules. We had become good friends. He told me that when he got thirsty and no water was around, he would find a pebble and put it in his mouth. This would create saliva and his thirst would diminish. With this in mind, I went searching for a pebble. After finding one, I put it in my mouth, and before long, I was not thirsty. It was remarkable how that worked. That sure helped.

Sitting down, I looked up at the horizon and saw the glare of lights so I figured I was close to Sinun-Ju, maybe fifteen miles away, or maybe less, the way the crow flies. I knew I had another seven plus days of traveling left. The ocean was nearby so I got up and started moving towards that glare on the horizon because I knew it was where the Port of Sinun-Ju was.

I continued to head in the direction of the Port of Sinun-Ju. In the last few days I had traveled up and down mountains. My body was beginning to show the effects of it. I ached and every muscle in my legs and feet were talking to me.

Two days had passed when the muscle spasms in my legs became so severe that I was forced to take a break. I started looking for an area that was safe so I decided to keep walking downhill. This had been a slow process due to my legs and the rocks that were all around. I had to either climb over them or go around. Another factor I needed to consider, were the cliffs that I would come across occasionally. The cliffs were neither visible or detectable, until you were right on them. This danger was more present in the dark. Some of these cliffs had drops from fifty to one hundred feet. This particular cliff I came across was an ideal place for me to rest my legs. I did not want to be in a hurry and fall to the bottom of the gorge.

While resting, I noticed lightning in the distance and figured there was a storm that looked to be heading in my direction. I did not hesitate in finding shelter. The wind was picking up and the temperature was dropping. It would only be a matter of time before the clouds engulfed the moon. That would cause me a delay in traveling because it was much too dangerous to walk in complete darkness.

I decided to continue my journey, hoping it would be several hours before the moon would diminish behind the clouds. I walked for close to two hours. It was dark by that time so I decided to call it a night. The rocks in the area would make good shelter from both the wind and the rain, should it arrive. I could not take the risk of getting wet and ending up with a cold, or worse – pneumonia.

I soon found a place where there was two huge rocks and some trees. I felt this would protect me from the rain and wind. I was going to remove some limbs off the trees to prop up in the opening of the rocks, but not having a knife, turned my searching towards dead limbs. I located some, then I propped them up in front of the rocks, creating half of an Indian tee-pee. It wasn't going to be a luxury suite at the Hilton, but for now, it was the best I could do. Inside was ample room to stretch my legs and get some needed sleep. This quick shelter was not enough to keep me real warm, but it would be comfortable and protect me from the rain and wind.

I took off my backpack and set it inside and realized that my flashlight was in it but I didn't think that I would need it right now. While I was squatting down to enter my shelter, I heard some noise. I couldn't figure where the noise was coming from but I panicked. Slowly, I entered the shelter then put the limbs at the entrance and then sat very still. Suddenly I felt the goose bumps all over and broke out in a sweat. What was it? I sat there, holding my breath, waiting for something to happen. I had my trusty pointed stick in my hand ready to plunge in to what ever was out there.

I heard the wind intensify and soon raindrops were hitting the leaves on the ground. Cautiously, I sat down inside the tee-pee and waited out the storm, keeping my ears tuned for that unknown noise. The noise had sounded like someone had jumped from a tree and landed hard on the ground. I decided to wait it out till morning knowing that this was going to delay my travels one whole night, but it was something that could not be avoided. I then thought I better get some shut eye but before doing that, I took a peek through the branches outside but saw nothing to worry about. I didn't know how long the storm lasted and by the time I woke up, it was getting light and there was no sign of the storm. I heard birds chirping as I slowly and quietly removed the limbs from the entrance. I looked through some of the branches that were left, then made my exit. I looked around and noticed that about ten feet from the shelter was a huge limb that had come down during the windy storm. I realized that the thud I had heard the night before had been a result of this limb falling. Once outside, I stretched my arms and brushed the leaves and dirt off my clothes. My thoughts returned to Tom, wondering how he was doing.

Since it was too light to travel I decided to stay put until dusk. Back in the shelter, I took out a pack of crackers to munch on. After finishing my snack, I put my knees to my chin. The weather had turned cold, and I started thinking what my future held. I started thinking about mom and dad and how they always worried about me. I was the most mischievous in the family. I wondered what they were doing and how they were handling their son Missing in Action. I knew how good it was going to feel to be home, but also knew this was premature, as I had to get out of this mess first. After spending the day in the shelter, I came out to check the surroundings and noticed the sun was going down. I returned to the shelter to retrieve my backpack and then continued in the direction of Sinun-Ju.

The ground was muddy, but not enough to slow me down as I had to make up the time lost in the shelter. Being careful and watching for any movement, I proceeded very slowly. I was hiding behind tree trunks whenever possible, so it took me some time to get to the bottom of the slope. I didn't see any activity, trail or path and it was very dark. It was at this spot where I decided to rest. I looked for a place so I would not be visible to anyone coming through the ravine below me. I found a place where there were rocks and a clump of trees so that's where I rested. I needed to give my legs a break.

From this area, I could see in all directions of the slope and most importantly, I could see the huge mountain I was going to climb. I also would be able to see if anyone was coming down the mountain. I was tired and very thrilled to have found this haven and not have to worry about being found. While I was sitting there trying to figure the best way to lay down, I saw some weeds, similar to our fern; so I broke off some of those and made a pad, where I would lay my aching body to rest. I finally laid my head down on top of my cracker sack and fell asleep; but not for very long. I was awakened by some jets so I looked up and saw jets engaged in dog-fights. Not having a watch, I looked up at the sun and it had moved approximately to 1500 hours.

Anyway, back to the dog-fights. They were chasing each other, firing at one another. I realized that they were Russian Migs and our F-86s. I watched them for about twenty minutes, and then I saw one get hit and it smoked as it went down. I saw the parachute and it went down about two to three miles from me. I kept an eye on the pilot but later lost him behind a mountain. I was hoping it was the Mig that had been shot down. After all the excitement, I just sat there and waited for darkness to engulf me so I could make tracks up the mountain. While I was sitting there, my entertainment was more dog-fights. I noticed that they were getting lower and I heard sounds like guns going off, then I saw black spots in the sky so I figured that this was an anti-aircraft emplacement.

I saw a jet come down but didn't see if the pilot had bailed out or if he had gone down with the jet. After watching all this I thought, "Wow!" This was a real treat to watch an actual dog-fight between a Russian Mig and an F-86. It never occurred to me that the gun emplacement was that close to where I was, so I didn't give it another thought.

As darkness came, I started up the mountain. I kept thinking how nice it would be to get close to the coast. I was sure I was heading in the right direction, but, I was also wondering what if the town was full of Chinese soldiers? Then what? What if there are no ships patrolling the coast? So I thought to myself, I'll worry about that when I get there. The only thing that kept me going was that I was so close to freedom and all I needed was the Lord's help for me to make it.

I looked up in the sky and saw a million stars and the moon was beaming down, lighting the way for me. There was no trail on the slope but I was making one. I was traveling at a normal pace, not hurrying because I didn't know the ridge and I tried not to step on something that would cause a sprained ankle or a broken leg from a fall. I kept thinking that if I did that, it would be the end of my escape and too much had been put into it to just louse it up now.

I wondered how Tom was doing and hoping he didn't go down to a village to get food. We had learned a very good lesson last time, that you can't trust anyone when you're running away and especially when the people in Korea hate you.

While looking up at the stars I suddenly saw one of the biggest shooting stars I have ever seen. It stretched for miles. When I was a kid, I used to sit in the backyard to watch the shooting stars before going to bed. It was exciting to watch them in the sky and then see them disappear.

I continued to move on, but it was getting harder because the slope was getting steeper. It was an encouraging feeling that soon I would be on top and see for miles. I was sure looking forward to that. I still had a few hours of darkness so I tried to take bigger steps so I would get to the top before morning. I moved quickly and stayed alert, hoping I didn't run into anything that I would get hurt from, or run into someone.

It was a blessing that Tom and I had been strong and fairly healthy on this escape. I don't know about Tom, but I wouldn't have done this well or gotten this far if I hadn't been in fairly good condition. As dawn was coming into view over the mountains, I tried to hurry and get to the peak as it was only another two hundred feet. But it was going to seem like a mile as it always does. The closer you get to something, the farther it seems. Another one and a half hours and I was on top of the world, or it seemed that way. In every direction I looked, I saw mountains. I looked to the west. I then had to look twice as there was a spot of blue on the horizon and my first thought was – it's the ocean! No, it might be the blue sky. I chose to believe it was the ocean. I jumped for joy and could feel goose bumps all over, my heart was pumping ninety miles an hour and then I said, "Thank you Lord. It was because of you that I made it."

I was so overwhelmed that I wanted to yell and tell the world I had made it to the ocean. I calmed down, then sat down, and thanked the Lord for guiding me here, and for my not running into any major problems. Even though the escape was not over, there was a lot of country and mountains I would have to cross before I got to the ocean. I sat there and said, "I'm home." I had never experienced that feeling as I had when I saw the ocean. It was a feeling of freedom. A feeling that I had accomplished what I had planned to do. As I was getting over the excitement, I realized that maybe it was a little premature to get excited. I still had many miles to go.

With this in mind, I looked for a place to rest and to figure out what my next move would be. After finding a safe place, I sat down and tried to decide whether to travel during the daylight hours or just stick to night walking. While I was sitting, another thought came to mind: Where and how far were those railroad tracks that I had seen on the map? I felt I was getting very close to them, but as yet I had not heard a train whistle. I figured that maybe over the next ridge I would see the tracks or hear something from the direction of Sinun-ju. Keeping a hold of this thought, I resumed my walking to the next mountain ridge. I walked cautiously, for it was daylight and I did not want to be seen, should there be anyone out there. Gradually making my way to the ridge, I heard a noise that I thought to be a train whistle, but was very faint. Not knowing for sure what the noise had been, I continued walking up the mountain. With all my aches, back pain, leg cramps and being very tired, getting to the top seemed to be an impossible task. However, logic re-entered my thoughts and I began looking for a rock or anything that would help hide my presence. I took a few more steps and decided on a rock with vegetation around the area. Sitting there, I looked around to see if I could see anyone on top of the ridge. I detected no movement. I felt safe at this point to remove my boots and massage my feet. It was a much needed stop because after all, my feet were taking the brunt of this whole ordeal.

Fifteen to twenty minutes had passed and I knew that I must move on. It took an hour or so before I got to the ridge. I hurried to the very top of the mountain because at this point, I was not taking anything for granted. When I looked around for the tracks, I did not see any. I gradually worked my way down to the ravine to get a closer look. Hopefully I would see the tracks.

I realized that once I found them, careful planning would be crucial. I did not want to run into Korean soldiers, or workers that might be guarding the tracks. It was to my disappointment that I did not see the train tracks immediately so the only decision left for me was to climb to the next ridge. As I walked, I remembered that the map had shown a railroad bridge somewhere in the direction that I was traveling. I had been concerned about the bridge because two months prior to this escape, Sinun-ju had been bombed and the tracks might also have been bombed. It was located close to Mig Alley.

I convinced myself not to worry about the railroad until I had found it. Another rest felt in order, but I did not want to make it a long stop as curiosity had set in regarding the tracks and bridge. A few minutes passed, and on my way I went. As I was descending from the mountain, heading for the ravine, I noticed that the elevation was dropping. I felt sure that meant I was getting close to Sinun-ju. I also noted that the lower I traveled into the ravine, the more vegetation there was. That meant that I would blend in with the vegetation due to the drab olive color, the same as the Air Force uniform I was wearing.

Another plus to the vegetation was its height. It would conceal me better, but on the other hand, I could only see ten feet in front of me. I had to remember to be cautious and not make any noise. The very last thing I needed at this time would be for someone to surprise me! I knew that it would be a very nerve-racking walk, but it was a must that I get to the bottom of the ravine.

By sundown I had accomplished the task. I walked about one hundred feet and I saw railroad tracks at the end of the ravine. I figured the reason that I had not seen the tracks before was that they went around the mountain. There probably was a cliff at the end of the ravine. At this point, I hid under the brush. I started shaking and realized just how scared I was.

I broke out in a sweat, so I decided to take a much needed break. I would look for a good resting place – a place near the tracks yet far enough away that no one could see me. I was nervous about finding the tracks yet it was a situation that had presented itself. There was no other way but to deal with it.

Dealing with it was no consolation to me; I was still scared. I didn't want to die in the hands of the North Koreans after coming this far. What if I ran into Korean soldiers? Would they shoot first and ask questions later? What if I can't cross the tracks for one reason or another? The negative thoughts were getting the best of me. While crawling on my hands and knees toward the direction of the tracks, I decided to stop and pray. I asked God to help me through this, whatever the consequences. Very quietly, I continued to crawl, and at the same time, looking for a place to stay and get some sleep.

As darkness was descending upon me, with very little light left, I was forced to find a place to settle down and I found a suitable place to stop. Out in the darkness and somewhere in the distance, I heard voices. I started to tremble. My thought was the voices were only one or two hundred feet away. Now what? Do I stay here? Should I try and find another spot to stay? Had they seen me? I thought I was in a very safe place, but once again, the fear of being captured was there. I focused on relaxing my body somewhat, because I needed to stay motionless, waiting to find out if something would happen.

I decided, after a few minutes, that I would move very slowly to a spot where I felt I would be shielded from the elements at hand. I did so very quickly. Not long after doing this, I heard voices again, but this time they sounded further away. That, in itself, made me relax a bit. I let out a big sigh of relief, but the danger of the unknown was still present.

I sat there and asked God to please help me in this time of need. A calming effect resulted after my prayer, as it usually did. I grabbed my backpack and retrieved a package of crackers. This would leave me with only one. All this time I was ever so cautious. I looked around to make sure I was safe from anyone seeing me. While all of my senses were on full alert, I thought that maybe those voices had come from the direction of the railroad tracks. With this conclusion, I knew that I must be close to them.

After finishing the crackers, I sat very still, listening for the voices to return. After several minutes had passed, I did not hear any noises or human voices. This was comforting. I was wondering what my next move should be. I recalled that there was a bridge somewhere close to where I was, but how far, and in which direction, I did not know. My first move should be to get to the tracks, find out if it was feasible to pass during the day, if there was anyone around, and keep vigil for at least a day. If any movement was detected, then I would not cross during the day.

I had to do this from some point on the cliff, where I would not be seen and where I would be able to see at least one hundred feet in either direction. I had since forgotten about the bridge. My concentration was solely on crossing the tracks at the bottom. This location was suitable for my crossing. The vegetation went all the way to the cliff so I would be able to see everything from there. I decided this is where I would cross to the next mountain. Darkness descended quickly, so I knew that I better find a safe place to rest. I would need to be alert in the morning while I kept a hawk-eyed watch for the next train. As I decided this, I grabbed my backpack and strapped it on my back. While I was sitting waiting for dawn, my mind drifted back to my mother and father. I wondered if they knew what their son was going through. A sound in the distance brought me back to the present. I started to move toward the cliff where I had seen the tracks.

A strong sense of urgency came over me. I knew that I had to make my move right then, so I very cautiously started crawling on my hands and knees. It would be difficult, but if I stood up, I would have to protect my face from the bushes. Plus, it would have been easier for someone to spot me if anyone had been out there.

I made good time, under the circumstances. The silence that surrounded me was almost eerie. I was thankful, but at the same time, I almost wished that I heard some other noise besides my heart. It was pumping overtime! I felt that I must get to a place where I would be able to see the train, should it make an appearance. Thank goodness for the rest that I had taken awhile back. I was alert and could move more swiftly, while dodging brush and rock. I thought about taking a breather, when low and behold, the train whistle sound filtered through the air. I canceled the idea of taking a break. As I was crawling, I saw a clearing ahead of me, about thirty feet, and I realized the end of the cliff was near. I paused for a bit to regain my senses. My knees and hands were hurting, so I massaged them. I decided to crawl to about five feet from the cliff. After doing so, I looked down and to my surprise, I saw the tracks. They were thirty to forty feet below. I turned around and crawled back, where I found a spot that I could wait for the train.

I laid down and watched for the train with no idea of how long this would take, I put my mind on the problem of crossing the tracks. Thank goodness the weather was cooperating. Just as I was about to ponder the crossing of the tracks, I heard the train whistle again, and it was coming my way. I got on my hands and knees, headed back to the edge of the cliff in time to see the train go by. I was still surrounded by enough vegetation that my being seen would be unlikely. I started to get nervous and all of my senses were back on full alert.

As I am laying there, watching the train pass by, I looked to see if there were any guards on top of the train cars. The train was moving at a good pace, so it was not long before it was out of my vision and I was left looking at the tracks for any movement. I lay motionless in my position waiting to see if anyone came around. I felt that I should stay there for a few hours and watch for movement and listen for sounds that caught my attention. By this time, the sun had just started to come up from behind the mountains.

Just as I was about ready to change my position to give my stomach a break, I heard a noise – like a truck. I had almost convinced myself that it couldn't be, when a truck came in to view. It was a Korean Army truck loaded with bags of rice. It was heading in the same direction as the train, south. I counted three soldiers on top of the bags and noticed that the truck was traveling on a road next to the tracks. The road did not look like it had been traveled much, for weeds and vegetation had taken control.

All of this activity had set me back, but only temporarily. I abolished the negative thoughts that had crept in and focused only on the positive. Nothing short of getting captured would have prevented me from crossing the railroad tracks. I kept looking across the tracks at the mountain I would soon be climbing.

My next decision was to find a place that I could get down from the cliff and then cross the tracks. A few hours had passed and during that time, I decided that I would make my move sometime tonight. While the hours slipped by, I wondered what might be up ahead for me. Would I be lucky enough to make it the whole way without being caught? How was Tom holding up? Had the guys that returned to camp received harsh punishment, or worse, death? If caught, what punishment would they give me? Would I find some food since I had depleted my cracker stash? Enough of this, I told myself. Get back to the problem at hand.

So many hours had passed without any noise or human sounds, so I decided that it would be safe to cross at sundown. Dusk arrived so I crawled to the very edge of the cliff, looking for a place to get down. It wasn't long before I spotted a crevice to the right of where I was. I felt that I could slowly climb down and still stay somewhat hidden from view. The crevice was about five feet deep, going all the way to the bottom of the cliff. It ended about ten feet from the railroad tracks – perfect.

I had to get down this cliff soon, as the day was being engulfed by darkness. I needed to see where I was going and time was ticking away. Before I started backing down, I said a prayer. Right after that, I put one foot on the side of the crevice and the other foot on the other side. With my hands, I balanced my body toward the middle of the crevice. It was a slow-paced ordeal and very hard on the muscles. I had gone about half way when I took a rest in a spot where I could relax my legs somewhat. I never let my senses go off alert. I continued down and about five feet from the bottom, my foot hit a soft spot. I nearly lost my grip and balance. I was able to lean to one side and regain my footing.

I slowly went down, inch by inch, until I got to the bottom. I then looked up and said, "Thank you, Lord." I quickly got on my haunches and looked in every direction. The darkness did not help but I felt secure that no one was out there. I proceeded toward the tracks, but in a quick second, I thought that I would stay at the crevice, take a rest, and not be in a hurry. It would be better to be safe than sorry. Not more than fifteen minutes had passed, when I decided to take the plunge.

The concern of getting caught by the North Koreans had resurfaced. I needed to rid my mind of such a thought and believe that no one or nothing would rob me of my freedom. Quietly, I crouched my body and headed for the other side, using whatever available resource for staying somewhat hidden from view. Once on the other side, I vanished into the brush.

I looked for a place to rest and determine if anyone had seen me cross the tracks. I found a good spot about ten feet from the edge of the hill. It was close enough for me to see the tracks and also I would see if anyone came toward me. While I sat, I wondered how much more pain my body must endure before I got to freedom? My legs had been cramping, and my back was burning with pain. But somehow thinking of my freedom overshadowed any pain that I was experiencing or had experienced on my quest to be free.

While I was resting, I massaged my legs and attended to some of the scrapes and scratches that I received while crawling through the brush. Not much time had elapsed when I felt it was time to move on toward the top of the hill before daybreak. Close to midday, I had reached the top. It had taken a long time. I had to fight the brush that was in my path, plus finding my way to the top.

Once on top, I took a look around for a suitable place to rest. I wanted one that would hide me from view if anyone should come around. I soon found a clump of huge rocks and that seemed good enough. I walked over there, took my backpack off and sat down. Since I had nothing left to eat, I decided to chew on my pebble, hoping to drown out my hunger. While sitting there, I thought back about crossing the railroad tracks without incident and what a relief that had been.

I got up to look around and see if there was a trail on the ridge. There was no trail and that was very comforting. That meant this area was not traveled frequently. I could sleep more at ease by not worrying that someone would find me. I returned to my spot of rest, laid down and dozed off.

When I awoke, dusk had arrived, sometime between 1700 or 1800 hours. I slowly got to my feet and then very quietly looked around to make sure no visitors had arrived while I was asleep. The danger of being found was always present.

Feeling safe, I continued on my journey. I was able to travel at a faster pace because I did not have to contend with the brush. Soon the moonlight would help me find the way around the trees and rocks. I finally reached the top so again I took a small break. I looked around and to the west, I saw the glare of Sinuiju. The light appeared brighter and to me that meant I was closer to the ocean. I sat down, leaned up against a tree and just looked at the glare. It sure felt good. Freedom was just a few miles away. I decided that I would wait for dawn. Time seemed to pass by quickly because before I knew it, dawn had arrived. I sat for a few more minutes wondering if it would be feasible to travel on the ridge in daylight. What were my chances of someone seeing me? The ridge of the mountain that I was on made a horseshoe turn so I would be able to stay on the ridge. I would not need to travel down the mountain and then go back up the next one. That in itself would save me time and a whole lot of leg work. I decided to walk along the ridge but be on alert at all times.

The thought of the ocean being near was enough for me to forget my suffering. I felt good and thought my pains were coming to an end. Freedom was just a few miles away. I kept telling myself this so I would keep going. I was exhausted by this time. I would keep going until I saw the ocean, and that in itself would earn me a nice long rest. I knew that my body would not take much more beating. I was taking more breaks and I would get the shakes. I needed to take care of myself. I waited for dusk, then I headed for the next ridge. I told myself that once I climbed it, I would get some sleep. I was very tired and my legs had been through a lot of mountain climbing. With that thought in mind, I started going up. I had found an easy way so I would not have to travel straight up. I started going up on a diagonal so I wouldn't be so tired after getting to the top.

After a few yards I realized that it was easier on my legs and so I was moving a little faster than if I had been going straight up. I felt I would reach the top within three hours so I kept climbing and soon enough, I made it to the top. I sat down and looked around. I rested my legs and thought about finding a place to rest as it had been a long haul. It was the early part of the evening by the time I got to the top so now it was time to sleep. I soon found a place where I would be hidden in every direction and I would not need to worry about it. I laid my head down and I guess I went to sleep in no time, because when I woke up, it was dark and the stars were out.

Off in the distance I heard some rumbling and thought they were bombing SinunJu but I couldn't see any planes or any glare from bombs exploding. I just couldn't figure out what it was. I could see the glare of the city but that was always there. I decided that I would get myself going so I could reach the ocean in the next day or so.

The mountain I was on had a lot of trees, in fact it was covered with them. That made me feel good because I could travel during the day without being seen from the bottom of the mountain or elsewhere. I leaned back on a tree, away from the top and decided that I would take a small nap. After an hour or so I woke up. I then tried to get myself focused on what I was going to do next. I stood up, looking in the direction of Sinun-Ju and there was one more mountain that I had to climb to see the ocean, so that is the way I decided to go. Making sure I was ready to travel, I strapped my backpack on and started down the mountain.

The weather was kind of nippy but the sun took care of that. There were a lot of trees plus going downhill was easy, but I had to be careful. I stopped once in a while, so as not to be surprised by some farmer or Korean soldier.

I seemed to be relaxing now that I would soon be out of this mess. Not only that, I felt secure somehow that everything was going to be okay. I was thinking that after running away from home at fourteen, I was more or less experienced at traveling alone. I think I was more scared of the Korean militia catching me than the Chinese soldiers. The Koreans had no mercy. I had seen the treatment that they had bestowed upon some of the POWs I took care of at Camp 1. With these thoughts, I was very cautious of running into any Korean.

I finally got to the bottom of the ravine where I took a ten minute break. My rest came to an end so I started up the side of the mountain as I did before, going at a forty-five degree angle. I had found out it was much easier on my legs and back and at the present time, I needed all the help I could get, to get to the top.

Climbing up and down the mountains had aggravated my back something fierce. My legs were cramping so I had to slow down, rest more, and massage them. There was nothing I could do for my back but just take it in stride. It had been hurting since the day of my capture but I wasn't going to let that stop me from escaping. I took comfort in my prayers and those that I knew my Mother would say for me. I also knew that God would see me through.

A few hours later, I got to the top. There it was with all its splendor – the beautiful blue ocean or at least I thought so. It would be better to believe that, than think it was the sky! I looked again and I could hardly believe my eyes! Ships were on the water. They would have to be, I said to myself. I started thinking that I need to get to the ocean at night, then I'll give them an SOS. "Wow" I said, "I'm going home!" It was getting late and being this close I was not going to hurry.

While I sat next to some brush and a clump of trees, I kept looking at that beautiful ocean. Even though I couldn't see the flags on the ships, I knew they were ours as they were quite a ways from the beach. Once I relaxed, I started looking around me to get acquainted with the terrain. This way I would know what was around me before I left for the ocean.

There were a lot of trees everywhere, so it was going to be hard for me to see anyone coming or for them to spot me. I looked for a place to lay down, away from where I was sitting. That wasn't going to be a problem because there was a lot of ground vegetation, and I could lay there with no problem of being seen. I made my place to lay on the ground and went to sleep.

By the time I woke it was almost dark so I laid there and rested for a while. Being dark and all, I went to the spot where I had stood and looked towards the ocean and also Sinun-Ju. I could see the glare from where I was. It was brighter. I then went back to where I had been laying and decided to lay back and maybe get some more sleep so the night might go faster. I wondered why I hadn't heard any jets flying around. I thought that maybe Sinun-Ju had been bombed the day before; or those ships on the ocean had shelled it, and that is where that rumble had come from. I told myself that I could assume so many things to which I would probably be wrong. I gave it up and tried to get some sleep.

I closed my eyes but just tossed and turned. I had too much on my mind about what could happen, like heading for the coast and trying to get towards the beach. What would happen once I got there and what if I got caught? I sat there trying to figure the best way to get to the ocean. It seemed like it was premature to try anything yet, as I would have to get closer. At that time, I estimated that I was about four miles away from the ocean. I still had to go up and down hills till I hit flat land, which would put me almost to the ocean.

The closer I got to the ocean meant more than likely I would encounter civilization, so I needed to be very alert so I would not be surprised. The hills towards Sinun-Ju were smaller and being that I was that close, I would have to travel slower. As the evening was coming to an end, I decided that I would sit there for a while and wait for it to get a little darker. I felt that I would run into someone on the mountains because the Korean peasants cook with wood stoves, and more than likely they would be out in search of this wood.

I decided that I would go to the next hill and stop there to find out which way to go. It started getting darker so I took off. While I was up on the hill, I had picked a direction of where to go. While going down the hill I said to myself, so close and yet so far. Close because I could see the ocean and far because I didn't know what I was going to run into. I was going slow trying to dodge rocks, trees and always stay on the look out for the unexpected. I was this close to freedom and did not want to take any unnecessary chances.

After several minutes I was at the bottom when I looked up and told myself, this is it. I should be able to see something in the morning when I get to the top. I figured that I would just lay there and wait until daylight and then decide what direction I needed to go. The hill wasn't too high but it was covered with trees as the previous ones had been. What I did like was it was covered with shrubs and ground vegetation so I could hide for days if need be.

While I was climbing, I kept telling myself that I cannot make a mistake. Think before you act, look before you leap and that kind of philosophy. I had been alone before when I ran away, but this was different. There was the enemy out there and so much at stake. When I was close to the top, I saw a tree with a broken limb and it had fallen across the tree resembling a cross. I walked over to it, knelt down then looked up and said, "Lord, no matter what happens, please help me to be a better person and whoever is out there, let him help me so I can reach freedom. If I should die for the sake of freedom, let me die as a Marine and with dignity. Thank you, Lord. Amen." I stood up and continued to climb. I kept looking back at the "cross" and wondered if God was trying to tell me something.

After seeing the cross, my mind drifted to my beautiful mother. She was always telling me about God. I remember, on one occasion when I was growing up, she said, "Son, don't ever be afraid of anything as long as you believe in God." Then she said, "God doesn't forsake those who believe in him." Then she kissed my forehead and patted me on the back. As I was leaving, she yelled, "Don't forget what I told you."

As I returned to the present, I kept repeating in my mind, those words of wisdom over and over. I soon had peace within and the strength to keep going, especially now. It was comforting to believe that I wasn't alone and that the Lord was with me and he would lead me in the right direction. That direction was to freedom.

Continuing to climb up the hill, my senses were on full alert. I also wondered what I would find once I was on top of the hill. After an hour or so, I got to the top.

Right away I looked for a suitable place to rest my body and wait for daylight.

Chapter Eleven
Russian Roulette

After resting and getting a couple hours of sleep, I sat up. I could see that dawn had started to break over the mountains, so I decided to stay put until daylight. I would then be able to make a survey of the area and figure out all my options. I faced a decision on how to head for the ocean.

One option was to head on to the Yalu River, which was to the north about three miles. Once I got there, I would look for a log large enough to hold me and float out to sea during the night. But then suppose I fall off the log, or worse yet, get caught by a Korean patrol boat? They would probably shoot me on sight. That in itself did not sound that great.

My second option was to leave where I was and head south, completely going around Sinun-ju. That meant I would have to backtrack about three miles and then go west another three miles. That didn't sound bad, but I didn't have any food, my body was completely drained and it would take another two to three days to reach the coast.

The third option was to continue the way I was heading, towards the outskirts of Sinun-ju and walk my way through the hills while staying away from the populated areas. I had to stay alert and pray that I would make it. This option would probably take me eight days, at the most.

As daylight was upon me, I decided I would make a survey of the area to see exactly where I was. I almost wished that the sun hadn't come out. Then I could be here forever and not have to make a wrong decision. That idea was frightening but I know that I had to get off the mountain and head for the ocean. After a few minutes, I settled down and looked over the area. Not wanting to be seen, of course, I crawled to the edge of the ridge, about fifteen feet, and then slowly got up. I moved the brush to one side so I would be able to see.

When I focused, to my surprise, I saw a valley down below. A few huts were scattered around in the area and they were about a mile from me. I abruptly let go of the brush and hastily sat down. The sweats and shakes had taken over my body. I realized at that moment that I had reached a point in my life where I had come face to face with reality. This was one time in my life that any decision that I should make would be the difference between life and death. That was not an easy thought to accept, although I told myself that I am here and I will see my self through. Having the Lord on my side was going to help.

I got on my hands and knees, then crawled back to my original position. I sat there and tried to get over the shakes. I had to rest and reason with myself that I would make it to the ocean, and ultimately be free. Having seen the ocean and village below had assured me that the third option was going to be the best.

I was hungry and thirsty but I was out of crackers and had not seen any water so I decided on the thirst pebble. That would just have to do for now, and I certainly hoped that it would. I prayed to God and thanked him for his hand in getting me this far and hopefully getting me to freedom – the ocean.

I was ready to continue on. As I walked out of the vegetation that had surrounded me, I veered off towards the clearing. Taking inch by inch, step by step, I continued to straddle the line of vegetation, so if I heard something close by, I would be able to hide back in the waist high vegetation. So far, so good. I took a few more steps when some movement caught my attention, so I looked up. To my surprise, two men were coming out of the clump of trees. They saw me and I saw them. All I could do was freeze right in my tracks.

Could my mind be playing tricks on me? Was I hallucinating? In a matter of seconds, my questions had been answered. The men pulled out guns and pointed them right at me! I immediately put my hands up in the air. Who were these people? Where did they come from? I hadn't heard any noises prior to this, so how were they able to just appear out of nowhere?

As I stood there with my hands up, they continued coming toward me. My thoughts went back to the Russians that had come to Camp 1. A second later, I realized these people were Russian as well. A feeling of fear engulfed me but for now, I would not let that show. One of them said to the other something in Russian. After putting his gun down, one of the men swiftly pushed me face down, grabbed my wrists, pulled them behind my back and tied them together. I had no idea at this point, what was in store for me.

They pulled me up, and with their guns pointed directly at me, escorted me to the clump of trees where I had planned earlier to rest. My mind was going a hundred miles an hour. I was also saddened by the thought that my escape to freedom had come to a screeching, abrupt halt. About the only consolation was that I was still alive. I didn't know for how long and only time would tell. As we approached the clump of trees, I realized why it was dark. They had an anti-aircraft emplacement covered with camouflage netting! There were ten to fifteen Russian soldiers under all the netting.

One of my guards summoned someone. I assumed that this was the officer in command of the unit because as he walked toward me, with a smile, he got face to face with me, looked me up and down and asked in broken English, "You are a F-86 pilot, aren't you?" At that moment I didn't answer because I had no clue as to what he was talking about.

I was then taken under the netting where my hands were untied. A few minutes passed when a soldier entered, holding handcuffs. The handcuffs were put on me then a few soldiers spoke in Russian. The officer, in a very harsh voice, asked me, "What is your name?" I replied, "Pfc. Nick A. Flores, USMC 1091431."

The officer then said something to a soldier standing nearby. After that, the soldier came to me and put a blindfold on me. I sat, nervously thinking what a terrible misfortune it was to have been caught, so close to freedom. Yet, maybe it was meant to happen for my situation could have turned out a lot worse. I could have been caught by the Koreans and tortured to the brink of death. I just wished I knew what was to happen next.

A few minutes went by when another officer, who spoke English, asked me, "You are an F-86 pilot, aren't you?" This person had authority because all the talking that had been going on, stopped abruptly as he spoke. The officer grabbed me by the shoulders and shook me, almost knocking me to the ground. He angrily said, "You are the F-86 pilot, and I want to know where you went down!" I did not answer which made him very upset.

He then took my backpack off and threw it to the ground. After showing that bit of rage, he began feeling around my collar, then pulled on it as if looking for something hidden. All this time he is talking to someone standing there next to him. Not finding anything of course, he stepped back, but even blindfolded I could sense that he was still there. I could tell by the sound of his voice that he was madder than hell. He then walked away, talking in Russian. He yelled to someone and a few minutes later, I heard a truck start.

At the same time, I felt two pair of hands grab me and then they stood me up. We walked about forty feet when I was halted. Two soldiers grabbed me from my arms and legs then threw me up on the truck bed. They got up on the truck and then dragged me to the front, just below the window. I sat motionless; I could not help but wonder what they were going to do with me. As many thoughts went through my mind, I heard soldiers laughing in the distance and they seemed to be very happy – maybe because they had caught a POW that had escaped, or they were pleased that they had an American F-86 pilot under their control. Whatever the reason, I was scared, confused and wondering what the Russians were going to do with me.

Sitting toward the back of the truck with the two guards standing by me, I heard the right side door slam. With the truck motor running, the driver stepped on the accelerator as if to check that the motor was running okay, and then I heard someone say something from a distance. In a little while I heard the opposite door from the driver open, words were uttered and the door slammed and away we went.

As the truck was moving very slow down hill, I felt this was going to be a long day. The truck seemed to be hitting every bump and pothole and my body was taking all the jolts. I didn't know my destination of course but I felt it was in the hands of the Lord just to be alive. As the truck kept moving, I kept leaning from side to side, bump after bump. It was a bad road wherever we were going, and I was definitely going to have a sore rear end. I thought how unfortunate it was to get caught so close to freedom – so near yet so far.

After going downhill a while, we came to a stop. The anti-aircraft emplacement would have to have been situated far up the mountain because it was a while before we hit a paved road. I would say it took us at least thirty minutes to get where we had started from the emplacement.

After stopping, we made a left turn because my body slowly leaned in the other direction and the guard pushed me as if to order me not to lean on him. As we entered the road, I felt the truck accelerate and it seemed like we were on a smoother road, maybe a paved one. We were moving along when I started hearing traffic going in the opposite direction. It seemed like a lot of traffic so I thought we were on a major highway. It sure was a relief not to bounce my body anymore as the trip from the top of the mountain had been very bumpy.

Moving at a good pace, we were encountering more traffic the farther we traveled. I don't know how far we traveled, but it seemed to me we were on the highway for at least twenty minutes. Just then I felt the truck slowing down. We came almost to a stop, then we turned to the right. I could hear horns blowing and also people talking as we were moving along. I felt we were traveling in a populated area. We kept stopping and going which continued for about five to ten minutes. I am sure we were going through intersections. After going through several more intersections, we came to a stop. I heard the door opposite the driver open, closely followed by conversation to either the guards or the driver. I could hear the person leave but he soon returned and got back into the truck. We moved on. It seemed to me that we were in an area of downtown, because where we had been parked, I could hear foot traffic.

We came to another stop, and the truck then proceeded straight. After about two to three minutes we came to another stop. I could hear someone talking to the person opposite the driver, and I heard some papers rustle like it was orders or other official paperwork. There was a lot of confusion close to the truck and at that time I really began to wonder where in the hell these people were taking me.

The truck finally began moving onto what seemed like a bridge because as we were moving, I would say twenty-five to thirty miles per hour, we were hitting expansion joints on the road every two to three seconds. Then I heard the side wall of the bridge. It made the sound of the truck echo and the bridge was at least the distance of three or four blocks long, in my estimation.

There I was bouncing around again and was glad when we came to a stop. At this point I was aware of different noises which got me curious and then I realized that water was nearby, possibly a river or lake. The truck came to another stop and I heard a Russian soldier talking to either the driver or officer. They exchanged a few words and then we slowly moved on. We came to a stop where the driver made a right turn then proceeded approximately a quarter of a mile where we stopped again. This time the driver and officer got out. I heard accents and language which I knew were Russian soldiers.

I felt that we had reached our destination for the driver and officer seemed to be getting off. The guards hadn't moved so I guess they were waiting for orders to take me off the truck. I sat there for a few minutes listening to conversation then the two guards yanked me on my feet and pulled me to the back of the truck where they sat me down. I realized how it felt to be manhandled and not be able to see, just like being blind. It is an awful feeling, plus it's real scary.

I heard the guards jump down and then they grabbed me from my arms and yanked me down from the truck, to the ground. I got up and stood there for a few seconds.

Someone with authority, by the sound of his voice, ordered, "Get down!" He spoke very good English. Then he asked me my name, which I reluctantly refused to answer after the way I was manhandled and loaded in the truck. I then thought better and gave in. "Nick A. Flores, 1091431, United States Marines."

"You are a F-86 pilot, aren't you?"

"No, I am not a pilot!"

He told the guards something in Russian, which I sensed was for the guards to escort me to an unknown destination. I heard jet engines in the distance. Was I at or near an airstrip? I was puzzled, so I asked myself what in the hell was I doing close to an airstrip or an airport? Thoughts came to mind; what are Russians doing in Korea? Where was I? Could it be Manchuria? Why did they insist that I was a pilot?

As I was being escorted, my hearing was on full alert. I now seemed to be inside an empty building or warehouse – or could it be a hangar? At this point, being handcuffed and blindfolded, I was confused to no end.

I heard echos in the distance from people talking in Russian. Had I been taken to a bunker at the air base? Continuing on for twenty feet I then felt like I was in a cave; it sure sounded like it. There were people moving around, then I heard something like ladders with wheels or dollies being moved about. All these noises were not helping my already nervous state.

My excursion came to a halt and I heard laughter in the background. As I stood there wondering what was next, I felt a chair hit behind my knees. I cautiously sat down then someone pushed me towards the back of the chair. I said, "Okay, okay!" very rebellious. That push really hurt and my patience was wearing thin. I asked myself, "What on earth do these people want with me?"

Then the officer in charge, I assume, said something to another person, and as he approached me, I could hear his boots hitting the floor. He got within two feet from where I was sitting and he said he was captain so-and-so I can't recall his name – at this point, he could have been Captain Kangaroo. He continued, saying that he was an interpreter and the colonel would be asking me questions to which I must answer truthfully. I knew that all I had to give them was my name, rank and serial number.

I was asked, "Your name?"

"Nick A. Flores, 1091431, USMC."

He repeated his question again with a very loud voice and told me that I will answer the questions they ask and it should be the truth. Did I understand? As he finished I heard a very strong voice coming from a few feet away. He spoke Russian and I could hear the clicking of the boot heels hitting the floor. While approaching me, he was still talking to the interpreter. He got to where the interpreter and I were, still talking to the interrogator. Then the interpreter said, "This is colonel so and so and he will ask you questions and I will translate in English. Is that understood?"

I didn't reply quickly so with his loud voice he again asked if that was understood? I replied, "I have no idea what you want."

The captain was getting hot under the collar because he gave me a slap in the face and got me by the shoulders then shook me. He told me, "You must confess!" The colonel said something to him and then he immediately let go of me. He then went behind my chair, put his boot on top of the hand cuffs, pushed down and my arms were pulled against the chair. I let out a big yell and he took his foot off but not for long. He repeated it again. With that I let out another big yell. Aaah! The pain took control of my body.

I screamed, "What the hell do you want with me? I am not a pilot!"

At that moment I thought, why are they making such a fuss about a POW escapee with a flier's uniform? I started to get scared because maybe someone had done something bad or killed someone and they were going to take it out on me. All kinds of unwanted thoughts came to my mind.

After the interpreter let go of my shoulders, I was trying to size up the colonel who kept asking me this question. He sounded like a very stout man, maybe forty-seven to fifty years old. I would guess he weighed about two hundred pounds and stood close to six feet tall. He got close to my face and said something in Russian. He then pushed my head back with such a thrust that I almost fell back, chair and all. I knew that my body could not stand much more of this treatment. I was exhausted and my body was racked with pain.

While I am trying to regain my senses, the interpreter yelled at me saying, "The colonel wants to know the location of your F-86!" I answered, "I am not a pilot. I wasn't flying an F-86."

"Where is your squadron based?"

I said, "Sir, I am not a pilot."

At that moment, the colonel moves toward me and said something in Russian. The next thing I hear is, "The colonel wants to know why you are wearing a pilot's uniform if you are not a pilot? You are lying to us. You must confess!" He then slapped me with the back of his hand, saying something in Russian. Then walked away.

Russian officers interrogating me after my capture by anti-aircraft personnel. (Sketch by Nick A. Flores)

They just didn't believe what I had told them. I tried, repeatedly, to convince them that I was not a pilot, yet it seemed the more I denied it, the more convinced they became that I was.

The colonel was speaking angrily to the interpreter. The interpreter then walked over to me and felt the uniform. I could not put my finger on why they kept touching my uniform. I braced myself, half expecting a slap on the face or a kick to my legs. I wouldn't put anything past these people.

"Did you come from a carrier?"

"No, sir. I did not come from a carrier. None of those accusations are true. I don't know a hill of beans about any aircraft carrier."

The interpreter yelled very loud, "You are lying!" The colonel said something to him.

I said, "I am a POW that escaped and I don't know anything about an F-86 jet or about being a pilot."

I was desperately trying to figure out why they were so sure that I was a pilot. I knew that I was wearing an Air Force overall and a jacket that belonged to a gunner on a B-29, but I sure wasn't going to tell them that!

After the colonel spoke to the interpreter, after which the interpreter asked me, "Are you spreading germ warfare? How many F-86s were in your group?"

I replied, "I am not a pilot, sir." As the colonel started to speak, I interrupted by saying, "I am Pfc. Nick A. Flores, United States Marine Corps, 1091431." I thought these guys were becoming a pain in the rear.

The interpreter then asked me, "Where did you hide the parachute?" I felt like saying, "Go look for it," and then decided not to. He had a strong, harsh voice. Again, he repeated the same words, I presume, in Russian, I did not answer.

He spoke with a lot of authority and there was not any noise in the background except the sound of jet engines way in the distance. He seemed calm, yet forceful. They had moved away from my chair and they were having a conversation between themselves. Then I heard both of them coming toward me. The colonel said something to me. He was very close to my face, then the interpreter said to me, "The colonel says you are an F-86 pilot and you must confess. He wants to know where your base is and where did you fly from?" Not this again! Getting out of a mess like this was not in the Marine Corps training. When I thought about it, I started laughing to myself. Apparently the interpreter saw me, because he grabbed and shook me while asking, "Why don't you confess? The others confessed!"

At that moment I realized I wasn't the only one that had been interrogated there. There had to have been other pilots who had been shot down in Korea and interrogated there. When the interpreter said that the others had confessed, the colonel yelled at him in a loud, harsh voice. I figured that he had said something he shouldn't have; sort of spilled the beans.

A few minutes later both of them let up on their interrogation and walked away, and I could hear five or six people talking to them. While that conversation was continuing, the interpreter returned and asked in a low voice that if I was not a pilot, why was I wearing an American Air Force uniform? I told him that it was given to me. Again he asked why didn't I confess? He said that I was lying to them. Then he came around to the back of my chair and kicked my hands. He then grabbed my hair and pulled it back then asked me once more where I was shot down.

The interrogation had lasted a long time and I was getting overly tired. The colonel said something to the interpreter and then he told me that I would be taken to a room where I would stay. They would come and get me after I had some food. Well that part about food was sure good news to my ears. Although it was late in coming, it was still welcomed as I was getting tired of getting slapped, kicked, and sitting here listening to the Russians trying to make me confess to something I wasn't.

While I was thinking about food, someone grabbed me and stood me up, then escorted me to a room that the interpreter had mentioned. We walked to the right a few paces, then we turned left. I heard a clanking noise, like a door to a cell, as in a jail. The whole time we walked, no one spoke a word. My guard pushed me in the cell and figured that since I was blindfolded, I wasn't able to see the bunk. He reached for my arm, took me a few feet and while turning me around, pushed me down from my shoulders and then I felt the bunk under my legs.

While sitting in the cell I thought about why the officers were so aggravated with my answers. I guess they couldn't figure out why they had run into a stone wall with me. As I heard the guards leaving, talking and laughing, they closed the door while I sat there blindfolded and handcuffed. I realized then that they had left the handcuffs on so I could not take off the blindfold.

My thoughts wandered back to the day that Tom and I started planning the escape. I never thought that I would be caught, let alone by

Russian troops. That in itself was incredible. This brought to my attention that if I were caught by someone, Korean or Chinese, they would have been convinced I was an F-86 pilot. The closest I got to an F-86 was about thirty thousand feet, when they were having dog-fights with Russian Migs over Camp 1 and in Mig Alley. The pain in my arms brought me back to the present. I felt like I had been put through a meat grinder but I would stand fast and not tell them anything.

I heard footsteps and then the cell door opened. Whoever had entered was now walking towards me and then I heard a female say, in English, that there was some food. I thought I would add some color to this nightmare so when she stated that there was some food, I asked, "Are we having tacos or enchiladas?"

She snarled back, telling me not to be funny.

She didn't seem to be amused at my comment because she told the guard something and then he pulled me from my bunk and stood me up. To my surprise, he turned me around and took off the handcuffs. He then sat me back down, put the handcuffs back on, with my hands in front, and put a small table in front of me. The woman placed the food on the table then grabbed my hand to show me where the food was. As if predetermined, she asked me if I was hurt. Then did you hurt yourself when you parachuted from the aircraft?

I said, "I didn't parachute, therefore I am not hurt from that." They didn't take my blindfold off and I sure wasn't going to ask her to remove it after my remark about tacos and enchiladas.

I heard the cell door close but didn't lock. I assumed that she had left and the guard was still there. As I am about to indulge in my scrumptious meal, I reached and felt a lump of dough that seemed to have been cooked ten years ago and the drink was water – bread and water – some scrumptious meal. As I was tearing the bread in half, I heard voices outside my cell; someone talking to the guard. Not knowing what was said, I waited for something to happen, then I heard the cell door lock, and I felt that I was alone. I decided that I would lift the bottom of my blindfold to see what was happening and also to see where I was. I found that the lights were out but there was a very dim light on in my cell. The guard was outside the door watching me so I would not take off the blindfold, I presumed. I kept munching on my bread and drinking my water. I decided to make a gesture to get up and see if they would let me stand up and walk around the cell, but the guard said in a loud voice, "No!"

At this point I wasn't too scared. I was more saddened for the fact that I had been captured just when I was so close to the ocean and to freedom. I told myself that maybe this is the way it must happen. Maybe it was just as well that the Russians had caught me because if the Koreans or Chinese had, I probably wouldn't be here. The Koreans hated American pilots because of the bombing of the North Korean cities. They felt that pilots were killing innocent women and children. The Korean treatment of American POWs was evident at Camp 1, when they brought thirty "death-warmed-over" POWs there. They were inhumanely treated, very brutally mistreated and starved to death. I knew that wearing this pilot's uniform I would be better off with the Russians. The North Koreans were known to shoot then ask questions, especially if you were a pilot.

While I was thinking about all that had happened, someone came into the cell and told me to get some sleep because the interrogation would resume in the morning. He added that I must not take off the blindfold and then he left. I already seemed to know that the interrogation would resume in the morning, with the same questions to be asked over and over again. I had made up my mind that they were going to get the same answers, no matter what they did or said. Sitting on the bunk, feeling around for a blanket, I laid down and hoped to get some sleep. I couldn't go to sleep though; I tossed and turned due to thinking about all that had happened.

I laid on my back, wondering if Tom was still moving through the mountains or if he was going through some of the same hell. I then put my thoughts to rest, turned over and finally fell asleep. The next morning someone came and rattled the door. I was already awake but didn't know what time it was. The interpreter informed me that they had brought me something to eat. Again the food was set on the table and the guard grabbed my hands and I felt for the food and drink. The food was like a cinnamon roll, NOT! The drink was like milk – not even close. God only knows what that stuff was. I started to eat when the interpreter, I presume, was going out and asked, "Are you ready for more questions?"

After swallowing, I replied in a soft voice, "You're going to get the same answers. I am NOT a pilot and furthermore, all I have to give you is my name, rank and serial number."

He said, "We'll see about that." My morning had just been made.

When I finished my roll and drink, the guard came in and escorted me to what seemed to be the place where I had been before. I was placed in the chair next to the interpreter, according to the direction of his voice.

I asked, "May I please go to the bathroom?" Someone said that I could and the guard grabbed me by the arm and took me to the restroom. Once there, the guard took off the handcuffs. I could hear the echos of voices milling around and I felt there were more people there. When I was finished I was brought back, handcuffed and sat back in my favorite chair.

It was a few seconds before the interpreter told me, "The colonel is here and he is going to ask you some questions. Do you understand?"

"Yes," I replied.

The first thing they asked me was, "What is the location of the base your squadron is stationed at?"

"I don't know. I am a truck driver, not a pilot and was captured by the Chinese, taken POW and detained at Camp 1. I escaped and here I am."

"Why are you wearing that Air Force uniform?"

"It was given to me at Camp 1, for my escape. I am telling the truth. I am not lying."

By this time I could tell by the voices that the colonel and interpreter were getting furious. It seemed there was nothing I could say to these Russians to let me off the hook. A few minutes went by and I could hear the colonel and interpreter move away from where I was sitting, discussing something. I sat there for about a half an hour when I began to get frustrated because I couldn't convince them that I wasn't a pilot. "Wow!"; can you imagine what pilots had to go through when they were interrogated? I am not a pilot and they are giving me the third degree. After a while they returned and informed me they were going to ask me to tell the truth. I told them that I had been and that I would continue to do so. By the colonel's tone of voice, he was very upset with me and the way this interrogation was going.

He asked me again, "Was your F-86 on an aircraft carrier?"

"No, sir."

"Were you armed with germ warfare?"

"No, sir."

"Do you know the function of the F-86 you were flying?"

"No, sir." I interrupted and asked, "May I say something? Sir, if I was a pilot, I would say so but I am not what you want me to be. I am a fighting Marine, nothing else."

He again asked, "Why don't you confess because we know you are a pilot?" The colonel said something then I heard them walk away. I sat there waiting for more questions. The truth only seemed to get them more furious. I never thought that this uniform would catch me so much hell.

The colonel was conversing with the interpreter as they returned. To my surprise, a woman came over to where I sat, grabbed my arm and told me, "You come with me." I could only hope that this was going to be the end of the interrogation that was leading to nowhere. While she was escorting me, someone spoke to the colonel and he was furious. Not a sound could be heard and the woman stopped in her tracks with me beside her. I was led back to my cell never finding out what happened. While I was being put inside the cell, the same woman asked me again, "Were you hurt from hitting the ground when you parachuted?"

Instantly I said, "I was not hurt *because I didn't parachute*. I had been apprehended by your army, in the mountains, while trying to escape."

She and the guard departed, locking the cell door behind them and once again I was alone. I felt they had sent her to see if she could trick me into admitting that I had parachuted. No such luck.

While sitting in the cell, bewildered and wondering what was going to happen next, I heard voices. Then I heard the cell door being unlocked. I was taken out of the cell and in a few minutes, ended up at the location where I had been interrogated. My escorts stood by, waiting. A few minutes went by and I heard, not far from where I was, someone start a truck. I prayed that it was all over for them and me and I would be going back to Camp 1. After walking a short distance, they loaded me on the truck then sat me down towards the front of the truck. I could feel the two guards right behind me and just then I heard the voice of the person that had brought me to the truck. I suspected it was the same officer that was taking me back to the Korean Headquarters. I heard him talk to the guards and then I felt hands on the back of my head, and to my surprise, they removed the blindfold. For the first few seconds I could not see. The sunlight was hurting my eyes so I put my hands over my eyes, then peered through the small opening in my fingers. It took quite some time for my eyes to fully adjust to the light.

At this point I figured that I was no longer a threat to them and this was the reason for my blindfold being removed. I looked back and realized I had been taken in to a big dome with huge doors. It resembled a bunker; its shape was the reason for my hearing echos inside. I turned to my left and saw two Migs lined up then I realized I was at an air base. It wasn't very long before we reached the main gate. We were in a good size town because there was a lot of traffic. As the truck was moving along, I kept trying to see the ocean from the road we were on, but I couldn't see anything. Just then we made a few turns on the main highway and then I saw the bridge. We went about a quarter of a mile and made a left turn onto the bridge. The sound was the same and I could feel the expansion joints of the bridge. Later I came to find out that we were crossing the Yalu River that divided North Korea and Manchuria, China.

When the Russians had first brought me there, I knew it had been a bridge but didn't know what river or what direction they had taken me. After crossing the bridge, we went for about thirty minutes when I heard the guards talking to the officer in charge. I felt the truck slowing and when it came to a complete stop, I saw North Korean soldiers all around the truck. I also saw them marching in the distance. While I am looking around, the Russian officer gets out of the truck and a North Korean officer joins him at the truck. When they approached each other, they saluted and the Russian officer then says something about the "American." I then knew they were talking about me. After the conversation, they went into the office and as they entered, the Russian officer yelled something to the guard. Probably he said to keep an eye on me. While this is going on, this young Korean soldier was still looking me over. I just then had a thought come to mind. If I spend anytime here with the Koreans, it's going to be hell. I had heard what they were like, and at this point I was very concerned why the Russians didn't take me to Camp 1.

While wondering what was next, I saw the officer coming towards the truck. The Russian officer is the same one who was at the anti-aircraft emplacement, so he spoke broken English but I could understand him. As he approached the rear of the truck, he spoke to the guard and then the guard grabbed my arms and stood me up. They walked me to the rear of the truck and I was told to sit on the edge of the truck. The Russian officer told me, "You will be taken back to Camp 1 in a while. A Chinese officer and a Korean lieutenant will accompany you. Is that understood?"

"Yes, sir."

They got me off the truck and then took me inside the building. A Korean officer and two North Korean soldiers sat me down in a corridor, with the guards watching me. Soon, three North Korean officers came down the hall and as they were passing me, one stops in his tracks and stares at me. He leaves the other two officers standing there and approaches me. He told me, "You are a very brave Marine. You escaped again?"

"Yes, sir" was my reply.

"You managed to get far without someone seeing you." He grinned and started to leave when he asked, "Is there anything I can get for you?"

I told him, "I would like some water." He turned to the guard and told him something and then the guard left but the other guard stayed to watch me. I was told that the guard went to get me some water and I thanked him. He left and joined the officers who were waiting for him. Before he disappeared into the crowd of officers in the hallway, he turned back and took another look at me. Little did I know that our paths would cross again. He was the same officer that shot the .45 by my ear.

The guard returned with a bowl of water and handed it to me. When I had finished with it, the officer asked me, "Are you ready to leave?"

I said, "Yes, sir, I am ready." The Korean officer joined him and told the guards to bring me along. I stood up and they escorted me to the outside of the building where there was a truck waiting for us. Also waiting was a large crowd of Koreans to watch me being loaded up on the truck.

Chapter Twelve
Mock Trial and No-Surprise Verdict

I could see the anger on the faces of the Korean people. I was glad to be going back to Camp 1, no matter what I had to face when I got there. I sat between the two guards and the Chinese officer, wondering what would have happened if I would have been caught by the angry Koreans. That thought was very unsettling.

As we moved away from the crowd, the truck started moving faster. After we got out of town, we finally started moving along the road to Camp 1. I don't recall how long it took us to get to there, but it was dark when we arrived. I had noticed that it was cooler at the camp. The Chinese were wearing their winter uniforms and while riding on the back of the truck, I was cold.

After all I had been through, I had accepted the fact that I would be punished and maybe severely so. When we finally pulled up in front of the Commanders' Headquarters at Camp 1, they were waiting for me. I didn't get to see the commander as another officer came up to me after getting off the truck and asked me if I was Nick Flores. I told him that I was. He then called two Chinese guards and said something to them. They got on each side of me and escorted me to a hut. This was about two blocks from the jail that I had been in previously. They put me in and then slammed the door. I heard them lock the door and the officer said something to the guard and I guess it was for him to guard the door.

It was cool in the hut, even with the Air Force uniform on. It was pitch black so I started feeling my way to the wall away from the door. I didn't know if anyone was in the hut so I asked aloud if there was anyone there with me. No reply. As I continued to feel my way around, I finally got to a corner away from the door. This was one of the farther corners in back of the room. I put my back to the corner and slid all the way to the floor. I brought my legs up into my chest, put my hands around my legs and I laid my head on my knees. Sitting there tired and completely exhausted, I felt like crying out, and at that moment I remembered my dear mother telling me that Marines don't cry; and when you find yourself in trouble, talk to God as he will hear you. I sat there and prayed, asking God to help me accept whatever my destiny was to be and give me peace in my heart, and that I hoped that he could get me out of this alive. Even with all the torture and beatings the Russians inflicted upon me, I never regretted escaping. I experienced a taste of freedom and it was worth it although I somehow knew that more torture was on the way.

With that thought and prayer, I found myself more at ease and secure. I decided that after feeling good about everything I should try to get some sleep. My mind kept going to the events of the last three days and it took me a while to go to sleep even though I was exhausted.

The next morning I was awakened by the guard and behind him stood a Chinese officer, Lieutenant Chew. He told me, "We must take the Air force uniform and boots away from you."

I asked him, "Why? It is cold in the hut."

He replied, "You will be given some hay and that will keep you warm." He stripped me of the uniform and left me with socks, undershorts and my Marine tee shirt. Then he threw about a half a bale of hay into the room and then left. I grabbed the hay and piled it in the corner. I made a bed and then tried to put some of it around me to keep warm. I started wondering what kind of hell they (the Chinese) were going to put me through. I knew that it was just the beginning with the worst yet to come.

I thought about Tom and wondered if he had made it. He had farther to go, more mountains to climb over, and a lot of North Korean territory to cover before he made it to freedom.

As the sun started peeking over the mountains, I noticed that there was a crack in the door where a streak of sunlight came in to my little corner where I lay. Then I heard some voices so I figured it was the changing of guards. I decided to get up and take a peek. I saw some Chinese soldiers putting poles in the ground, five to six feet apart. I leaned back and asked myself what those could be for. I stood there and tried to figure out where I had seen these type of poles before. I recalled back to when I went to my grandfather's ranch in Mexico and the Indians used to do that to roast wild boar and then they would take off chunks of meat as it was getting done. Well, you bet your life I wasn't going to let them roast me!

I went back to my little corner and sat there thinking, no, they wouldn't roast me – or would they? I didn't know if that is what they were going to do but I got up again to keep an eye on what was happening. I noticed that they were putting a pole across both poles and tying them to the V shape at the top of the poles. I then knew that this contraption they had out there was for me and they were going to hang me "out to dry." If you are a POW and you escape, I guess you can expect the enemy to throw everything they have at you. I was going to try to accept the fact that they would do this to me and go from there.

The fact was, the commander of the camp had warned me about escaping again, and being that I did, he had been embarrassed. He had stated in one of the first assemblies we attended that no one escapes from the camp, and because I had, this had made him lose face among his officers and his people.

With no other choice, I decided to sit and wait for the outcome. I didn't have to wait long for I heard the door being unlocked and it was the guard and Lieutenant Chang, who was there at camp when I escaped. As he opened the door he got on his knees, about three feet from me, and asked me, "Do you know where Tom is or where he went?"

To that I replied, "No, I do not."

"When was the last time you saw or talked to him?"

"About a week ago," I replied.

"Where was he going?"

"I do not know."

He told me, in no uncertain terms, "You have shamed the Chinese Peoples' Volunteers and they have tried to make the POWs as comfortable as they could and then you do this to them."

I replied, "Yes, but how can you answer for all those who have died at the beginning because of the garbage you fed us? We lost a lot of men needlessly for the lack of good food and medical treatment. What do you have to say about that?" He started to get up then I told him, "I am not sorry that I escaped and I will take whatever is coming to me as a POW that did his duty." As he went out the door, he looked back but said nothing. About ten to fifteen minutes later the door was unlocked again and a soldier came in with a bowl of rice and some water. They forgot the spoon so I guessed I would have to eat it with my hands.

Later on Lieutenant Chang told me "You will have one meal a day consisting of a bowl of rice and some water." I guess this was my breakfast, lunch and dinner all in one. At this point I was very, very hungry and the rice didn't even put a dent on my hunger. After eating my rice I decided to take a nap as I was exhausted. I laid myself down on top of the hay not thinking I would go to sleep any time too soon but I did, and when I awoke the sun was almost behind the mountain. It was getting dark so I tried to rearrange my bed for when I was ready to hit the sack. Trying to get warm was a difficult task as August was a cold month, especially at night, which I could definitely feel. Night fell and it really got quite dark in my little world. I decided to truly "hit the hay." I eventually stopped thinking about how cold it was and drifted off to sleep.

The next morning I was awakened by some loud rumbling noises and at first I thought it was thunder. When I looked outside, through the crack in the door, I saw the sun. I then heard jets, which I knew were F-86s bombing somewhere close and low because one plane came overhead and it sure made a lot of noise going by. I dragged myself back to my corner and sat down. I wasn't there but for a few minutes when I heard the door being unlocked. It was Lieutenant Chang, followed by the commander of the camp, accompanied by two Chinese guards. They told me I was to go outside. I had been rubbing my legs to restore the circulation when they had entered, so I got up, staggering forward with as much haste as I could manage. After being escorted outside, the guards grabbed me and tied my hands and feet. I knew what was just about to happen. They were going to put me on that pole and let me hang. The two guards grabbed me, one by my underarms and the other from my feet. After they had lifted me up, the officer ran the pole through the ropes and the three of them hoisted me up on the pole. As I hung there, the commander said to me, "Flores, I told you that if you escaped you would have to suffer the consequences."

They stood there conversing for a few seconds and then left. Needless to say, the view upside down wasn't impressive. Not only that, if they had at least given me some clothes to hang with, I wouldn't have to have my rear end showing while I was hanging there. After they left, I started thinking, what's next? There I was, seeing the world upside down and it wasn't fun, especially alone and cold. I thought it would be nice if Tom was here alongside of me, but then I told myself, what a heck of a thing to think. My next thought was, "Now I know how animals feel when they are hanging for slaughter." There was only one consolation. The weather was cool but at least the sun gave a little warmth. It felt good even if I was hanging upside down.

I decided that if I was going to hang there till who knows when, I would accept it and not think of the pain going through my arms and ankles. I tried to think of back home and my teen years when I had fun. I wasn't going to let them know that I was hurting and I wasn't going to let the pain overtake me either.

As the day was wearing down I heard voices nearing me and when they got close by I turned my head to see who it was. It was the officer and two of his thugs talking. When they were finished with their conversation, the guards grabbed each end of the poles and laid me on the ground and untied me. While I was struggling to get up, rubbing my wrists and ankles, the officer told me, "I hope that you have learned a lesson. Also, tomorrow you will have the same done. Are you hurting?"

I did not answer right away because I was trying to decide what answer I should give him. If I said yes, maybe they wouldn't put me out there again. If I said no, to demonstrate that I was a tough Marine, they would continue hanging me till I broke. I decided to tell them, "I am hurting very much." They walked me back to my cell, looked contemptuously at me and then left. Somehow I got the impression that whatever I had answered would have gotten me the same reaction.

I decided to do some exercises so that I might warm up as it felt like the inside of an icebox in my room. Even though exercising would aggravate my aches and pains, I felt the end result would be worth it. After that, I tried to get comfortable on my hay bed. That didn't last long, so I got up and walked around my domain. Then I heard voices outside. I was alerted to the familiar sound of a lock being unlocked. Then the guard quickly handed me my one and only daily bowl of rice and a bowl water. After taking them, I went to my little corner and indulged. When I was finished, I knocked on the door and then handed my bowls to the guard. I then went to my corner where I sat down because soon it would get dark and be the end of another day. I did not look forward to night setting in because I knew that the room would become cold. The night-time temperatures dropped to thirty two to thirty eight degrees.

The second day came and went. It was like the day before, they hung me on the rack, then I ate my one and only meal, did exercises and then went to sleep. Today, being the third day, started out the same. I was hung, and then returned to my room. I was informed that food would be brought to me. This was late in the evening so I just sat there and waited. A few minutes later my meal was delivered. As I was taking it to my corner I realized how much my body hurt and how exhausted I was. I felt like I had been stretched a couple of inches from hanging twelve hours a day for three days. With the meal over I got myself ready for bed, laid down on the hay and knew I wouldn't have any problems sleeping.

The following morning I was awakened by a commotion outside my hut. I went to the door and took a peek and couldn't believe my eyes. It was Tom Cabello! They had caught him and were going to put him in a room next to mine. I sat down and all I said was, "I'll be darn." Still sitting by the door I then yelled at Tom in Spanish, "*Como te pescaron Tomazito?*" That means, "How did they catch you, Tom?" In the meantime he was walking to the room next to me with his hands tied and the two guards beside him. Tom hadn't answered me and he said nothing after he was inside the room. I figured I would talk to him after he was settled in his quarters.

I went to my little corner and sat down to try to figure out a way to talk to Tom. After a while I started looking around to see if there was a way that I could make a hole in the wall so we could talk to each other. I needed something I could scratch a hole with in the very bottom of the wall so the Chinese wouldn't see it. It was dark so that was like looking for a needle in a haystack, as the saying goes.

The wall was made of tree branches that were tied to poles about one and a half inches in diameter. Once the wall was formed it was plastered with mud.

I figured I had four to five inches to penetrate before I could make a hole all the way through. The mud was so hard that my fingernails wouldn't even scratch the surface. I had to find a way to dampen the mud so I could dig with my fingers. Then a thought came to me; when they bring my rice and water, I'll spill some water where I am going to dig and it might soften the mud.

With this idea in mind, I leaned back and decided to rest for a while. I wished they would hurry up and bring the food. I was anxious to try my idea of putting water on the wall to soften it. I didn't know what time it was but my stomach was telling me it was time to eat. I waited impatiently to get my food and a few minutes later they brought it.

I was not looking forward to more rice, but the water had a new importance for me. There were times that I wished they would bring me seaweed even if it was tasteless. It would have been a change anyway. I ate the rice, and saw that the guard was away from the door so I spilled some water on the wall. When I did this, I was scratching with my fingers to see if I could make a dent in the mud. After doing this, I put hay on the spill so it would not be noticed by the officer who came in once in a while to check on me. I put the bowls by the door, knocked on the door then sat down quickly so when he opened the door to get the bowls, he wouldn't suspect anything unusual going on.

I tried to see if I could scratch the wall with my fingers but to no avail. I gave it up and decided to take a nap and maybe something would come to me. I laid in the hay and went to sleep.

I gave myself a few minutes to wake up then returned to the problem of making a hole in the wall. After several tries at trying to make the hole, a thought came to my mind. I had become desperate, so why not ask the guard for chopsticks to eat my rice with? When I did, the answer was "No!" I didn't think they would but I thought it was worth the try.

I was not going to give up, so I began searching the room for anything that I could use to assist me in my endeavor. I was coming very close to calling it a hopeless cause, when I happened to look up and there was my answer! The Koreans used a layer of branches, followed by a layer of mud then topped off the roof with hay. I soon realized that I would have to jump up and try to grab a twig on my way down. After all that I had been through, this seemed to be an easy task. I followed through with the plan and before long, I had just what I needed in my hand.

I continued to scratch away at the wall and although it seemed like it took forever, I did manage to scratch a hole all the way through. I then got down on my stomach and put my face close to the hole so the guard wouldn't hear my voice. I said in a very low voice, "Tom! Are you there? If you are, come over to where the twig is showing on your side."

Before long, I heard Tom moving around then he asked, "Nick?" We greeted each other by saying, "Hi." Then Tom asked, "How are you doing? How long have you been here?"

"I have been here five days. This is the fifth day and they have been hanging me upside down each day."

He chuckled then said, "I hope they don't do that to me!"

"Tom, do you have your clothes on?"

He replied, "Yes."

I told him, "I only have on my skivvies and a tee shirt. How do you feel?"

"Fine" he told me, "But I feel bad about getting caught. Do you know what they are going to do with us?"

"I don't have any idea about what to expect from the commander. I know that it won't be easy, because we made him look bad after telling him we wouldn't escape."

After talking a while, softly so the guards wouldn't hear us, we decided to get some shuteye. It was dark, so we didn't know what time it was. When I got tired of thinking is when I would lay down and sleep.

The next morning I was awakened by one of the Chinese officers. As he unlocked the doors, he came in handing me my clothes and told me, "You are going to an assembly."

I asked him, "Is there a chance of washing up?"

"No."

As I walked out, Tom was outside waiting with two guards, and another two guards tied my hands in back. We walked to the playground and there I saw all the POWs from Camp 1, sitting facing a platform. On this platform was the commander and four Chinese officers. At that moment I didn't know what this was for, but I figured this was so we would confess to our crime against the Chinese Peoples' Volunteers.

As we were approaching the platform, the fellow prisoners gave us a standing ovation, clapping and hollering "Okay, Nick and Tom!" It gave me a good feeling and a sense of mission-accomplished even though we had been caught. After we were taken to the platform and put behind the commander, the guards stood behind us and at our sides. The commander stepped up to the microphone and said what was on his mind. Then Lieutenant Chang interpreted, "This is an event that won't happen again. Nick and Tom have committed a crime against the Chinese Peoples' Volunteers and it won't go unpunished. We told them not to escape after the last time, but they refused to obey. They must admit their mistake and confess their crime. We have tried to make you all happy since being POWs and they didn't appreciate what we have done for them." Just then the POWs started booing him. He continued, "You will hear from the men who committed the crime as they will confess."

The guards escorted me to the microphone where I said, "All I am going to say is that I am not sorry that I escaped. I escaped because as an American and a Marine, it's my duty to try to escape. My country expects me to do so." One of the officers came in a hurry and put his hand over the microphone. I then said in Spanish, "These Chinese have another thing coming. As far as I'm concerned, they can go to hell!" The officer then asked me what I had said and I told him that I was sorry I hadn't made it. A lot of POWs yelled, "Good for you Nick!" Some British soldier yelled, "Good show, Nick."

The Chinese officer grabbed me, then pulled me back and told me in English that I would be punished for my crimes. After the officer put me with the guards, he told Tom to go to the microphone. Tom very slowly got up there and said, "That goes for me, too – what Nick said." Then he did his usual shrugging of his shoulders.

After Tom finished, they took us back to our huts. I could see that the Chinese officers and camp commander were upset. As we got to the huts, they pushed us in and they said something in Chinese, then left, locking the doors behind them.

I was surprised that they didn't take my clothes but I wasn't going to ask them why. As soon as we went back to our corners, Tom and I started whispering. Tom wanted to know what was next. I told him, "I don't know. I don't think that it's going to be nice what ever they do."

We were stuck back in our hut for two days. While we were there, we talked about our travels. Tom said, "I don't have any idea where I was apprehended. There were a lot of Chinks." I started telling him about how I got caught. I think we talked about everything and anything. When we did this, the time went faster.

The regular routine was bringing the food and water by the Chinese officer who would stick his head in and ask how I was doing. These two days that we were there, after the assembly, things had changed. The food was put on the floor when the guards opened the door and the officer wouldn't say a word to Tom or me. This attitude confirmed how upset they were.

Tom knocked on the wall and I put my ear to the hole. He asked, "What is going on?"

I told him, "I don't know but something is happening out there that has to do with us. I feel there's something in the air."

Tom added, "I hope it isn't for us, whatever it is."

By this time, I felt that I had accepted almost anything from the commander of the camp. When he called me into his office, he had warned me that if I escaped again, I would suffer serious consequences. I believed that whatever was coming were the consequences he had threatened.

I started praying and I said, "If it was his will for us to die, then let me die, not Tom. I had talked Tom into escaping with me, whatever is to happen to us, don't let us suffer." I felt that I was to blame for the predicament we were in. After speaking to God, I had peace of mind and I said "What will be will be." Then I told Tom, "I guess they feel we have to pay the price."

I knocked on the wall and told Tom that I was going to take a nap. Tom told me that sounded like a good idea. We didn't know the time of day, except when the sunlight hit the crack of the door, we knew it was daylight. Other than that, it was dark continuously.

It was not long after I woke up from my nap that our food was brought to us. After finishing, I set the bowls by the door and knocked on it so they knew to pick them up, but this time no one came. I walked a couple of feet, peeked through the crack in the door and to my surprise, I couldn't see any guards. I rushed to the corner, knocked on the wall and put my head close to the hole. I said, "Tom, there are no guards out there. That proves something is going on out there for them to remove the guards from here." If there was a guard, he had to be somewhere away from view. They were usually five to ten feet from the doors at all time.

I felt that these Chinese were going to give us a big surprise, and they were keeping us in the dark until it happened. An hour or so passed when we heard someone unlocking the door. Whoever it was, grabbed the bowls and closed the door again. It was odd because it was like he didn't want to be seen. I then quietly told Tom, "Let's not worry about it. Maybe we are worrying for nothing. Maybe they're having problems at camp."

By this time, dusk had arrived and shortly darkness would be upon us. All I could think about was what the commander had said, "You escape and you will have to pay the consequences." It was something we had talked about, and decided that escaping to freedom overshadowed anything that might be put on us later. With that thought, we decided to get some sleep and leave the worrying for the morning. That was probably easier said than done. How does a person sleep when your existence is balancing between life and death? There is a very thin line between living and dying but I had prepared myself for the worst, or so I hoped. I could only hope for the best. I said a prayer and then tried to get some sleep.

The next morning, I was awakened by a knock on the door. I then heard a voice saying, "It's Lieutenant Chang," as he entered. "You need to walk outside." I was stopped five feet from the door and then joined by one of the guards. Just at that time, Tom was being escorted out of his room and joined me. Lieutenant Chang then informed us that, "You will stand trial for your crimes. You will be taken to the theater, where the trial will be held."

They led us out of the small compound and headed for the main street of town. As we were being led to the theater, I noticed that we had a few Koreans watching from the roadside. I saw, on both sides, guards placed about fifty feet all the way to our destination. I thought that maybe this was to protect Tom and I from the Koreans throwing rocks at us, as these people just didn't like us. I looked at Tom and then I made a gesture with my head for him to look at the Koreans. Tom just shook his head and grinned.

The walk to the theater took about thirty-five minutes. On the way, I saw Koreans put up their fists as to say, "We hate you Americans." We were taken into the theater and saw POWs sitting down, lined up against the wall, with some yelling and clapping their hands and some just looked worried for us. Some who knew us said Hi and waved while some just waved. At that moment, many thoughts entered my mind. Would I survive this? What would the penalty be for escaping? Could the punishment be any worse than the treatment the Russians gave me? Would Tom handle all of this, whatever this was? The one thing I did know, I had God on my side and that alone gave me strength and courage. I would hold my head up high and proud and let the pieces fall where they may.

As we were escorted to the stage, we walked up a few steps. At the top were two guards who walked us to the middle of the stage. They motioned for us to move back away from the microphone. While standing there waiting for Lieutenant Chang and the commander, I felt a hot sweat come over me. Trying not to focus on this, I looked around. I noticed the tense look on some of the guys' faces as if they were getting very impatient for this whole ordeal to end. There were no empty seats and guards were lined up against the back wall. No escaping this!

While I was trying to find some of the guys that had helped us get food to the mountain, I noticed there was a group of POWs to my right. They seemed to be separated from the rest. Were they our jury? These men were mostly sympathizers or better known as turncoats. Oh boy, were we in trouble or what? What a hell of a jury this was. I quickly realized they had probably been hand picked by the Chinese because these turn-coats would do or say most anything for special treatment.

The commander was introduced by Lieutenant Chang and all of a sudden you could hear a pin drop. Everything came to a standstill as the commander stepped up to the microphone. He began by saying, "These men, who you know very well, ignored my order for them not to escape. They did so, and now they must be punished."

After the commander finished talking to Lieutenant Chang, he informed everyone that the commander had told him to read the charges against us. The charges are as follows:

1. Nick Flores conspired against the Chinese Peoples' Volunteers and escaped two times after he said he wouldn't.
2. Nick Flores, prior to the escape, stole a flashlight and map to aid in his escape.
3. Nick Flores lied to the Chinese people.
4. Nick Flores talked five other men into escaping with him. We have the evidence. He was the leader for both escapes.
5. Tom Cabello conspired against the Chinese Peoples' Volunteers and escaped two times after he said he wouldn't.
6. Tom Cabello lied to the Chinese people.

The commander got up from his chair then walked up to the microphone, accompanied by Lieutenant Chang. The commander looked over at us and then started his speech. You could feel the anger in his voice when he looked at us, talking about what we had done. The commander moved two paces to his left and Lieutenant Chang then moved up to the microphone. The auditorium was quiet.

Lieutenant Chang grabbed the microphone with his left hand and with his right hand, pointed to where Tom and I were standing. He said, "These two men broke the rules of the camp. They shamed the officers by breaking the rules. We have tried to make your stay as pleasant as possible, with what we have here at camp. You are eating better, you get clothing, shoes, tobacco, and you get to write letters to your family. Is this the way you pay us back? By breaking the rules and escaping? These two men must be punished for their actions."

He then stepped away and the commander spoke again. When the commander was thru, Lieutenant Chang returned to the microphone, to translate. "I want everyone here to know that anyone escaping from this camp will be severely punished, as these two men will be. They escaped not once, but twice and there will be no mercy! They made me lose face with my superiors and the Chinese Peoples Army. Therefore, they will be punished accordingly!" Lieutenant Chang then gave a jester with his hands for the officer to give the charges to the jury.

Some one yelled, "They are innocent!" Then some fellow prisoners started stomping their feet. The guards moved in and got them quieted down. You could hear the whispers among the guys. Just then some pieces of paper were passed to the jury. A few minutes went by and someone in the crowd yelled, "You'd better vote innocent!" as we waited for the jury to give the verdict to Lieutenant Chang, wondering, yet knowing, what it would be.

A jury member stood up and said, "Tom Cabello, you are guilty as charged and you will spend six months in hard labor camp." I looked at Tom, grinning, and then said to myself, thank God for that. You could hear the guys whispering amongst themselves about the punishment for Tom.

A few minutes went by and then I saw one of the jury members retrieve a piece of paper from Lieutenant Chang. He returned to his seat and showed the rest of the jury the piece of paper. He then stood up and read the verdict, "Nick Flores. You have been found guilty as charged. Your sentence will be to serve twelve months solitary confinement, and that starts today." After I heard that, I thanked God because it could have been a lot worse!

I could hear some of the POWs disagree with the sentence while some shook their fists at the jury. I was just relieved that this whole ordeal was behind me. Twelve months of solitary confinement was a small price to pay for the days of freedom that I had experienced.

The commander finished by telling everyone, again, that this would serve as an example for those who may plan to escape or who are thinking of escaping. The guards then escorted us down the stage. Every one of our friends wished us good luck, and job well done. I felt good as Tom and I were walking out, due to the praise of the fellow POWs. Some British friends said, "That was a good show." Tom was very quiet as they were taking us out of the theater.

Chapter Thirteen
Solitary Confinement

Tom and I were being detained on the steps of the theater while Lieutenant Chew instructed the POWs to form a column, in rows of four, then they started moving down the street. The commander walked out of the theater, with his guards, and stared at me long and hard. I knew I had shamed him and his officers by escaping.

As the column got about fifty feet down the street, Lieutenant Chang told both the guards and Tom and I to move along behind it. Lieutenant Chang walked in front of us with the two guards on each side of us. As we were walking Tom said, "Nick, do you think you can make it for twelve months in solitary?"

With a little skepticism I replied, "With my mom's prayers for me, the Lord on my side, I just know I'll make it. Not only that, Tom, we are both healthier this time around and hopefully a little wiser." I had no sooner finished when the guard poked me in the rib cage with the butt of his rifle, shook his head, indicating not to talk.

As I was walking, I started to think about if we would have made it. Or one of us would have. The trial had been held to show an example for the rest. Sergeant Pettit had escaped but never got out of camp. What was it that we did to be able to get out of camp with no problems? One must suppose that careful planning and the tools for the escape were essential. I felt that freedom was worth paying a price for and that in itself was the key. Especially since we were ready to pay the price no matter what happened if we got caught. A man has to do what his heart tells him to do and do it to the best of his ability.

I noticed, as we continued walking, that the townspeople looked more settled, not raising their fists or throwing rocks at us. I guess by now, they had heard the outcome of the trial. Just as Tom and I were approaching the camp, Lieutenant Chang separated us from the column and headed us towards the huts where we had previously stayed. I thought we would be housed next to each other. Wrong. The guards escorted Tom to his hut, where he was before the trial, and then Lieutenant Chang told me, "Flores, you follow me. I am taking you to the place where you will serve your sentence."

Off I went, walking two short blocks and then turned left and then continued on for another block. I saw this huge barn or warehouse in front of me. We got closer to the barn when Lieutenant Chang said, "Flores, this is where you will remain for the duration of your sentence." The guards opened the doors and they escorted me inside. Once inside, I looked around and I could see daylight through the cracks in the boards. At that moment I thought, "Wow! I'll have the whole barn to myself. I'll be able to do some running and exercises." Wrong again. At the far end of the barn was a small room the size of a closet. The guards escorted me to the door of that small room and Lieutenant Chang informed me, "This is where you will spend your sentence."

After he said that, I realized just how scared I was. I thought that this would probably be my coffin. I'll probably go crazy in this little room. As the guard opened the door, Lieutenant Chang grabbed my arm and escorted me inside. Again he repeated that this is where I would spend my sentence. He added, "Meals will consist of rice and sometimes a side dish of sea weed, no more than two bowls a day. If you need to go to the latrine, knock twice on the door and the guard will know what you need and let you out." The latrine consisted of a hole in the corner of the barn, with slats across it. You had to straddle the boards. The latrine was about ten feet from my little room.

Lieutenant Chang warned me, "Do not make any trouble with the guards and especially do not talk to any POW if they happen to come to the window. If that happens, we will take measures to remove you from camp. Do you understand?"

"Yes sir." As Lieutenant Chang and his thugs were getting ready to leave, I asked, "Am I going to get winter clothing?"

The Lieutenant replied, "I'll find out," then he was gone.

I heard the barn door close and then heard a lock being put on the door. I then said, "That's a hell of a way to treat a guest!" Oh well, I was going to make my stay as pleasant and happy as I could, no matter what. But it wasn't going to be easy.

There was still light inside the barn so I surveyed the room. I noticed that they had left me more hay than in the previous quarters, so I decided I would spread the hay to cover the floor and save some for my bed and to cover me with. I still had the summer clothes that they gave me for the trial but I just hoped they would not take them from me.

My room was about eight foot long, four foot wide and seven foot high. The wall facing the street behind the barn had a window but it had been boarded up with only a few cracks between the boards. This allowed me to tell when it was daylight. As I was finding out all about my room, I said, "Where else can you get a room like this; rent free, food catered to your door, sleep whenever you want and do whatever you want to do?" I started to laugh in trying to put a little humor into a very bleak situation. Twelve months was going to be a long time in here and I just hoped I would not lose my sanity.

I went to the corner by the window and sat down. I tried to understand what was happening to me. My mind reflected to my teen years when I had a problem that I didn't understand. My mom would give advice, "Son, if you find yourself in trouble and there is no one to help, there is someone to help and that is God. You tell your problems to him and he'll be there to help ease the pain and give you peace."

With those very comforting words I began to pray, "Lord, please give me peace and tranquility so that I can serve my sentence and go home to my family. Thank you, Lord. Amen." Serenity took over me and I then knew I would be strong enough to endure the sentence that was handed down to me.

I heard a knock on the door, then the door opened and it was Lieutenant Chang. He ordered me to take off my summer clothes and hand them to him. I told him, "I don't have a blanket or clothes. The only thing I have is my underclothes." I know he heard me but took the clothes and then shut the door behind him.

There I was, confronted with twelve long months of being alone so I decided to put the past behind me and concentrate on what was ahead of me. I spread the hay so it would be comfortable for sleeping. I put a little hay here and there, managing to make a little nest. Visualizing what my room was like was difficult because of the darkness but that didn't stop me from making a place to sleep. It was cold in the barn and it was only August. I had to look forward to spending the cold winter in there without clothes. I told myself not to get excited. Sit down and relax. I checked to see if there were any holes in the floor or in the walls. I wanted to know if there were rats or other animals for which I should look out for. Then I thought, well this room is inside the barn so that should protect me from the wind and cold. That's the way to think – positive.

I had been preoccupied about everything else that I hadn't looked out the window. I got on my tippee-toes and looked at what was outside. I saw, through the cracks, people walking around in the playground about one hundred feet from the window. When the guards escorted me to this barn, I had not looked at the surroundings. At least I knew where they were holding me. I could yell at someone if they came close enough and

What I felt I looked like after ten and a half months in solitary confinement.

let them know I was here. I sat and started thinking about the events of the day. I had known that my sentence was going to be more severe than Tom's because I had been warned not to escape. I had promised that I would not and had broken my word. In addition, for the fact that I had stolen the map and flashlight, I would be made an example to the others.

In my mind, this was not a heavy price to pay for freedom. I had to think of a way to keep busy for twelve months. I knew it would not be easy, with nothing to do, one meal a day and a half of a bale of loose hay to sleep on. My shorts and tee shirt wouldn't keep me warm but maybe the hay would keep me from freezing to death.

I kept telling myself to think positive; not to get down in the dumps. I knew I couldn't just sit there for twelve months. I would have to do something to keep fit and not go stir crazy. How about exercise? I'll make a daily routine of exercises such as pushups, five every morning, sit ups and bend over touching my toes. Then, looking around the room, I said, "Lord, this is my domain. Let me cope, and watch over me. Let me serve the sentence so I can go home to my family. Thank you Lord." I kept reassuring myself that I was in good hands.

I wasn't afraid, but more concerned about my idle time. Being in the dark did not help at all. I heard the barn door slam and then a few moments later, someone came to my door and unlocked it. I was told that they would bring my meal between twelve and one o'clock but today they would bring it in a few minutes. I asked what time it was and the reply was four thirty. I thanked him.

I wasn't hungry after everything that had happened but I knew I had better eat. It had been a long time since I had eaten anything. I leaned back and waited for my meal. I soon heard the barn door slam and seconds later there were knocks on the door. After the door opened, I was informed that my food was here. When I asked what it was, they responded with rice and a side dish. These side dishes consisted of seaweed, pork or some kind of vegetable. I was handed a spoon and bowl of water. I was told to knock when I was finished and the guard would come get the bowls. I realized I had to take the officers' word about what I was about to eat because it was to dark for me to see anything. As I sat down to eat, I realized that this was a change because they had not given me a spoon before. I did not have to eat with my hands and I noted to myself that it was a nice change.

I had decided I was going to make the best of it and not worry about anything. I would let time pass the best I could and with the help of God, I would make it. I ate my meal, and then sat a few minutes wondering if

Tom was doing okay. I just hoped that he would make it through hard-labor camp. I got up and knocked on the door. The rice wasn't bad, it did have a little flavor, but wasn't enough for having only one meal a day. In a few minutes the guard opened the door and then took the bowls. When he locked the door, I sat back and waited for a few minutes before starting my exercises. By this time, the sun had gone down behind the mountain and it was getting dark outside. I looked through the crack and I couldn't see anything. Not even the playground. I knew it was getting close to bedtime so I felt around, moving the hay around to make my bed.

Once I was finished with that, I did some sit-ups and then turned around to do my push ups. I did about five each and I would add one every other day. When I finished with my exercises, I sat there thinking how I would get along for twelve months without a bath. I was going to look like a fish – scales all over me. I hadn't shaved for at least six months. Thinking back a year ago, we were shaving with half of a razor blade. Someone at camp had gotten an idea that the rounded portion of a broken bottle would sharpen the blade. This is how we shaved. It was a while before the blade got back to you as it made rounds around camp.

After thinking about that, I wondered what I was going to look like when I finished serving my time. When you're in solitary, your thoughts go back to childhood and I found myself thinking about when I was three or four years old. I tried to stop thinking so I could get some sleep. I leaned back into my corner and scooted my body down so I could put hay over me as a blanket. I closed my eyes and fell asleep.

The next morning I told myself that today would be a great day. I talked to the Lord, asking him to bless me and help me to make this a good day. I ended up by thanking him for just being alive. It took a few minutes to wake up fully but when I did, I did my exercises. This was my second day in my little room and so far so good.

Almost two months had passed with the routine staying the same. I was marking the days on the wall, making little marks for each day. This way I was able to keep track of how many days I had been there and how many to go. It was the end of October and we had our first snowfall. I could feel the temperature dropping. I tried to figure a way to keep warmer but all I had was hay. There was nothing I could do except cover up with it. I then thought that I would ask whatever officer showed up if I might have a blanket. Maybe they would lighten up and give me one. All they could do was say no. I was still doing exercises, getting up to fifteen each. I was doing half in the morning and the other half at night before bed.

November was almost half gone. I was laying there, after I had finished eating when I heard a knock on the window. I was surprised that someone had found the place where I was. I then heard a voice say, "I say there, Nick. Are you okay?"

I replied, "Yes, under the circumstances." I knew that the person speaking to me was Dawson, a British soldier whom I met when the British POWs came to our camp. We had become good friends.

I got closer to the window and asked, "Is that you Dawson?"

"Yes, mate. What a bloody room to put you in, those bloody Chinese." He then told me that if he could, he would try to slip a pencil and paper to me so if I needed anything, they would try to get it for me.

I told him, "Thanks a lot. Just talking to someone is a blessing from God."

He replied, "Take care, mate," and then he left.

Hearing a voice from a fellow POW was so encouraging. At least they knew where I was and that sure made my day. I didn't ask him how he knew where I was. That didn't matter, what was important was he took the risk of talking to me and chanced getting caught. From that day on, someone came occasionally and asked me if I was all right. Knowing that some were concerned for me would make my loneliness easier to take.

It was now December, with only a few days left before Christmas. Before I knew it, it was Christmas and I knew that because a group of British and American POWs had gotten together and came by my window to sing. They sang about five Christmas carols and I started to cry. I then said, "Thank you. That was a great Christmas present you guys."

Dawson spoke for the group, "Merry Christmas, mate, from all of us 'Blokes' here at Camp One. You're a hero to us and it took a lot of guts to do what you did, mate." Before they left, Dawson wished me a Merry Christmas again and told me to they had to go sing throughout the camp.

After they left, I could see through the cracks of the boarded up window that it was cold. Everyone was wearing winter clothes. I could also see that the snow had turned to ice. I only got cold when I got out from under the hay, so I crawled inside the hay and laid down thinking how nice it was of those guys to make my day on Christmas an enjoyable one.

I then thought back to the Christmas of 1949 and how all the family had gotten together. It was enjoyable to sing Christmas carols and go shopping for mom and dad. That was the last Christmas for me with the family. I remember that my dad always received socks, ties or handkerchiefs for Christmas and he would ask us, "Is that all I'm getting from you kids?" It did seem like that was all he ever got.

Reality now surfaced and I wondered where my food was. Not much time passed when the guard brought my food. I was glad. I was hungry enough to eat a horse. I was aware of the fact that I didn't know what they were serving me but this is where trust comes in, whether you liked it or not. After the guard took my bowls, I decided to take a nap.

I still couldn't believe how hay could keep you so warm. I had never known this until they put us in a barn during our march to Camp 1. The weather had been thirty below zero so I crawled into some hay and kept warm. I was thinking of this as I was rearranging they hay in order to bed down. I laid back, covered myself and soon fell asleep.

When I woke up, I decided to sit up while keeping the hay around me. I had a sort of vision that I was aboard a troop ship and all my friends from the POW camp were with me. I could see people waving so we waved back. I heard the ships air horn blow as he got close to the docks. On this dock I saw people crying, and waving their hands and handkerchiefs. I was trying in vain to look for my mom and dad but the ship was still too far away for me to see them. I looked around and asked where we were. Then the vision left me and I found myself in the little room, covered up to my neck in hay.

I sat there trying to unscramble my vision. What ship was it? Why no buildings in the background? Why didn't I see mom and dad? I said to myself that maybe God was telling me that I was going home. Maybe that is the way it was going to happen when the war was over and I was released. It was so vivid that I couldn't believe what I had seen. I sat there wishing that it would happen that way.

New Year's had come and gone. I looked at my scratches in the wall and we were already in February. The guys at camp came by to ask how I was. I always replied, "Okay, I guess." My visitors never said much. They would walk by my window acting like they were looking for something, then when the guards weren't looking they would talk to me. The Mexican guys, friends of mine, would drop by occasionally. Dawson was my most frequent visitor, however.

I sometimes wished that I could say more or carry on a conversation with them but my guard was just outside my door. Most of the time I would say, "okay; I don't know; thanks for coming" or "how's everything out there?" Not only that, but my vision was not that good through the cracks. Dawson had tried to get me paper and a pencil but was unable to fit it through the cracks. At times I wished I had a knife so I could carve a hole big enough for them to slip through. The Chinese had nailed the boards too close together and I was not able to pry them loose. I did my exercises and after finishing, I looked at my body and knew I was losing weight. One meal a day would not put meat on my bones.

When I woke up the next morning, I did my exercises and noticed that it was sunny outside. Since we had snow two weeks into February, it was still very cold and that was probably why no one was outside. The sun was melting the snow, then at night it would turn to ice. The bitter cold wind that came from Manchuria made the conditions outside unbearable.

I decided to lie down while I waited for my food. When it arrived, I would ask for some hot soybean milk. I didn't know what they would say but it would be worth asking for. The guard soon brought my food. When I heard the door being unlocked, I asked, "Sir?" When he said yes, I asked if there was any way I could get some hot soybean milk. He harshly responded that they were punishing me. I had lost all of my privileges and I would get only what I have been getting till my sentence was over. I thanked him and then in Spanish I said, "Your mother wears Maggie's drawers!"

Being bitter cold in the room, water didn't even taste good but it did help to get my food down. While I was eating, I looked at my calendar wall and soon it would be March and I would be twenty-one years old.

Well, time went on and it was still very cold. My exercises were getting fewer and fewer. I sat there and tried to figure a way to not get in a negative state. I kept thinking, suppose I don't make it because I felt my health wasn't up to par, as far as strength. What happens if the war was not over soon? What then? Then I told myself to think positive and I would make it out of here. I then looked up and asked the Lord to give me strength, tolerance and fortitude that I need to finish my twelve months so I could go home to my family. Please, Lord, that is all I ask. You took care of me while I escaped, don't let go of me now.

I tried not to think negatively so I wouldn't get down in the dumps, but when I did I would do more exercises or think about when Tom and I escaped the first time. It was strange because while I was sitting there, I would get visions of myself and my parents, including my whole family. It was like looking through a window of my house and I could see mom, dad and myself doing things when I was eight years old. Sometimes I would see myself returning from school with a friend. After a few minutes, I would try to unscramble what was going on in my mind. I just sat there dumbfounded. This would happen often. I decided that I would not worry about it and let it be. The day finally ended so I started getting my bed ready.

Day in and day out, nothing changed. I looked at my calendar and it was three days after my birthday. I peeked outside and found that the snow had melted but I could still tell it was cold. The moon was shining and I could hear the guards outside the barn. I guessed that they were checking to see if anyone was by the window. I then crawled into bed, covered up with hay and thanked God that I was alive and well and for him being there for me. With this thought I turned on my side and fell asleep.

It was now April 1953. I noticed this as I was marking my calendar. I realized that I had put almost nine months of my sentence behind me and that I would soon be free. I jumped up yelling and rejoicing that there were only ninety more days. That was great! A knock on the door disrupted me. The guard opened the door, saying something while his finger was on his mouth, as if to say *ssshhh*. Then he told me, "No." I told him that I was happy and added, "You go to hell!" He then quickly slammed the door shut. I immediately got down on the ground and did some push-ups. I looked outside and saw that the sun was shining on the hut next to the playground and the POWs seemed happy. I guess it was because of the weather.

A few more days went by and I didn't need the hay to stay warm. The weather had changed for the better. There was something strange going on at camp. I looked outside and could see that the guys seemed more relaxed. When my next visitor arrived at the window, he asked how I was doing and I replied, "Okay. Say, what's going on out there?" He told me that there wouldn't be anymore wood detail and he thought the war was coming to an end. All I could say was, "Wow!" He then said he'd see me later and to hang in there.

No one knows what that did to me. I got chills and goose bumps all over and then I cried, I got on my knees and said, "Lord, let the war be over so I can go home as I have suffered enough. Thank you." I was on cloud nine. I felt my face and there felt like about five inches of beard. My hair was ten to twelve inches long so I told myself, you're going to look like a cave man. I then added, I don't care who sees me like this. I'm going home!

It was May and I knew something good had happened because I had just finished my meal when I heard a knock on my window. I then heard a voice belonging to Dawson. He said, "I say there, mate. Nick, can you hear me?"

I said, "Yes, Dawson."

"Hang in there, mate. The war is going to be over sometime next month. Do you need anything, mate?"

I responded, "No, that is all I needed – what you just told me."

Chapter Fourteen

Repatriation

It was great news that Dawson had just told me. On the other hand, we had been told that before. After Dawson left, I sat in my little corner and tried to visualize the war being over and going home. I didn't want my emotions to come out, in case the news had been incorrect. In 1952, the Chinese told us that the Koreans and Americans would meet soon and bring the war to an end. Two years later, we were still there.

My mind was overtaken by so many thoughts and questions. Was the war really over? Was it some kind of a sick joke or mind game? Was this another way to make my punishment worse? No, Dawson would not do something that heartless. He must have believed that the war would soon be over and therefore, he wanted to share the great news with me. Now, I wondered if I would have to stay in this room until I was repatriated or would they release me back into camp? I can only pray that I will be free of this room. After a few minutes I sat up and my thoughts turned to my mom and dad and how happy they must be to know that their son would be coming home. I could not stop my tears from flowing. I thanked God and told him that this would not have happened without him.

A few days had gone by, making today the tenth of May, Mother's Day. I found myself thinking about what I was going to do when I arrived home. Only a few minutes had passed since doing my exercises when I heard a knock at the door. The door then opened. My visitor, realizing that I was in the dark, identified himself: "I am Lieutenant Chang. The commandant has given the order for you to be released to Camp 1."

I could not believe what I had just heard. I just could not believe that I was going to be taken out of here and that they had ended my sentence. I broke down and cried. Lieutenant Chang informed me that the remaining three months of the sentence would be forgotten. I had completed my punishment. He also added that since I had been in the dark for ten months they would be putting a blindfold over my eyes to protect them from the sun. They would then take me to a new squad and that is where they would remove the blindfold. I was warned not to go out into the sunlight for at least two days. Lieutenant Chang asked if I understood and to this I replied, "Yes, sir." I was still overwhelmed by all the great news and just wanted to shout it all to the world. I had hung onto the thought that one day I would be leaving this corner of the world and re-enter the world of Camp 1.

I said my goodbyes to the little room that had sheltered me for the past ten months. As I neared the door, the guards grabbed me and took me out side. There were many people outside the barn although I could not tell who they were. Also present were some guards that I could hear convers-ing with Lieutenant Chang. I was still very much in awe about everything that was happening to me.

A POW that had been standing next to me grabbed my arm and said, "Let's go, Nick." I asked who it was and he responded, "You don't know me, but I know of you. You're going to be in my hut and I'm the leader of the squad. My name is Bill." Then I heard Lieutenant Chang tell Bill that I was not to take off the blindfold. Nevertheless, he could go ahead and take me to the hut. I walked along slowly but it felt good to have that fresh air in my face.

As we were walking along, I could sense that we were nearing the huts for I heard people saying, "Hey, Nick is here!" Just about that time men were all over me, shaking my hand, putting their arms around me, welcoming me back. It was truly a glorious day for me as solitary con-finement was all over. No more suffering, no more living in the dark. I could feel all these guys close by and walking along side of me. As we got to the hut, I heard one voice say, "Welcome home, mate." Yes, it was good ol' Dawson. He shook my hand and suggested that I get some rest. Bill then added, "Fellows, let's let Nick rest a while and when his blind-fold comes off, you can come back and see him."

I felt like a celebrity with all the guys around me making a fuss. I don't think they knew how important their caring meant to me. Coming out of a situation like solitary confinement, one never knows how the others will react, but they showed me that I had nothing to be concerned about. Bill quickly took me inside the hut, sat me down on a bunk and then said, "This will be your bunk for as long as you're here. That won't be much longer, I hope. Nick, did you know that the war is coming to an end?"

"Yes. Someone told me and then Dawson repeated the news. By the way, do you know Tom Cabello? Do you know where he is?"

"I heard they took him to another camp when he got out of hard labor camp." He had not heard where Tom had been taken. He felt bad that he was unable to supply me with any information.

For the first few days I had a lot of company with a lot of questions being asked. One of the most frequent was, how far did I get before I got caught? Another was, what had I done for the ten months that I was in solitary? To that I answered, "I prayed a lot and asked God to let me live through it." After they took my blindfold off, I realized how precious one's sight is. I was so thankful to be able to see all that was around me. I can sympathize with the blind and how important it is not to take anything for granted.

It was now June and the time seemed to go faster on the outside than when they had me cooped up in a small, dark room. The Chinese told us that we were going to have an assembly the following day and all the POWs must attend. Lieutenant Chang went around telling everyone that the camp must be cleaned up. All huts must be cleaned and ready for inspection. We knew something big was about to happen because they were sure in a hurry to get the whole camp cleaned up.

The next morning we gathered at the playground and even the men at the medical clinic had been brought to this assembly. Lieutenant Chang told us that the commander would be saying a few words to us. The commander then told us that today was a great day for us. The war would be over in ten to twenty days so they decided to issue new clothing to all of us. The International Red Cross would be at camp when the Peace Treaty was signed and they, the Chinese, would try to get us as presentable as they were able to. They also asked that we clean up the quarters we lived in, plus the surrounding area because the Chinese Peoples' Volunteer Delegation would be arriving in a few hours. We were to be prepared for questions regarding our treatment since our arrival at camp. With that, he told us good luck and have a safe trip home.

With the Chinese delegation coming, plus the Red Cross later, I decided that I wanted to look presentable. I asked around if I could get someone to cut my hair and maybe a shave. I started asking the people from my hut and a response came from a roomie, "Nick, I know a guy that has a pair of scissors and a razor. I'll ask him for you, maybe he'll do it." He was only gone a few minutes and he brought someone with him. His reply was, "He'll give you a cut and shave."

This guy said, "Ready, Nick?"

I replied, "Let's do it." After he was finished, I felt like a new man.

The news of the war's end left men speechless. Some men took off toward their hut while others threw their hats up in the air and yelled, "We're going home!" Yes, it was finally ending.

The men from the hut where I stayed, plus myself, headed to the hut and started cleaning, some outside, the rest of us inside. I noticed that

This is one of 12 letters I wrote to my mother while a POW before going home.

some were getting rid of the things they had made while at the camp. After the cleaning had been completed, I sat by the door. It was not much time later when I noticed some vehicles drove up to the commanders' office. I figured the occupants belonged to the Chinese Delegation. They got out of the car and went into the office. It was not long before they resurfaced and headed toward the clinic and through the streets where the huts were. Most of the POWs were walking around and some were playing cards while talking about what they were going to do when they got home. The delegation spoke with some of these men, then went to others who were standing by the woodpile. When I got up to return to my hut, I saw them go into the recreation room, and then into the kitchen. I did not want them asking me any questions so I went inside. At this time they probably would have received nasty answers!

In a while the whistle blew for lunch and as usual, the squad leaders went with the pans and returned with rice and a side dish. After eating our lunch, people went back to what they had been doing. The Delegation had left so now all we had to wait for was the International Red Cross. The guys were still excited about the war being over. That was the most popular conversation around camp.

The day came when they told us to assemble at the playground. We all waited impatiently as POWs were still trying to get there. The commander stepped out of his office with four officers standing beside him. He did not have a microphone this time but said that this was a great day for everyone. The Americans and North Korean Army had signed the Peace Treaty. Therefore, we would be going home in the next few days. This was truly a day to rejoice and celebrate. In the next few days they would issue us new clothing and then we would be ready for the trip to Kaesong. When he finished, a lot of us cried for joy that the war was really over. Plenty of men were jumping around telling the world that the war was over and they would be going home. I enjoyed watching them and wished I could have joined in but was still to weak from my months in solitary confinement.

A few days later, I decided to take a walk and visit some of my friends who had taken the time to visit me while I had been confined. I thanked them for coming to my window to check on me and to see if I was okay. We still had some sick men in the camp so I went to check on them. I stood there looking at these men and I couldn't help wondering why the Chinese and Koreans had not had the proper medical treatment that was needed at Camp 1. When they told us that the Chinese would do everything to make us comfortable, they were lying. The worst part is that we cared, but were unable to change anything.

I talked to some men, giving them words of encouragement. I asked them to hang in there and soon they would be in an American hospital. After seeing these guys, I was hurting so badly for them. I somehow felt like they wouldn't make it for the trip home. It was so depressing to see that. When I was finished talking to them I headed to my hut. Once inside, I prayed for all the men in that senseless condition. "Lord, please help these men who can't help themselves. Give them life at least until we get back to our people. If they are to die, let them die on American soil."

What a wonderful sight it was when the trucks drove in to Camp One. The sick and wounded were loaded first and then some of the POWs that had been selected were loaded onto other trucks. After several loads of POWs had left, I realized that the ones whom they left had at one time or another given the Chinese a bad time. We either didn't attend lectures or had done something against the Chinese officers. I guess they were going to make us sweat it out for not being the "good guys." About ten days went by before finally the trucks came for us.

We were loaded up in the morning. As the trucks rolled out, we looked back for the last time at a place where we had spent thirty-three months and eighteen days of our lives. Leaving the playground, I took a glimpse at the cemetery. I felt sad for those who didn't get to make it home. I told myself that they were with the Lord but somehow felt bad leaving their bodies behind. I don't think anyone felt the sorrow that I felt for the men who had died. Some had been friends while others I didn't know but they were all God's children. I felt I had left something behind.

Traveling down the road toward the railroad station, seventy-two miles away from camp, I looked up at those huge mountains and ravines which Tom and I had walked. Memories came flashing back. I thought about Tom and wondered where he was and if he was all right.

There were eight trucks carrying about one hundred and sixty POWs. We entered a good-sized town and stopped about half way through it. The reason for this was unknown at first. We sat there waiting for something to happen when, in a few minutes, seven trucks full of POWs got behind our eight trucks. Shortly we began to roll again. I didn't know where or what POW camp they came from but the trucks were loaded. We were moving about forty-five miles per hour. We had been informed that the railroad station was two and a half hours away.

Once at the railroad station, we were told to get off and line up. When I looked toward the front of the convoy, I could see more POWs lined up. It looked to be about eight or nine hundred men waiting for the train to arrive. We sat down while staying in line. There were several men asking about their buddies, trying to find out if someone knew them, what camp they were from and what happened to so and so. We were soon informed that the train was on its way so there would be another fifteen or so minutes wait. I don't believe this mattered to anyone since we were going home. We sat down and waited for the train.

We heard the train whistle and the Chinese guard motioned with his hand for us to stand. Once on our feet, we were told to get in a single file line until the train reached its stopping point. We started loading from the rear of the train. Lieutenant Chang had been with us all the way and now his last assignment was to put us on that train. After everyone boarded, we started traveling along the countryside of North Korea. That enabled us to see the destruction the war had left. The reality of it all was devastating.

The place where we were to disembark the train was a good-sized town. After leaving the train, we were loaded onto trucks. We arrived at Panmunjom where we were turned over to the American forces. Waiting for us at the exchange gate were several Military Police. It was a great feeling to know our suffering was over.

After unloading, we were put into single file ready for exchange. As we moved through the line, a group of officials took our names, rank and serial numbers. We then entered a large tent where we disrobed. Standing by were service personnel with fumigation guns. We were each sprayed to 'delouse' us, then after showering and drying off, we headed to another section of the tent to get issued GI clothing.

As I went through the line, with only shorts on, an officer came up to me and asked, "Are you Nick Flores?"

"Yes, sir. I am." I began to wonder why he wanted to know this.

He then told me, "General Pate would like to speak with you." I was then escorted to a table where the "Big Man" of the 1st Marine Division was already seated.

General Pate looked at me and said, "Flores, sit over here by me." I did not hesitate. After I was situated, he continued, "Your country is very proud of you, the Marine Corps and myself included. We have heard stories about your heroism while a POW. Also, what you did for the other POWs and your escapes."

Sitting in the nourishment section, having ice cream and milk while talking, are Major General Randolph McCall Pate, Commanding General of the 1st Marine Division and returned prisoner of war, Private First Class Nick A. Flores, son of Mr. Pablo Flores, 343 N. 8th St., San Jose, California. Pfc. Flores was captured November 29, 1950, while serving with the 1st Service Battalion, 1st Marine Division.

I told him, "I did it because it had to be done, to take care of the POWs."

Then he said, "I know that our country will give you the highest honor that you could receive for your heroism while a POW."

I responded, "Thank you, sir."

He asked if I was proud to be a Marine to which I told him that I was very proud. The conversation ended by, "Well, I want you to know you're a fine Marine. Call your parents when you finish debriefing."

"Yes, sir," I replied.

General Pate then got his cane and as he was walking away, turned around and had one final say, "Welcome home, Marine."

I left so that I could finish getting dressed before I was led into the debriefing room. This is where I told them about my escapes and what I did while a POW. They asked me if I knew of any Marines or Army POWs that had collaborated with the enemy. I gave them some names and then I was told to go call my parents.

The Red Cross had a tent where the phones had been installed. Before I left, I was informed that I would be interrogated again aboard ship. They welcomed me home and with this said and done, to the phones I went. There was a lengthy line, which was to be expected at a time like this.

I called mom and dad, telling them I was fine. They said they were so happy to hear from me and thanked God for bringing me home safely. Our conversation was kept short because many men were still waiting to use a phone.

With everyone now finished making that very important phone call, we were loaded up in helicopters. Our next stop was Freedom Village and what an appropriate name that was. Here, we received our long overdue haircuts. This alone made me feel 'human' again. We were also given three hundred dollars and with this money in our pockets, we anxiously waited for our time to head home, via San Francisco.

It was very exciting to have money and to eat what we wanted. Most of the guys wanted nothing other than hamburgers and hot dogs. I invested in a camera so I would be able to take pictures of my buddies and also of Freedom Village. It was a place that would always be close to my heart. It had been much too long since I, and all the others, enjoyed that wonderful thing called freedom.

We were taken by bus from Freedom Village to where we would board the ship. Once everyone was all gathered, as many as sixty to seventy men were taken to the ship on landing craft. The *Marine Adder* was the ship that would take us to San Francisco. After we went up the plank, mingling

Free at last ... our "Gate to Freedom"

with the other men was the thing to do. We were eventually shown our quarters and that evening, headed for San Francisco. We were fed like royalty – the best food – and everything was just superb.

Shortly after we had gotten underway, the captain's voice came on the loudspeaker. "It's an honor to be the captain of this ship and having you aboard. Welcome home. We will try to make your trip to San Francisco as pleasant as we can. The whole crew will try to help you and make you comfortable. Thank you. Now the colonel will speak to you."

"Welcome home, men. It is a pleasure to be here with you and as the captain said, we Marine and Army officers will answer any questions you may have. We will try to make your voyage a pleasant one. Thank you."

After the welcoming, we were on our own to do whatever. There was a game room, theater to watch movies and ample paper and pens to write letters, if that is what we chose to do. All of this treatment was overwhelming and very much appreciated. Our debriefings were held as we knew they would be.

After getting settled and all the salutations and welcome home speeches were over, we were told to report to the mess hall. There, I found several POWs sitting, waiting for an officer to start speaking to us. He informed us that our parents had been notified regarding the day and time we were to arrive at Pier 40 at Ft. Mason in San Francisco. Then a Naval officer spoke to us, "I am a Naval Intelligence officer and I, along with several others, will be debriefing each and every one of you, starting tomorrow. You will be escorted by a Marine Sergeant to one of the twelve dorms that we will be using for the debriefings. There will be a number on each door, and the Sergeant will take you to the appropriate room. You will be asked questions and you will provide the answers. This procedure is exercised with any POWs, after a war. Let me say again, welcome home. It's good to see you."

Everybody seemed to return to what they were doing before the speech. I didn't have long to wait before my name was called. I believe I was the fifth one called. After being escorted to the correct room, I entered and saluted the officer. He introduced himself, then told me, "At ease. Please sit down." As I sat down, the first question I was asked was, "How do you feel?"

I said, "Fine, except for my back is still hurting and a few aches and pains. I'll be okay."

I answered all the questions that I had answers for. Several of his last questions dealt with my escapes and how I was treated afterward. He instructed, "Tell me, in detail, about the escapes." I did so and his reaction was one of surprise about the last escape, when I was apprehended by the

Back on friendly ground at Freedom Village with my buddy Bob Dyer.

SAN JOSEAN HEADED FOR HOME – Marine Pfc.
Nick A. Flores, left, son of Mr. and Mrs. Pablo G. Flores,
343 N. Eighth St., boards ship Marine Adder in Inchon
on his way home to United States. Flores was released
by Communists in Korea after two and a half years of
captivity. Other Marines, left to right, are Pfc. George
Cowen, Oklahoma, Corp. Donald Williams, Missouri,
and William E. Schultz, New York. – AP Wirephoto.

Russian soldiers. He wanted to know more, to which I obliged. He ended the sessions with, "Flores, I will definitely call you again. Later today or possibly tomorrow."

I, as well as many others, couldn't truly believe that we were going home, and our suffering was over. There was such a "high" in the guys that this in itself was a great morale booster.

Two days had gone by when I was called again for debriefing. This time, there were more questions and I was asked to give more detail. After an hour or so, I was asked, "Would you consider re-enlisting and if you do, would you consider training to be a spy agent? This would entail trying to locate the missing pilots and men who disappeared. You do not have to give me an answer now, but think about it."

My final debriefing was just three days before we docked in San Francisco. I was summoned by the same Naval officer. "I want to know what you have decided to do."

I replied, "Yes, I have come to a decision. I feel that the injuries I sustained while a POW and the beatings from the Russians were enough for me. I would rather not. Thank you sir for the offer. I have suffered enough."

"I understand. Thank you for your cooperation in this matter. You may now go, Flores. Good luck."

"Thank you, sir."

Our trip home aboard ship lasted fourteen days. Our journey would be over soon. It was brought to our attention that we should expect to dock in San Francisco the following morning. Excitement could be felt and seen all over the ship. Some wondered if their parents would be there while some just thought about their girlfriends. My thoughts involved my parents and I was so very anxious to see them.

That evening, before getting to San Francisco, we put all our belongings together. Two days before, we had been issued new uniforms so that we would be ready to meet our loved ones. It was complete chaos aboard ship because a lot of us were very nervous, not knowing what to expect once getting to Ft. Mason, San Francisco. That night we went to bed but very few of us could sleep so we ended up watching movies or playing cards.

The next morning started at 6:00 o'clock. We went to the mess hall where we ate ham and eggs, our last meal aboard ship. A few hours went by then the Captain's voice came over the loudspeaker saying, "Gentlemen, if you would like to come up on deck, you will be able to see the

Arriving back home at Pier 40 in San Francisco, California.

great Golden Gate Bridge." Of course we all rushed to the upper deck and there it was. Wow! You could see it off in the distance. As the ship got closer, a banner attached to the bottom of the bridge read, "Welcome Home." I cannot imagine that there was a single POW aboard ship at that moment that had not been taken by this. It was an extremely emotional time.

This was a glorious moment in my life. I had goose bumps all over and tears in my eyes. While standing on deck, I thought about the vision I had while in solitary. I thanked God that this was coming to life for me. I turned around and told another POW that I had met earlier on the voyage about the vision.

He asked, "You knew this was going to happen before it did?"

I told him, "Yes, more or less. The vision was just like what is happening now."

He shook his head and said, "I'll be darn."

As the ship, *Marine Adder*, was going under the Golden Gate Bridge, we were all summoned to the bow to witness a spectacular demonstration. Tugs were shooting colored water fifty feet high. There must have been roughly twenty tugs doing this. Jets were flying over the bay. It was quite a welcoming home celebration for all the POWs. While the ship was getting close to Ft. Mason, I saw some tug boats getting close to the ship. One of the tugs came close and a few Marine and Army personnel came aboard ship. In a few minutes, they were approaching some of the POWs.

To my surprise, at a distance of about thirty feet, no other than my motor transport Tech Sergeant Opiot came toward me. He said, "Welcome home, Marine" and then embraced me and gave me a big hug. He asked, "How are you?"

I replied, "Great! This is a beautiful day to get home."

He then informed me, "Your mom, dad and family are on the dock, waiting for you. I called them to tell them you were arriving today. They were so thrilled to hear the news. I heard what you did at the POW camp. I'm proud of you and so is your company commander, Lieutenant Banks. I can say that your whole outfit is as well."

As I looked at the tugboat escorting the ship to the dock, I could see thousands of people waving. When the ship finally reached its birth at Ft. Mason, Elsi Norwood was singing on the dock while the plank was being lowered. I looked to see if I could spot mom and dad but couldn't locate them in the crowd. I truly believed that this totally amazing welcome was a time that most would not soon forget.

Chapter Fifteen

Home at Last

As I reached the bottom of the gang plank, I was greeted by a marine Lieutenant who said to me, "Flores. Follow me. I will take you to where your family is waiting." He escorted me to the main section where all the families were desperately waiting.

As I was approaching, I could see mom and dad, looking worried, along with the rest of my family. When I got close to them, I could not hold back my tears. I ran the last ten feet, met mom with her open arms and we embraced. Neither one of us wanted to let go. My heart was pumping and so was hers. She finally let go, pushed me slightly and said, "Praise the Lord, son. You're home. God brought you back to me. Let me see how you look – a little skinny but that can be taken care of when you get home."

After she finished, dad came to me, giving me a big bear hug and said, "We missed you, son. Welcome home." Following dad was my two brothers, Paul and Armando, my oldest brother's wife, Lupe and their son, my sister Susie and her husband Carlos.

After being there for a while, the Marine lieutenant told me I must report, in fifteen minutes, to the POW section and get my orders. After a little time had passed, I told my parents that I would be back and then we could go home. I reported to the POW section and the Marine officer handed me a manilla envelope containing my orders. He told me, "You will be given a thirty-day leave, and then you need to report to Oak Knoll Naval Hospital for observation. That should take about four to six weeks. Is that understood?" He ended by saying, "Welcome home, Marine." I stepped back, saluted him and then he returned the salute. I quickly went back to my family and moments later, headed to the cars.

I felt uneasy. Don't get me wrong, I was glad to be back on American soil and back with my family. I felt like I had been reborn and beginning a new life. Now that I was home and in the hands of my family, it seemed that all the torture and hell that I went through seemed to be a myth. But in my mind, I could not forget the men we left behind. I could not erase the thoughts of the men I had taken care of and the men who died because of the lack of medical care. It seemed so unfair for me to celebrate with my family and yet what about those families who had loved ones that didn't come back? It felt selfish to be celebrating when others were grieving.

As I was walking arm in arm with my parents to the car, my mom looked at me and very concerned asked, "What's wrong, son? It seems like your mind is a million miles away."

I looked at her and responded, "I was thinking back to the men who didn't come back."

She gently squeezed my hand and said, "They are all in good hands. They went to heaven and they are safe there."

We continued walking and my dad asked, "Are you hungry?"

I quickly told him, "Yes, dad."

We arrived at the cars, piled in and started on our way home. Dad told Paul to stop at a restaurant so we could all eat. Traveling along the El Camino Real through San Mateo, Paul saw a restaurant sign and pulled off. My father asked curiously, "Why did you stop here?"

Paul replied, just as surprised, "It says restaurant."

My dad questioned Paul, "What kind of restaurant is it?"

My brother could not figure out why dad was asking all these questions. He looked up at the sign, now noticing it was a Chinese restaurant, *Ching Ling Chinese Food*. All Paul said was, "Oh my God."

My dad added, "Don't you think he has had enough Chinese food to last him the rest of his life?" We all laughed. What else was there to do?

Paul quickly turned the car around and then we headed down the road until we found an American Restaurant named *Ricky's*. We went in and dad asked me what I wanted. Before I answered, he said, "Get the biggest steak in the house." I did just that and we all ate a very delightful meal and the thrill of all the family together again was very prominent.

During and after eating, I noticed my family members staring at me. It seemed to me that they were wondering if they should ask me about being a POW but instead they asked me about the trip home aboard the ship and what we did while coming home. They also wanted to know how Japan had been. "That is enough questions for now. Let him rest and when we get home, if Nick wants to talk about it, he will," my mother said.

We arrived home shortly after leaving the restaurant. I was thrilled to be home. As soon as I stepped out of the car, my dog, Duke, came to me and just went wild, licking me, and wagging his tail. I guess he was showing me that he had really missed me, as I had him. I had Duke since he was a puppy when he used to follow me on my paper delivery route.

As my mother and I were walking on the porch, I took hold of her arm and we continued inside. Once inside, she broke down crying and said

A picture with my mom after I arrived home.

with tears streaming down her face, "Praise the Lord. It's good to have you home, son."

I embraced her and then told her, "I missed you something terrible. I missed dad and everyone else. It is so nice to be back with my family."

The following day, a photographer came over and took pictures of me, mom and dad. Our neighbors also visited, bringing their "welcome home" greetings. They also informed me that they had kept a vigil of all the names of POWs that were coming home. It was comforting to know that so many people were following the news and concerned enough to do so.

I decided to make the best of my thirty-day leave, so I stuck around the house and enjoyed my family. I figured there would be projects that both my mom and dad would need help with. Some of the chores I helped with were watering my mother's flowers, going to the store for her and also taking dad to work.

My mother surprised me with what she prepared for the first meal we shared as a family since I had returned. She fixed enchiladas, which was usually saved for Sundays but she informed me that this was a special meal. I enjoyed that meal very much and while over in Korea, I had thought often about sinking my teeth into one of my mother's homemade enchiladas.

The second day after my return, several friends and relatives dropped by to visit. They told me how happy they were to see me home. After all the greetings, I decided to visit my old school chums from Peter Burnett Jr. High. I also ended up visiting my past teachers who were still there. That excursion brought back a lot of memories.

Eight days of my thirty day leave had gone by and I was still having a ball with my friends. When I wasn't with them, I was occasionally kicking back in a recliner that mom and dad had bought for me. I must admit, I don't think that I spent a total of five hours in that chair due to my time spent in solitary confinement. I could not sit still nor did I like to be confined indoors. I told mom, "Who wants to rest after being cooped up for three years in prison?" She laughed, and as always, that made me feel good inside.

My leave was drawing to a close all too soon. I received my orders to report to Oak Knoll Naval Hospital in Oakland, California. Since I would be spending some time there, I decided I would stay home and be with my family for what was left of my leave.

Why is it that a day that you do not look forward to comes much too quickly? I spent thirty days at the hospital and I was found to be of sound mind, comprehensive and I reasoned well. I departed for home, where the happiness of my family became as important as anything else.

On or about the third day back home, I received a letter that requested I report to 100 Harrison St., Marine Barracks. It would be at
that location where I would be formally discharged from the Marines.
On the morning of October 5, my brother drove me to the Marine barracks in San Francisco. Once we arrived at the proper location, my brother
dropped me off, went and parked the car, and stayed there until I was
finished.

I crossed the street and saw the sign, Marine Barracks – 100 Harrison
St. I then entered the building and went directly to the desk and presented
my orders. The clerk directed me to the door on which the nameplate
read, Commanding Officer. I knocked and soon after, I was told to enter.
The commanding officer asked me to sign some papers and then he handed
me a manilla folder which I suspected held my discharge papers.

At that time, little did I know that the manilla folder contained a time
bomb; the ruining of my life for 41 years! At that time, I was just happy to
be home, missing no limbs and my sanity was intact. I could have easily
been shot by either the North Koreans or the Russians after they captured
me. I really had a lot to be thankful for, and I never forgot that so many
others were less fortunate.

After the manilla folder was in my hand, the commanding officer said,
"Good luck, Flores." I quickly left his office. I was about to walk out of
the Marine Corps for good. Up to this time, I had not opened the folder to
look at my discharge papers. Walking back to where Paul had parked the
car, I was curious about the discharge but did not take the time to look at
it. I knew that Paul was waiting and I wanted to hurry back to the car.

As I opened the car door, I said, "You are now looking at a civilian!"
He reached for the folder and asked me if he could open it to which I
replied, "Sure. Open it."

When he pulled out the discharge paper, he exclaimed, "General Dis-
charge!" I saw his face turn white and in anger, he asked, "Why didn't
they give you an Honorable Discharge? After all you went through as a
POW, this is how they are going to repay you?" His face was flushed and
I noticed tears running down his cheeks. Looking directly at me, he said,
"Thirty four months as a POW, you went through hell and you get this?
Why?"

I didn't have an answer. I found out in later years, how important it
would have been to be able to answer his "Why?" Society looked at the
recipient of a general discharge as a dishonorable one. I was seen as a
nobody, a screw up Marine that wasn't fit to be a Marine.

I could see that my brother was hurt so I told him, "I am alive and in good health. That's all that matters."

He replied, "I know, Nick, but this is the thanks you get from the Marine Corps for being a POW?" He soon composed himself and we left San Francisco behind, heading for San Jose. My brother didn't speak a word all the way home. It hurt me to see him so upset over something that I felt powerless to change.

A few days later, I found out that Paul had spoken to my father about my discharge. My father had cornered me and asked if he could speak to me. I told him, "Sure."

He started by saying, "Let's go to the living room." As we walked he asked, "What's this I hear about you getting a General instead of an Honorable Discharge? Don't you think it needs immediate attention?"

I replied, "Yes, sir. I am going to look into it." I knew that my family looked down on me for accepting a General Discharge. "Dad, I promise that I'll look into it even if I have to go to Washington and have them look at it. Hopefully they would agree that it shouldn't be."

A few months went by and I was having a great time being a civilian. I had received a partial payment for my back injury. I was thrilled to get it. I decided that I would buy myself a car. I saw this beautiful powder blue Ford convertible. I said, "Dad, I want this car."

He replied, "Let's look around and maybe you'll find something else you might like." I accepted his suggestion for now but I knew I would be back to buy that Ford. After searching for two more days and not finding anything else, I went and bought the 1953 Ford convertible.

A couple of weeks later, my mom, dad and I went to Mexico to visit my aunts, uncles and grandfather, Abraham. He is the one that I was named after. They had been very anxious to see me. Two years later, I am sad to say, my grandfather passed away and I was again heading to Mexico for the funeral. I loved him very much and missed him dearly.

After my mother and I returned from Mexico, I stayed around the house for a few days. I got the inkling to go to Del Rio and search for Mito. I told my parents of my plans and I left, with their blessings. My dear mother added, "Be careful, son. God be with you."

I arrived in Del Rio and inquired around, asking friends if they knew where Mito was. I soon found out that she was working at a gas station as a cashier. I found the gas station and there she was, as pretty as ever. I walked through the opened door and the first thing she said to me was, "Abraham! I thought you were dead!"

I jumped over the counter and told her, "You're coming with me and we're getting married."

She hesitantly replied, "I can't. I'm already married. Plus, I'm pregnant."

That devastated me. My world had just been turned upside down in a matter of seconds. I looked at her and said, "Thanks for waiting for me!" I went to my car, spun out of the driveway, heading for California. I never saw her again.

After getting home, I decided that I would look for a job and put my life in order. What Mito had told me, about being married and pregnant, had such an impact on me. I didn't know if I could handle it.

I found a job working for a trucking company as a parts clerk. After eight months, I started looking for another job. I ended up working for different construction companies. In 1956, I went back to the VA hospital and requested that my back injury be checked again, as my back was preventing me from working. Adding to that was my experience in the POW camp, the hell that I had gone through regarding my General Discharge, and to top it all, losing my childhood sweetheart. It was all more than I could handle. I was unable to put my life together. The only consolation was that my beautiful mother was always there to give me advice, and to reassure me that everything would be all right. Bless her heart.

I was at the Palo Alto Veterans Hospital. While there, the doctors performed a milogram, spinal tap and various other tests. I remained at the hospital for three months. I was told during the seventh week that I would be having a conference with the doctors. I went to the conference, anticipating the diagnosis of my back. The doctors had all the data from the tests and examinations. To my utter disappointment, all of the doctors agreed that there was nothing wrong with my back! They all agreed that my problem was a nervous disorder. One of the doctors explained, "Flores, this does not mean that there is nothing wrong with your back. It is that we are saying we can't find any damage to your back after all the tests that were performed." I was dumbfounded. My back caused me a lot of pain, yet they could not find anything wrong. Now what?

A week after the conference, I was put in a ward and classified with a very acute nervous disorder. That diagnosis did not hold water with me, but at the time there was nothing I could do. The nurses were administering uppers and downers to me. I felt like a zombie as a result of the medication. What made the situation worse was that the ward I was in was under lock and key. All I kept hearing from the doctor was that I needed to stay in that ward until I got well.

I soon realized that this ward was for the mentally ill. I witnessed what war does to men who are unable to cope. It is truly a reality check. Men would disrobe, urinate on the beds and talk to themselves. I woke up one day to find a guy urinating on the foot of my bed. I realized that I did not belong in this ward, nor for that matter, did I belong in this hospital. All I wanted was the doctors to find out what was wrong with my back, not to be committed to this institution.

The following day, I thought of a great plan to get myself out of there. I called the orderly through the wire cage that was placed between the office and the lobby.

The orderly came over and asked, "What's wrong?"

"I have severe pain on the right side of my stomach" I answered. He then opened the gate, let me out and I then proceeded to let out a yell, as if I was having another severe pain attack. He ran into the orderly's office and found no one present. I let out another yell of pain and added, "Hurry up man! The pain is severe!"

The orderly responded, "I am the only one here. I can't take you to the doctor across the way." The doctor's office was about twenty feet from our front entrance to the ward. He asked me, "Do you know where the doctor's office is located?"

I answered, "Yes." So I was given permission to go to the doctor's office, but to wait because the doctor would be there shortly.

I walked through the lobby, down the stairs and right past the doctor's office. I walked around the building, across the lawn and down the road to the gate. The guard at the gate waved at me and I waved back. I quickly went six blocks to Highway 101, leading to San Jose. I got a ride after an hour or so and went home.

Approaching the front steps to the house, mom stepped out of the house and asked, "What happened, son?" I told her everything that had happened and her response was, "You'll never go to that hospital again."

A few weeks had gone by and I was still trying to forget about what I had gone through at the VA hospital. It had been a nightmare. One day, while sitting on the porch, dad came home from work and approached me. He asked me, "Would you like to work in construction?"

I replied, "Anything, dad. I'm desperate to go to work."

"Your Uncle Paul said he could get you in as a laborer where he works."

I was so excited. I asked him, "When can I start?"

"He wants you to call him so you can follow him to work. He'll talk to his boss." That was like a shot of adrenaline. With that good news I got on the phone and called my buddy Russell Pernice. I had met Russell in elementary school. He stood about five-foot-eight, medium size, dark hair, light complected and had brown eyes. He was the type of person that would go out of his way to lend a helping hand. From the first day I met Russell, we were inseparable. I asked him to meet me at the Holland Drive-In for coffee. I was going to tell him the good news then.

Now that I had a job, I would be going out drinking and dancing with my friends. Dancing became my favorite past time. One of my favorite nightspots was Knight Kap. They had live music seven days a week. One Friday night, Russell, his brother and I went to the Knight Kap to dance and have a few drinks. We planned to go home early but it didn't turn out that way.

I noticed a girl, across the dance floor, sitting with another couple. I found out later that they were her cousin and his wife. While dancing with some lady friends, she glanced at me at the table I was sitting. She kept looking at me, so I decided I would ask her to dance. She was very attractive with a round face and brown eyes. She had shoulder length brown hair, stood about five-foot five and had a very nice figure. She accepted my invitation to dance by saying, "I'd love to." She was a very good dancer and we danced all night, until the club was ready to close.

While we were dancing, I found out that her name was Wilma Johnson. She was a single mom with a little boy named Steve. She worked in San Francisco at Wells Fargo Bank. After the last dance of the evening, I asked her if she would like to join me and my friends for breakfast. After a few minutes, she convinced her cousin that she would be okay and her cousin granted her permission to go with me.

After that night, we saw each other on a regular basis. Several days later, we each met our respective parents. We all got along great and Wilma and I went dancing as often as time permitted. Eight months later, we decided to get married.

My daughter, Jeri, was born within the first year of our marriage, in 1960. Before Jeri was born, I had been out of work for two months, and still was. It was not easy, especially for me to have to depend on the county to foot the bills for Jeri's birth. A short time later, we found out that Jeri had been born with a hernia. That meant surgery, a hospital stay, and medications. I still hadn't found work and I was resigned to the fact that I needed the county's help to make sure that my daughter received all necessary surgeries, medications etc.

My unemployment continued for a few more months, and then I received great news. I was called to go to work for the City of Campbell, just outside San Jose. This was a tremendous relief for me as debts had piled up, and we owed the county about three thousand dollars for the delivery and surgery. I worked for the city about eight months, then my back went out. I couldn't even sit down due to the severe pain. I was forced to quit my city job. I went to the VA and told them what had happened, and I was given an appointment for further evaluation of my back.

As I suspected, the doctors did not find anything wrong with my back. They scheduled me to see a psychologist. I saw the doctor, a "shrink" as they were called. The first visit was spent getting to know the doctor. A few visits later, the doctor told me that he was crazier then I was for seeing me. He continued to tell me that I didn't have a mental problem.

After all my scheduled appointments ran out, I decided to fight the Veterans Administration. I fought them for fourteen years. I was going to keep going to the VA until they corrected my back, or gave me compensation for my disability. The VA finally scheduled me for an appointment at the Veterans Administration Regional Office in San Francisco.

I was scheduled to see a doctor at the VA for a complete physical. This doctor was elderly and was not very friendly. He examined me and said that he would make a report to the judicial committee. In his report, he stated that there was nothing wrong with me and that I was a Mexican laborer looking for compensation to live on.

That in itself was damaging to my self-esteem. I decided that I would never step foot inside that office as long as I lived. I went home and told my wife. She was just as upset by the report as I had been. I vowed not to let it bother me. We went on with our lives and did the best we could.

The problem with the VA and my General Discharge was not helping my marriage. We were in debt up to our necks; the VA had given me a ten percent disability that amounted to forty dollars a month, which was not enough to buy groceries, let alone pay rent and utilities.

I decided, come hell or high water, that I was going to get a job. I started looking, and to my surprise, I found a job selling carpet, screen rooms and aluminum siding. By this time, my wife was ready to take the kids and go live with her parents so they could be cared for. I talked her out of it, and told her that with this job, we would get out of debt and live like normal people.

She asked, "But, how long will it last?"

I told her, "I don't know but I am going to give it all I have, and go for broke."

She stuck it out, and within a few months, we could breath again. With everything that had transpired, our relationship was still rocky. I was doing well with the company I worked for. However, after only a year, the company closed their doors and I was out of a job again.

There was no other option for me but to look for another job. I was worried sick about ending up in debt again, paying for our necessities, and just the ordinary day-to-day things. To add to my worries, my wife informed me that we were going to have a baby. This news made me both happy and yet, devastated me. I was in shock, I guess. How was I going to pay for the medical bills that go along with having a child? I found myself heading to the garage, where I knelt down and prayed. "Lord, please help me to find a job, and let me save my marriage. I have a son to be born soon, and I have to provide for him and my family. Amen."

A few weeks had passed when I found a job doing construction work. That was a definite boost to my morale. My thoughts began to be more positive about life, which was a welcome blessing. The all-too-familiar thing happened once again. The particular job ended in three months and there was no other work available with this company. I came tumbling down the ladder once again.

I couldn't handle the stress anymore and had a nervous breakdown. I ended up in the Palo Alto VA hospital again. Because of this, I presume, I was awarded one hundred percent disability, making my monthly benefit three hundred dollars. Out of that check, I would keep fifteen dollars and send my wife the balance. That was enough to pay rent and buy food for the kids. I came home on the weekends so I could see the children and my wife. She had put up with a lot and was really trying to find a reason to stay in the marriage. I came home one weekend, and we had a talk. I asked her, "Please stay till I get out of the hospital." She agreed to stay until I was released from the hospital so we could try and work things out.

While at the hospital, I decided to write the Commandant of the Marine Corps and tell him what I had done while a POW. I also wanted to discuss that upon my release from the Marine Corps I had received a General Discharge and it was ruining my life.

Prior to my release from the hospital I discussed the doctors' findings with them and I asked them, "Does this mean that there is something wrong with my back?" They answered, "No. We are going to classify you as unemployable – that you are unable to find work. So, take it and don't come back."

My son, Michael, was to be born July 18, 1965. I asked for a pass for the week so I could be with my family and attend the birth. I wouldn't have missed it for the world. I was summoned to the VA hospital in Palo

Alto for another evaluation. While I was there, I decided to write my Congressman and ask for his help in fixing my General Discharge.

The birth of my son, Michael, was a blessing from God. I became so determined to find a long lasting job so I could be a good provider and husband. I wasn't going to let the VA put me down as a Mexican laborer not wanting to work! I told myself that I would do everything within my power to walk tall and get out of this mess.

I found a job selling carpet and I was doing well. We started on our way to recovering from the financial cloud. A few years went by and we were out of the hole, so we decided to move away from San Jose. We picked a small town east of Sacramento, called Penryn. The way we chose where to move was kind of funny. We grabbed a straight pin, closed our eyes and moved the pin over a map of California that was spread out on the table. With the help of my wife, Steve and Jeri, we lowered the pin down on the map. Penryn was where it touched.

It was not all that easy to just pack up and move, but I wanted to start a new life with my family and that made it a little easier. My wife had put up with a lot over the first seven years of our marriage. She was the best mom the kids could have ever asked for. She deserved a fresh start. Plus, there were just too many memories in San Jose, and I wanted to leave them behind.

We rented several houses while the kids went to Penryn Elementary School. I started looking for a job. I was receiving my disability check but we still did without just to make it. We eventually found a five-acre ranch for sale. The owner just wanted to get rid of the place. She told us she would take five hundred dollars down, and ninety dollars a month. The total price she was asking for the ranch was ten thousand dollars. We decided to go ahead and buy it. We ended up borrowing the five hundred dollars from Wilma's parents and three weeks later, we moved in.

After a few months at our ranch, I started going for coffee at the local coffee shop. I continued to pass the word around that I was a carpenter, doing remodeling, cement work and anything in the home improvement field. Things started happening for me. I was getting calls everyday, which resulted in our financial security. We slowly fixed up the house, making it our home. The children loved the country and were doing well in school. I bought a few calves, chickens and goats.

While at the ranch, we were surprised by a visit from an officer of the Marine Corps. He told us that my presence was requested at the Marine Corps Headquarters in Sacramento. It was there that I was awarded the Navy Commendation medal. This was made possible by Congressman

Prisoner During Korean War

A Hero Is Honored – 14 Years Late

Former Leatherneck Cpl. Nick Flores, right, is presented the Navy
Commendation Medal by Marine Maj. G.B. Tucker of Sacramento.
Flores' family looks on approvingly. (From the May 12, 1967 is-
sue of *The Sacramento Union*)

Gerbser. It was brought to my attention that he had passed my letter on to the Secretary of the Navy, who in return, granted the medal. This whole episode came as quite a surprise to me. I so appreciated all the effort that Congressman Gerbser put into this. It was a great feeling to me that at least a few people listened and believed in me.

The calls for carpentry work slowed down and eventually stopped. Again, I was unemployed. In just a couple of days, I found a job, but my bad luck soon found its way back into my life. I fell off a ladder at work, breaking my arm, and ended up with a cast from my shoulder to my hand. That really did me in. We were forced to sell the ranch. We moved to El Paso, Texas, in 1971 where my mom and dad lived. We ended up staying with them for about a year and then moved back to Penryn. The children loved Penryn and we were going to stay there, no matter what. We rented a place and the kids were happy to be back with their friends and in the same school.

With all that had happened in recent years, I still kept my faith. I felt that God had something for me, and that if I could handle being a POW for three years, I could handle the misfortunes that kept finding their way back into my life.

After working for some contractors, I got to know a few people in Roseville, which was only twelve miles from Penryn. I started to get calls from various areas that were close to Penryn. Keeping very busy, I started to see the clear sky. It was a great relief for me. Maybe, just maybe, I would stay working and be rid of the financial worries.

An old problem resurfaced one night when I arrived home from work. My wife told me that she was divorcing me. It didn't surprise me because our marriage had been heading for rock bottom for a while. I moved out, rented a local motel room and had to eat out. At the same time, I gave my wife money for rent, food and whatever the children needed. I often went without so I was able to see that my family's needs were met.

One morning I decided to ask God for help. I prayed and decided to leave all my problems in his hands. I was managing to get a few jobs, which kept me afloat. One morning, I went to the coffee shop and I was sitting and talking to some other contractors. A gentleman whom I had never met before, came up to the table, asking if I was Nick Flores. When I told him that I was, and he said that he wanted to know if we could talk, pointing to an empty table at the corner of the coffee shop. He introduced himself and asked if I could build a house for him. He added that I came recommended from a friend. After discussing all the details, I signed an agreement that I would build this house. I was to receive three thousand dollars to start and he would lease a pick-up truck for me. The whole meeting overwhelmed me and I wasn't quite sure what to think. Slowly, the joy of this unexpected meeting flowed through my body. I didn't question how long this would last. I decided I would take it one day at a time.

I ended up building an additional two houses for him. This boosted my self-confidence. To meet someone that trusted me to build houses for him was wonderful. To this day, that man does not know what he did for me and my life.

In 1979, construction all over came to a halt. Contractors were filing for bankruptcy left and right. I had just completed the third house when the building industry hit the skids. I found myself out of work, and as a result, tried to figure out what type of service was needed, even though construction was at a standstill. Then it hit me – a janitorial business. I fixed up my 1963 GMC flat-bed truck, bought a mop, bucket and a vacuum cleaner. In about six months, I was doing fourteen hundred dollars worth of accounts a month. I was working only at night, after the businesses closed. By the end of three years, I had fifty five hundred dollars coming in from my business. I had two vans and was doing well financially.

My children were still a part of my life. Steve had married in 1977 and Jeri got married in 1980. They were both living happy family lives. Michael was working full time while living with his mother in Roseville, California. I loved my kids very much and didn't want to hurt them anymore through the unpleasant problems happening between their parents. So, I decided that Texas was the place for me, plus I could take care of my mother and be there, should she need me.

As I headed west on I-10, I found myself alone again, and flashbacks of my past were once again in my mind. Korea was very vivid. I thought about the men who died on the "death march," the forty-below temperature, the three months of hell; the escapes, the trial and torture for escaping, my solitary confinement, and the torture I had received from the Russians. As if that wasn't enough, I had to come home and be presented with a general discharge. That was the icing on the cake. I feel that the discharge ruined my life forever. Don't get me wrong. I don't regret anything I did while a POW. I love my country and I loved the Marine Corps. I figured that freedom wasn't free and I paid my dues.

After putting the past behind me, I ended up in Las Vegas. I worked there for a couple of years. In between jobs I went to El Paso to check on my mother. I also decided that I would go to California and try to make amends with my kids.

After leaving my wife and 20+ years of marriage, I had not called or seen my family for about three years. I felt it was time to put my bitterness behind and start a new relationship with them. I was in Roseville, California, for about two weeks. It was very uncomfortable, but nevertheless, I felt good within myself for taking the first step.

After going back and forth from El Paso to California, and Las Vegas to California, I decided to stay around Roseville and be close to my kids and grandkids.

In 1993, on one of my fishing trips, I met a lady, Marijane Kolher. Over the course of four days, we had many conversations. It was through these that I became aware of her plans to go to her father's house in Indiana, but was unsure of driving that distance by herself. I suggested to her that she follow me to El Paso, and then drive the rest of the way to Indiana by herself. From the start, we had gotten along well, so I was not concerned about any trouble occurring on the way.

We set off for El Paso, July 5, 1993. We reached El Paso, got settled in a trailer park, then took on the task of watching over my mother, who was in a convalescent hospital by this time. We weren't in El Paso but for a week or so, when I got a message to call Wilma. She informed me that an agency from Washington, DC, was looking for me. After getting the number to call, I returned the call. I quickly discovered that I had called Task Force Russia, an agency of the Department of Defense. Through that contact I became acquainted with Peter Tsouras who was associated with finding out the fate of POWs and MIAs of the Korean War. My experience with the task force was both rewarding and inspiring. It also changed my life, but I'll let you read about that in the last chapter of my book that was written by Peter Tsouras.

Peter was the one who first encouraged me to write down the story of my life so it could be passed onto my family. Over the next several years following my trip to Washington, I did just that. Both Marijane and myself put in hundreds of hours of work on it. Without her moral support, dedication and devotion, I wouldn't have had the strength to continue on and this book would not have been written. I also had the help of my family and friends who are all a part of making this dream come true for me. Thank you.

Chapter Sixteen
Semper Fi

In late March, 1993, Major Werner Hindrichs, Lieutenant Colonel Huang, and myself, Peter Tsouras, were reviewing the Navy/Marine Corps classified Big/Little Switch debriefing files at the downtown U.S. Archives. It was slow laborious work reading each file, and we had not found a great deal of useful information, when Major Hindrichs exclaimed, "Bingo!" We looked over to see him grinning from ear to ear. He had just found what we were to discover as a key to the Soviet handling of prisoners destined for a one-way trip to the Soviet Union. He was looking at the file of one Corporal Nick A. Flores, USMC, who had been captured at the Chosin Reservoir in November 1950, and repatriated in Big Switch in September 1953.

The notes of Flores' American interrogator aboard the ship that took him and all the rest of the Big Switch repatriates to the West Coast, revealed that during an escape attempt from a Chinese POW Camp, Flores had been captured by Soviet antiaircraft personnel and immediately transported by truck to the Soviet headquarters at the MIG base just across the Yalu River and into Andong in Manchuria. He had been mistaken for an F-86 pilot whose plane had been shot down in the area barely an hour before. The fact that Flores had been wearing USAF uniform items given by fellow POWs to enhance his survivability seemed to confirm his identity to the Soviets. While in Soviet custody he was intensively interrogated for about 48 hours. Only when the Soviets confirmed his true identity by checking with the Chinese was he returned to the camp.

We concluded that Flores had accidentally slipped into the special POW category destined for transfer to the Soviet Union. None of the other repatriated pilots ever told of such special handling by Soviet captors. He was able to slip out of the system when it was confirmed that he was not a pilot but a Pfc. For the Soviets, he was then a nobody who could be safely returned to a camp. That was their mistake. They ejected him from a highly secret operation because he was an aberration. They should have either sent him on to the Soviet Union or disposed of him in order to not let anyone see inside their special system and live to tell about it. But they didn't, and forty-one years later, we picked up the lead.

Having had our appetites mightily whetted by the Big Switch file, we were eager to find out more about Flores. Was there a fuller account of his experience with the Soviets? Was he willing to be interviewed? The first thing I did was to call Wendy Hollingsworth, our POC (point of contact) at the national Personnel Records Center in St. Louis and ask her to retrieve his official file. A few days later she called back to say she had found it, but that there might be a problem. "He has only a general discharge." That set me back. Was there a problem that could affect Flores' credibility? So I asked Wendy to send me a copy of the whole file to review. A week later as I read through the thick file, a tragic story unfolded to my increasing dismay.

There was nothing in his file that reflected unfavorably upon Flores except the general discharge itself. I could find nothing that seemed to reasonably be the cause of such a discharge. If anything, there was a great deal of material that showed Flores to be, if anything, a hero. There was a letter from him in 1965 to his congressman and the retired commandant of the Marine Corps asking for some recognition of his conduct while a POW and a relook at his discharge. After two years of internal correspondence the Navy issued him the Navy Commendation Medal for his conduct above and beyond the call of duty while a POW, but nothing was done about his discharge. There were many letters in this correspondence from other POWs who affirmed that Flores had acted with great courage and selflessness, that he nursed back to health many POWs abandoned by their comrades, that he was a major-hard case for the communist camp authorities, and that he had escaped no less than three times. He had served thirty-three months as a POW and about a year beforehand.

Looking through his file closely, I discovered a service computation form used to establish the type of discharge. A numerical rating was given for each period of service, but only the period before his capture was taken into account.

Unfortunately, he had several cases of nonjudicial punishment for AWOL and failure to report while a peacetime Marine in the States. There was nothing about his exemplary participation in the Inchon Landings and the subsequent campaign of the 1st Marine Division across the Korean Peninsula up to his time of capture. The quickness of his return to the U.S. and his decision there not to re-enlist ensured that his record in the camps would not catch up with him to his credit. And so, I'm sure, some clerk at his discharge station had tallied up the form, it was signed by an officer, and his life was ruined. The 1965 letter was a cry of the heart for justice. He had written from the VA hospital where he was undergoing treatment for back injuries caused by all the beatings he had received from the communists for his escape attempts. He had also undergone extended counseling attempting to deal with the shame of a less than honorable discharge, something not to be made lightly of in the 1950s.

Major Hindrichs read the file and immediately came to the same conclusions I had that we had stumbled across a major injustice and blot upon a good name of the U.S. Armed Forces. We also showed this to Mr. Pokrovsky who became as equally exercised. Nick Pokrovsky was an Army Master Sergeant attached to Task Force Russia. He acted as a liaison with other agencies of the government. The three of us determined to do something about it, irrespective of whether Flores would cooperate if and when we found him. I inquired of the Board for the Correction of Naval Records and was told that this case certainly seemed to warrant positive reconsideration. There this matter rested while we tried to find Flores himself. Our last address found him in Las Vegas. I telephoned the number listed under Nick A. Flores and talked to a Mrs. Flores only to discover that I had stumbled upon someone of the exact same complete name. I had disconcerted this poor woman by referring to her late husband's general discharge from the Marines and was told in no uncertain terms that he had been honorably discharged from the Air Force. Wiping the chagrin off my face, I apologized and kept looking. We finally traced Flores to two post office boxes in Roseville, California, outside of Sacramento. We sent registered letters to both, and both were returned addressee unknown. At this point something on the order of the miraculous occurred. Mr. Pokrovsky looked through his police channel connections and by sheer chance found someone who knew the Flores family, not through any police record or anything since Flores had none. He talked to Flores' ex-wife who told us that he was on his way to El Paso, Texas, to visit his mother, and gave us the trailer park telephone number he would be staying at. Mr. Pokrovsky made contact and asked if he would mind talking to us. He replied, "Sure, I'll do anything for my country."

We were struck by his unalloyed patriotism, even after all he had suffered. I remember how noble it sounded when Nick Pokrovsky related his conversation. But we were off to El Paso to interview him, Major Hindrichs, Mr. Pokrovsky, and I. Nick Pokrovsky went to meet him at the trailer park while Werner and I set up in a motel room for the interview. When Pokrovsky came into the lobby with Flores and both were laughing, Werner and I new we had struck gold. Pokrovsky was a master humanist, and his ease with the man was a good sign. Flores was everything we could have hoped for – the salt of the earth, genuine, and with an incredibly good memory.

Pokrovsky had to return to Washington shortly after arranging our meeting with Flores, but first set into motion our conspiracy. Before the three of us had left Washington we had attempted to get the Board for Correction of Naval Records to unilaterally change Flores' discharge. Everyone at the Task Force was wholeheartedly behind this effort. I distinctly remember how excited and supportive Lieutenant Colonel Freeman, acting Deputy Assistant Secretary of Defense for POW/MIA Affairs, was. Pokrovsky prepared a beautifully crafted letter to the Secretary of the Navy to be signed by Mr. Ross requesting him to initiate proceedings to upgrade the discharge. Ed Ross was a Department of Defense Senior Executive Service employee. Pokrovsky briefed Ross who gladly signed the letter which Major Hindrichs hand carried to the office of the Secretary of the Navy. To our surprise and initial disgust we were told that the Government could not on its own change the discharge; the individual or NOK (next of kin) had to petition for such a change. Then the reason dawned on us. If the Government could change it for well, it could also change it for ill. So the petition was a necessary safeguard. Then our problem became how to get the poor man to sign a petition without making a promise that it would be changed. After all, we were not put in a position to guarantee the outcome of an official board. Instead, Pokrovsky nonchalantly at lunch with Flores and us had mentioned that we had noticed he had only a general discharge and asked why. Flores said he really didn't know and hadn't been able to find out. Later in the room, Pokrovsky mentioned that we could look into the problem with the discharge if he didn't mind. Flores said he didn't, whereupon Pokrovsky flashed a form and asked Flores to sign it, explaining casually that it was only Flores' permission to look into his case because of the Privacy Act. Unbeknownst to Flores, he had just signed his own petition. Within an hour Pokrovsky was on the plane back to Washington. Immediately upon his arrival back at the Hoffman Building, he faxed copy to the Board for the Correction of Naval Records, which had been standing by for it. That afternoon they convened a special board, which upgraded the discharge to honorable.

Back in El Paso, Major Werner Hindrichs and I spent the rest of the day interviewing Flores and found him very credible. It was an education to watch Major Hindrichs conduct a highly professional debriefing. It was highly instructive watching him smoothly extract the right information. At the end of the evening we were satisfied that we had indeed found our looking glass into the special Soviet POW handling operation. We invited

Task Force Russia Team

Right: (l. to r.) Army Master Sergeant Nick Pokrovsky, me and Peter Tsouras.

Below: (l. to r.) Second Lieutenant Timothy Lewis, me, Major Werner Hindrichs and Peter Tsouras.

*Assistant Commandant Gen. Walter Boomer presenting
me with my honorable discharge and POW medal.*

Flores to Washington to undergo further debriefing and an official video-taping. He agreed eagerly. I suggested that he bring a good suit. He showed up at the Hoffman Building all ready for the videotaping. Major Hindrichs told him that our room at the Pentagon had just been pre-empted, but that we had found a suitable room at the last minute at the Navy Annex nearby. Werner drove him there while Pokrovsky and I went by a different car and met him in the lobby. As we walked down the long corridors of the navy Annex, it was obvious that we were in USMC territory. Flores became visibly nervous as he noticed the sudden increase in the quality of the surroundings to paneled walls adorned with oil paintings of past commandants of the Corps. When Mr. Pokrovsky led him up to the pol-ished mahogany door with its gleaming brass plaque announcing that we were entering the office of the Assistant Commandant of the Marine Corps, his eyes bulged. Inside was the elegantly appointed waiting room filled with people from both the Task Force (Lieutenant Colonel Free-man, Major Taylor, and Second Lieutenant Lewis) and the Clarendon of-fice (Mr. Ross, Colonel Schatter, Mr. Kass, and a few straphangers). The Clarendon office was a large government leased office building that housed the Deputy Assistant Secretary of Defense for POW/MIA affairs and the Defense Intelligence Agencies POW/MIA office. They worked hand in glove with the office of the Deputy Assistant. There were some mighty long minutes as no one spoke and poor Nick Flores' eyes darted nervously around the room at the gathering, most of whom he didn't know.

Then, to his further consternation, General Boomer walked into the room and went straight for Flores and shook his hand, saying how proud they were to have him there that day. Then he shook everyone else's hand, thanking them for coming, and looking each one right in the eye. If ever there was a soldier who had an innate sense of leadership it was Boomer, a handsome, martial man who had led two Marine Divisions to victory in the Gulf War.

Finally he welcomed everyone into his private office. He stood in the center of the room with Flores and began to explain why everyone was assembled. First he recounted Flores' record of service in the Marine Corps, having earlier read a long document prepared by Mr. Pokrovsky and re-membered every bit of it. Finally, he talked about how Flores' discharge had been surely the error of a clerk and that the Marine Corps wanted to put things right. "I want to make amends," he said. Then he took the hon-orable discharge off the table and presented it to Flores who had tears welling in his eyes. He followed this with the POW medal. There wasn't a dry eye in the room, I thought. Next he had a Marine photographer take a photo of the two of them. After that, he suggested that Flores have his picture taken with all the people that had helped him. It was an unalloyed joy to watch Flores savor his vindication, even so many years after the fact. He called his son, Michael, to join him from California, and the two had a wonderful few days together in Washington. The DOD Public Affairs Office also arranged for Nick to be interviewed by two reporters, Gigit Fuentes of *Navy Times* (1) and Bob Burns of the Associated Press (2). They both ran great stories on him that were picked up by his home town press. Bob Burns also was allowed to interview me on the story to round out the details. He immediately picked up on the importance of the F-86 connection to the Soviets' interest in Flores, and I unraveled some of the background on our growing hypothesis. Burns wrote the expected human-interest story on Flores and a second story on the F-86 Connection:

U.S. investigators view the new information as especially important because it is the first documented case of a returned American POW who was captured by the Soviets in Korea and sent directly to a Soviet military post in China for interrogation. U.S. investigators are pursuing the notion that the Soviet military singled-out downed American F-86 pilots in Korea for interrogations and – bypassing the Chinese-run POW system in Korea – possibly transferred them to the Soviet Union (3).

(1) Gigit Fuentes, "Honor at last for POW," *Navy Times*, August 30, 1993.

(2) Bob Burns, "41 Years Late, A Marine Gets His Due," Associated Press, 24 August 1993.

(3) "Ex-POW's story indicates Soviets seized U.S. flyers," from the Associated Press, *Washington Times*, 22 August 1993, p. A6.

Index

Notes

Notes

Nick Flores enlisted in the United States Marine Corps at the age of 17. Within 18 months, he found himself right in the middle of the Korean War, a prisoner of the Chinese army. After enduring over 33 months of hell in the Chinese POW camps, including 10 months of solitary confinement, he was repatriated on August 20, 1953. He now lives in Nevada where he spends his time fishing, relaxing, and visiting with family.

Printed in the USA
CPSIA information can be obtained
at www.ICGtesting.com
JSHW022324140824
68134JS00019B/1279